Toxic Silicone Poisoning - The TRUE Breast Implant Stories

The TRUTH of the GREATEST TRAVESTY AGAINST WOMEN in the 20th century

By

Susan A. Pope Helman, Ph.D.

authorHOUSE

1663 Liberty Drive, Suite 200
Bloomington, Indiana 47403
(800) 839-8640
www.authorhouse.com

First published by AuthorHouse 07/09/04

ISBN: 1-4184-2191-X (sc)

Library of Congress Control Number: 2004093963

Printed in the United States of America
Bloomington, Indiana

This book is printed on acid-free paper.

INTRODUCTION

Toxic Silicone Poisoning-The TRUE Breast Implant Stories THE TRUTH OF THE GREATEST TRAVESTY AGAINST WOMEN DURING THE 20TH CENTURY

Written by a woman whose life has been drastically and profoundly affected by silicone/ polyurethane breast implants. A professional woman by trade whose career was marketing, management and research in the medical arena. I am not a professional writer or a medical expert but a woman with a steaming desire to bring forth the actual stories about breast implants and the women affected by them.

My goal is to reveal to the "people" what has actually happened to these women before and after implantation and their sufferings and realizations concerning the manipulation of general opinion and media interests by large corporations and the major cover-up that has taken place in this "medical device" industry. Their triumphs too.

DEDICATION

TOXIC SILICONE POISONING - The TRUE Breast Implant Stories

Is dedicated to all of the hundreds of thousands of husbands and families who love, support, understand and comfort, and take care of those affected by silicone toxicity.

Is dedicated to the women who have suffered and continue to suffer from the effects of breast implants. Many having faced loss of career, family, insurance coverage, and some even complete medical and financial devastation. Even DEATH!

Is dedicated to my Mother, Anne H. Pope and my Father, Joshua David Pope, who instilled in me the necessities of conviction, morals, and always tell the TRUTH!

Is dedicated to my husband, whom without, I don't think I would have survived.

Is dedicated to my best friend, Benita, for her love, support and encouragement for success in this whole process.

Facing the issues and challenges of these illnesses alone can be and is most difficult. Special love and heartfelt support go out to all of those who have lost loved ones because they were unable to cope with the myriad of difficulties and hardships, or accept and support the multitude of illness and problems arising from silicone poisoning.

"The TRUTH Shall Set You Free". By Printing these TRUTH's that these women actually experience; hopefully, will come an outpouring of support, understanding and help for each and every one of these women. An understanding of what caused them to chose implants, what happened to them after implant, and most of all, what is to become of these women in the future?

ACKNOWLEDGMENTS

Gratitude and thanks go to each and every woman who shared her story. What courage and strength all of these women demonstrate.

Particular gratefulness goes to those families who lost their loved ones due to the highly TOXIC substances found in silicone, silicone/polyurethane, and silicone/saline breast implants.

They have passed on to another place where there is no pain, no anguish and they are free at last!

A very special thank you to the doctors, especially Dr. Frank Vasey, and others; Dr. Samuel Epstein, Dr. Everold Haffizulla, Dr. Marguerite P. Barnett, and Dr. Ernest Lykissa who are included with the early pioneers like Dr. Pierre Blais, Dr. Eigelman, Dr. Robert Gary, Dr. Gary Weiss, Dr. Michael Middleton, Dr. Henry Jenny, Dr. Andrew Campbell and Dr. Sidney Wolfe and Ralph Nader with Public Citizen, who realized early on that there exists a correlation between breast implants and neurological and rheumatological diseases or disorders. Placing their professional and personal careers "on the line" because they took a stand on this a very controversial issue.

Thank you again......you treated these women with dignity and respect and continue to give them the treatment and medical support they so desperately need.

For my children, who no longer live with me but have families of their own and have been so very patient with my ever changing moods, personality changes and still love me.

Lastly, thank you Craig, my husband, my support, my strength. Who during the last ten and a half years has never failed me. Who has picked me up when I was down....Who has literally fed me, clothed me, washed me, and comforted me when we thought I was dying..............I LOVE YOU!.

DISCLAIMER

The author neither endorses nor recommends any person, organization, service, clinic laboratory, product, book or treatment listed herein.

All of the stories presented here are TRUE stories written by the women themselves. Only their names have been changed to protect them and their families. The author cannot be held responsible for any litigation that currently exists or could arise from the printing of these stories. If there are any similarities the author apologizes, for they are purely coincidental.

To order additional copies of this book contact:

TABLE OF CONTENTS

Section One - Purpose for writing this book

TOXIC SILICONE POISONING---THE TRUTH OF THE GREATEST TRAVESTY AGAINST WOMEN IN THE 20TH CENTURY

Fifty years ago I was adopted by a very "prominent" attorney and his wife, a bookkeeper- Who knows why? All of the records are "sealed or missing"? I am just one tiny person, but if this can happen to me imagine what can happen to records of large corporations if their attorneys choose to cover-up or hide information? Even though the adoption laws have been changed in the State of Tennessee, I will never know who my biological parents were! The "papers are sealed"! I even had a judge tell me, "Susan, your daddy buried those records so deep," "You will never be able to find out"!

For comparison purposes only, let us consider what has transpired in the on-going TRAVESTY of silicone/polyurethane, silicone gel, and silicone/saline breast implants. What happened to my records of adoption and what

2

continues to happen to the records of the large breast implant manufacturers run a similar parallel........From cover-up to misinformation to misrepresentation and purposeful deception!

There are thirty-eight known chemicals in the manufacturing and contents of silicone gel filled breast implants! These thirty-eight chemicals are all toxic alone if inhaled, ingested, or even handled; some causing cancer, some causing neurological damage; organ damage or tissue damages. Combined all together; however, they become a "chemical soup" that the F D A, the government, the National Institute of Medicine, the Judicial System, the manufacturers and their public relations' firms, their lawyers, and the medical community have allowed to be classified as a "medical device" and "suitable for implantation" in the human body! In the "informed consent" papers one must sign before having the surgery for implantation of these "medical devices" no where does it state any information about this "chemical soup", no where

3

does it state any of the damage that could take place with these toxic "things" in the human body! This travesty is unparalleled at least in my opinion only by the clitoral excision done to females in parts of Africa, even to this date.

Our image and appearance as a society continues to be of utmost importance. To be accepted "as we are" and for what "we are made of" rather than how we are built and what we wear has not existed since we were a "cave dwelling" society! Even then, tattooing and tanning of leather and curing of fur was done for identification, beautification and edification purposes.

While watching television, reading magazines and newspapers, and even billboards along the roadways seem to define what we should look and act like! Using beautiful, thin, large busted women to advertise products intended for use by the average looking person! This type of advertising makes us all question

our appearance and "do we measure up"? Our culture seems to demand that we look, act, dress and be the epitome of this perfect human being.

After hearing from women all over the world, talking with them, and writing to them, interviewing them one on one for the past ten years, and involvement with thousands of women in support groups, I decided to try and write down what I have learned. I have spoken with professional women with great careers they have abandoned because they could no longer work; women who had wonderful families until they became too ill to care for them and their husbands left them because they could not deal with the health problems their partners experienced. Women with small children who were also affected with illnesses caused by the toxins in their mothers' milk from breast feeding while they had implants. I have experienced personal devastation from knowing women who have committed suicide because they could no longer handle the day-to-day pain, debilitation,

hopelessness and frustration they experience as a result of these breast implants. The women I know come from all "walks of life", all professions.... from secretaries to doctors, receptionists, nurses, yes even attorneys! They were all deceived, they are all ill, and they all believed what the surgeon, the manufacturer, and the governing body....the F D A said was TRUTH! Breast implants are SAFE! All testing has been done and breast implants are completely safe......" they will last a lifetime"!

The information I present here to you is from association with many of the doctors who are treating these women, the lawyers who represent these women and from the many support groups and personal relationships I have with these women. Having silicone/polyurethane breast implants myself, they feel comfortable talking with me and understand I have promised to change all of their names in order to protect them and their families from any repercussions

It is my understanding that one of the manufacturers, DOW, will be released from their bankruptcy in about one year, which they sought after so many women became involved in the "MDL 926" Class Action litigation in the 1990's. In writing this all down I hope to bring forth the TRUTH that these manufacturers continue to hide from the public......

As you will see in most of these stories we are all suffering with many of the same illnesses.

The manufacturers "say" they are conducting studies "breast implant research", they "say" there are "clinical trials" (which show breast implants are 'totally' safe), they "say" they are "tracking" each person who receives breast implants. THEY SAY many things but no one is keeping track of any of us! Who is keeping lists of those with specific illnesses? How many of us have Lupus? How many of us have Multiple Sclerosis? How many of us have Fibromyalgia,

7

Connective Tissue Diseases, Sjogren's Syndrome? How many of us have Cancer or Heart problems? The manufacturers don't know! The F D A doesn't know! The Government and the Justice Department don't know! Neither do the Centers for Disease Control! How many of us have died or committed suicide? THEY DON'T KNOW! Not a doctor, a manufacturer's representative, nor any one from the F D A or Centers for Disease Control has ever contacted me or any of us that I know of to see how we feel!

We women, hundreds of thousands of us are trying to keep "track" or make lists of these things but we are many and we're spread out all over the world! We cannot possibly be expected to maintain an accurate list, but---we are trying! Just in the month of September, 2000, personally I know of six women who passed away from illnesses directly related to breast implants! It seems to me the only thing important to the manufacturers is to SELL as many of these TOXIC

DEVISES as possible. Get them inside a woman's body, and go on to the next "victim"!

When there is a death of a woman with breast implants the pathologists and the physicians do not list the implants as a factor or possible cause of death! Why? We women want all of our medical records released and opened for us so that we might have a TRUE MEDICAL EVALUATION. We also have requested that the "gag order" be lifted from the breast implant court cases which were settled long before the MDL 926 Class Action Suit transpired. These cases contain information that the manufacturers don't ever want the public to see, regarding studies which were completed with negative outcomes showing the very symptoms and illnesses we are all afflicted with.

The manufacturers continue to say their breast implants are safe....Then tell us why we continue to receive new inquiries each and every day from women who have received these NEW implants saying they are sick! Their symptoms are the same as ours. Can these implants be safe when women are still becoming ill? Explain to me how a woman could have been surgically implanted with breast implants in August, 2000, and four weeks later, September, 2000, she's DEAD? What did she die from? The attending physician surely knows what caused her death! Of course, she was most likely poisoned by the "chemical soup" contained in the implants which were put into her body!

Hundreds of thousands of women have been subjected to this same "chemical soup"! They purchased implants, trusting the physicians, the manufacturers and the F D A who all stated they were 100 percent safe! Well, tires, pharmaceuticals, transmissions, baby food, beef, all are supposedly safe if they are on the market for human consumption......But if they are not safe they can be recalled; unlike breast implants, when proven unsafe by unbiased science, are already in the body, doing their damage! They are not recalled! The TRUTH is simply coined "junk *science", or worse, covered-up, or misconstrued, even ignored! Breast implants are classified as "medical devices", they have NEVER been given a safety stamp of approval by the government or the F D A. So how did they become salable? They were "grandfathered in" back in the 1970's with the understanding that all safety testing would be completed. The testing was done but the results were skewed to favor the manufacturers' not the F D A standards. When negative results were obtained by their research scientists this was covered-up and/or the evidence destroyed!*

*For years, we women have written to our government agencies to include but not limited to: The Justice Department, The F D A, The Centers for Disease Control, The Institute of Medicine, Medical Journals, The National Cancer Institute, The Lupus Foundation, The National Multiple Sclerosis Society, to local and national media, including television and radio and newsprint......
.....Still, We ARE NOT HEARD! How many women will become ill from the TOXINS in breast implants*

11

before the year 2005? How many will die before someone somewhere decides, as we have, that there have already been FAR TOO MANY

NOW!

Just as it seems we women begin to move toward recognition internationally the manufacturers' public relations firms, paid millions, seem to once again manage to cover-up the TRUTH and go on with their deception and lies to the public.

If you didn't know of someone or have a family member affected by these breast implants personally, you probably wouldn't be reading this book! The general public has no idea what is going on and may not even care! That's been the cause for concern all along! The public must not find out what is going on! The manufacturers might be held accountable then! How in the world would they cover that up?

In the sections that follow you will see how this whole scenario plays out! The manipulation of and by the doctors, the public relations' firms, the media and even the medical journal contributors! Also you will be shown TRUE research and current findings by the F D A and the National Cancer Institute. Sections are also contributed by some of the physicians' who treat us daily and by attorneys who have given so much of their time and efforts trying to help all of us in this real travesty that has been allowed to go on for decades. Will we ever uncover all of the facts? Will we ever know all of the TRUTH? Will the laws change? Will the manufacturers ever be held accountable? Keep in mind the 'power' that huge corporations have......Keep in mind and remember the unanswered cries for help from all of the women you are going to read about!

Many different issues are at hand with silicone related illnesses. Not only are we the recipients of the silicone gel, polyurethane/silicone gel, and saline/silicone

Breast implants affected but so are our families, our bosses, our friends......all those who once knew us as vibrant and full of life now have trouble understanding we are sick. We mostly look the same but inside we are not the same! Most days are spent in considerable pain and exhaustion. Some days we can do so much but the next day, and the next and the next we might not be able to get out of bed. We might exhibit feelings of anger, despair, we may feel discouraged, we may lash out at the one we love the most.... not understanding why ourselves, and even worse unable to control it!

We find it difficult to think, sit, talk, walk, sleep, even be sociable, on the other hand; however, we might appear normal. Just because we did something once doesn't mean we can do it now! These toxins in our bodies affect every organ, every tissue, every muscle, even the brain....we have been chemically poisoned! We women as a group are pleading for "UNBIASED" medical research regarding our illnesses and pray someone finds a way to DETOX our bodies. Things could have been so much easier if the manufacturers had accepted responsibility for their mistakes and tried to help each of us get better so that we could continue to be productive members of society. Also, I believe they now, should be required to medically take care of each and every one of us for the rest of our lives! We have no idea what illness or disease will befall us next. Most of us now are receiving Social Security Disability and some of us Supplemental Security Payments as well. This could have all been avoided!

The American Taxpayer did not have to be responsible whether we eat or have clothes, or pay electric bills or house payments! We were all actively pursuing a life! Now most of us are in bed or confined to a wheelchair or to our home, if we have one! Please hear our CRY now!

Section Two - Facts Years 1964 through 2000

FACTS:

1954 - Dow Corning/Chemical finds that silica in silicone implants has a GH order of TOXICITY!

1954/55 - Dow Chemical was informed …..by scientist, H. C. Spencer (1954) that silicone causes health problems, and by Dow Chemical scientist, V.K. Rowe (1955) that silicone spreads throughout the body and causes organ damage!

1960 - Silicone injections were classified as a criminal offense!

1968 - A secrete study conducted by Dow, revealed that dogs were implanted with silicone gel filled bags and the silicone leaked and dispersed through their systems!

1968 - Cock roaches went into the silicone fluid "only"……and…..never got more than a few

inches from the dish before DYING!   (Texaco & Shell studies obtained from Dow Corning)

1975 - "I don't know who is responsible for the decision (to put faulty implants on the market) but it has to be right up there with the Pinto Gas Tank!!! (Bob Schnabel, Dow salesman in a letter to his boss)!

1975 - Plastic surgeons complained to Dow Corning that the implants were OILY and seemed to be LEAKING, salesmen were instructed to wash and dry the implants before showing them to doctors. (Buyers)!

1975 - Dow Corning's' company training video for plastic surgeons is edited ....to delete... ...references to implant RUPTURES!

1976 - Thomas Talcott, Sr., Dow Corning Materials Engineer, leaves Dow Corning in a dispute over the safety of silicone!

19

1976 - Dow Corning reveals that the lining of silicone implants loses strength when sitting on the shelf!

1976 - Art Rathjen, a Dow Corning Technical Services Specialist, complained about the lack of any scientific evidence for safety of silicone!

1978 - Dow Corning MISREPRESENTS in a patient brochure, that laboratory studies prove that implants last a lifetime!

1978 - William Boley, (Dow Corning's Chief of Biomaterials Safety) said that it is HIGHLY PROBABLE, that a woman's onset of LUPUS IS CONNECTED to silicone implants!

1978 - Dow Corning started receiving COMPLAINTS from salespeople and surgeons, that implants can spontaneously RUPTURE!

1985 - William Boley and other Dow scientists conclude, that the preponderance of available data suggests that silicone can produce immune mediated diseases!

1990 - At hearings in December 1990, Dow Corning MISLED the House Committee on Government Operations by testifying that silicone posed NO SAFETY problems or health risks! In addition, Dow Corning also REFUSED to provide KEY documents requested by the Committee...... Representative James Traficant!

1992 - The F D A LIMITS future sales of silicone breast implants!

1993 - Dow Corning acknowledges, that silicone may NOT be INERT!

1993 - Chief medical officer for Dow Corning said, "It clearly raises my concern that silicone gel MIGHT CAUSE IMMUNE SYSTEM DISEASES"!

1994 - Plastic surgeons file lawsuits against Dow Corning for MISREPRESENTING the quality of the implants!

1994 - If you have or had a ruptured silicone breast implant or breast implants PERIOD.......you WILL be denied health insurance coverage!

1999 - The Institute of Medicine's National Science Panel found no "known" link between silicone breast implants and connective tissue disease or systemic diseases

2000 - Spring of 2000, Representative Bliley of the United States Congress, launched a full scale "criminal investigation" regarding the testing of breast implants

Section Three - Profile of Chemicals Used in the Manufacture of Silicone Breast Implants

THE CHEMICAL PROFILE FOR BREAST IMPLANTS From the Environmental Health Information Service via National Institutes of Health:

1. *METHYL ETHYL KETONE*
2. *CYCLOHEXANONE*
3. *ISOPROPYL ALCOHOL*
4. *DENATURED ALCOHOL*
5. *ACETONE*
6. *URETHANE*
7. *POLYVINYL CHLORIDE (liquid vinyl)*
8. *LACQUER THINNER*
9. *ETHYL ACETATE*
10. *EPOXY RESIN*
11. *EPOXY HARDENER*
12. *AMINE*
13. *PRINTING INK*
14. *TOLUENE*
15. *DICHLOROMETHAN (methylene chloride)*
16. *FREON*
17. *SILICONE*
18. *FLUX*
19. *SOLDER*

20. *METAL CLEANING ACID*

21. *LOFOL (formaldehyde)*

22. *TALCUM POWDER*

23. *COLOR PIGMENTS AS RELEASE AGENTS*

24. *OAKITE (cleaning solvent)*

25. *EASTMAN 910 GLUE (cyanoacyrylates)*

26. *ETHYLENE OXIDE (ETO)*

27. *CARBON BLACK*

28. *XYLENE*

29. *HEXONE*

30. *HEXANONE-2*

31. *THIXON-OSN-2*

32. *ANTIOXIDANT (rubber)*

33. *ACID STEARIC*

34. *ZINC OXIDE*

35. *NAPTHA (rubber solvent)*

36. *PHENOL*

37. *BENZENE*

38. *PLATINUM II (non-organic) (one of the most toxic heavy metals known)*

CHEMICAL LIST of ingredients used to manufacture silicone and silicone/polyurethane breast implants................

People working in the plants that manufacture these chemicals LIMIT their exposure to them. It is unbelievable that as "intelligent" human beings we have allowed this type of "internal" chemical exposure.

(These are via the National Institute of Health via the NTP Chemical Repository [Radian Corporation, August 29, 1991])

1. METHYL ETHYL KETONE - Clear Colorless Liquid

SAX Toxicity Evaluation - THR: Moderately toxic by ingestion, skin contact and intraperitoneal routes. Human systemic effects by inhalation. An experimental teratogen. Experimental reproductive effects. A strong irritant. Human eye irritation @ 350 ppm. Affects peripheral nervous system and central nervous system. Uses: This compound is used as a solvent in nitrocellulose coating and vinyl film manufacture, in smokeless powder manufacture, in cements and adhesives, dewaxing of lubricating oils, "Glyptal" resins, paint removers, organic synthesis, cleaning fluids, acrylic coatings; intermediate in drug manufacture, manufacture of colorless synthetic resins; swelling agent of resins, intermediate in the manufacture of ketones and amines; and printing catalyst and carrier.

ACUTE/CHRONIC HAZARDS: This compound may be harmful by inhalation, ingestion or skin absorption. It is a severe irritant of the skin and eyes. It is also an irritant of the mucous membranes and upper respiratory tract. When heated to decomposition it emits TOXIC fumes of carbon monoxide and carbon dioxide.

When working with this chemical, wear a NIOSH-approved full face chemical cartride respirator equipped with the appropriate organic vapor cartridges. If that is not available, a half face respirator similarly equipped plus airtight goggles can be substituted. However, please note that half face respirators provide *a substantially lower level of protection than do full face respirators.*

STORAGE: You should store this chemical in an explosion-proof refrigerator and keep it away from oxidizing materials.

SYMPTOMS: Symptoms of exposure to this compound may include severe irritation of the eyes, irritation of the skin and upper respiratory tract, headache, dizziness and nausea. Other symptoms may include weakness, fatigue, possible respiratory arrest, diarrhea, vomiting, stomach and/or intestinal irritation and unconsciousness. It may cause irritation of the nose and throat, diminished vision, mild vertigo and narcosis. It may also cause central nervous system effects and neuropathy. It may irritate the mucous membranes. Prolonged exposure may produce central nervous system depression. Repeated exposure is reported to cause permanent brain and nervous system damage.

Eye contact may result in slight conjunctival hyperemia developing to severe anterioruveitis. It may also result in corneal injury. Prolonged skin contact may defat the skin and produce dermatitis.

2. CYCLOHEXANONE - Colorless Liquid

SAX Toxicity Evaluation - THR: Poison by intravenous route. Moderately toxic by ingestion. A systemic irritant by inhalation and ingestion. A skin irritant.

ACUTE/CHRONIC HAZARDS: This compound may be harmful by inhalation, ingestion or through skin absorption. Vapor or mist is irritating to the eyes, mucous membranes, upper respiratory tract and skin. It may also be irritating to the nose and throat. When heated to decomposition it may emit toxic fumes of carbon dioxide and carbon monoxide.When working with this chemical, wear a NIOSH-approved full face chemical cartride respirator equipped with the appropriate organic vapor cartridges. If that is not available, a half face respirator similarly equipped plus *airtight goggles can be substituted. However, please note that half face respirators provide a substantially lower level of protection than do full face respirators.*

STORAGE: You should store this chemical in an explosion-proof refrigerator and away from all mineral acids and bases. STORE AWAY FROM SOURCES OF IGNITION.

SYMPTOMS: Symptoms of exposure to this compound include dizziness, nausea, loss of consciousness, skin rash, central nervous system depression, upper respiratory tract irritation and chemical pneumonitis. In high concentrations it may cause narcosis. It may cause defatting of the skin and a dry, scaly, fissured dermatitis, mild conjunctivitis, excitement, loss of equilibrium, stupor, coma and death as a result of respiratory failure.It may also cause gastrointestinal disturbances. Other symptoms of exposure may include vomiting and irritation to the eyes, skin, nose and throat. It may cause kidney and liver damage. It may also cause eye redness, swelling of the mucous membranes, tearing, redness, swelling and pain or thickening of the skin, hyperactivity, rapid breathing, difficulty breathing, fatigue, headache, incoordination, tremors, anesthesia, increase in respiratory rate, diarrhea, circulatory collapse, pulmonary edema, confusion and weakness. It may also cause hepatocellular degeneration and toxic glomerulonephritis.

3. ISOPROPYL ALCOHOL- Clear Colorless Liquid

SAX Toxicity Evaluation - THR - Poison by ingestion and subcutaneous routes. Moderately toxic to humans by an unspecified route. Moderately toxic experimentally by intravenous and intraperitoneal routes. Mildly toxic by skin contact. Human systemic effects by ingestion or inhalation. Experimental teratogenic and reproductive effects. Mutagenic data. An eye and skin irritant.

ACUTE/CHRONIC HAZARDS: This compound is an irritant of the skin, eyes, mucous membranes and upper respiratory tract. It is flammable and flashback along the vapor trail may occur. When heated to *decomposition it emits acrid smoke and toxic fumes of carbon monoxide, carbon dioxide and unidentified organic compounds. This chemical has not been tested for permeation by "Radian Corporation"; however, the Gloves+ expert system was used to extrapolate permeation test information from compounds in the same chemical class. The Gloves+ system uses permeation data from literature sources; therefore, extra safety margins should be used with the estimated protection time. If this chemical makes direct contact with your glove, or if a tear, puncture or hole develops, replace them at once.*

The Gloves+ expert system is a tool that can help people better manage protection from chemicals; however, this tool cannot replace sound judgment nor make technical decisions.

Our Gloves+ expert system is designed to offer initial advice and assistance in glove selection while the final glove selection should be made by knowledgeable individuals based on the specific circumstances involved.

When working with this chemical, wear a NIOSH-approved full face chemical cartride respirator equipped with the appropriate organic vapor cartridges. If that is not available, a half face respirator similarly equipped plus airtight goggles can be substituted. However, please note that half face respirators provide a substantially lower level of protection than do full face respirators.

STORAGE: You should store this material in a refrigerator. STORE AWAY FROM SOURCES OF IGNITION.

SYMPTOMS: Symptoms of exposure to this compound include irritation of the skin, eyes, nose, throat and respiratory tract, dizziness, nausea, central nervous system depression, giddiness and headache. It can cause flushing, decrease in pulse rate, lowered blood pressure, anesthesia, narcosis, mental depression, hallucinations, distorted perceptions, dyspnea, respiratory depression, vomiting, corneal burns, eye damage and coma.. It can also cause abdominal pain, *hematemesis, areflexia, oliguria followed by diuresis, generalized tenderness, induration and edema of muscles. Prolonged skin contact may cause corrosion. Drunkenness may also occur.*

4. DENATURED ALCOHOL - Clear, colorless, very mobile liquid

SAX Toxicity Evaluation - THR - MODERATE-LOW via oral, intravenous and dermal routes; probably also via inhalation routes. MUTATION data. It is rapidly oxidized in the body to carbon dioxide and water, and no cumulative effect occurs. Concentrations below 1000 ppm usually produce no signs of intoxication. It is a central nervous system depressant in humans. It causes teratogenic effects, equivocal TUMORIGENIC effects, gastrointestinal effects and glandular effects in humans.

ACUTE/ CHRONIC HAZARDS: This compound is harmful by ingestion, inhalation or skin absorption. It is an irritant of the eyes, nose and throat. It is also an irritant of the skin. Flashback along the vapor trail may occur. When heated to decomposition it emits fumes of carbon monoxide and carbon dioxide.

Recommendations based on permeation test results are made for handling the undiluted chemical. If this chemical makes direct contact with your glove, or if a tear, puncture or hole develops, replace them at once.

When working with this chemical, wear a NIOSH-approved full face positive pressure supplied-air respirator or a self-contained breathing apparatus (SCBA).

STORAGE: You should store this chemical in an explosion-proof refrigerator, and protect it from moisture. STORE AWAY FROM SOURCES OF IGNITION.

SYMPTOMS: Symptoms of exposure to this compound may include irritation of the eyes and nose, drowsiness and headache. Other symptoms may include stupor, nausea, mental excitement or depression, vomiting, flushing and coma. It can cause *irritation of the respiratory tract, intraocular tension, ataxia, sleepiness, narcosis, impaired perception and incoordination. It can also cause lowered inhibitions, dizziness, shallow respiration, unconsciousness and death. Eye contact results in immediate stinging and burning, with reflex closure of the lids and tearing; transitory injury of the corneal epithelium and hyperemia of the conjunctiva. Other symptoms may include irritation of the throat, lassitude and loss of appetite. Vapor exposure may cause watering of the eyes. It can cause mild redness and burning of the skin, sensory and motor disturbances, mood swings, overconfidence, dulled then lost discrimination, memory, concentration, and insight; vasodilatation, increased sweating and heat sensation. It can also cause drunkenness, slow comprehension, numbness and fatigue. Slurred speech, visual impairment such as blurred or double vision and slowed reaction time may result. Other symptoms may include nervousness and tremors, Chronic symptoms may include weight loss, cirrhosis of the liver, gastroenteritis, anorexia, diarrhea, polyneuritis with pain, motor and sensory loss in the extremities, optic atrophy and loss or impairment of other abilities, excitement, acute and chronic gastritis, malabsorption syndrome, acute and chronic pancreatitis, anemia due to acute or chronic blood myopathy, alcoholic cardiomyopathy, lactic acidosis, hypomagnesemia, hypouricemia, hyperlipidemia, pulmonary aspiration and respiratory infections. Chronic exposure may also result in serious neurological and mental disorders. (e.g. brain damage, memory loss, sleep disturbances, and psychoses) Other symptoms include mucous membrane irritation, central nervous system depression, giddiness, jaundice, pain in upper abdomen on the right side and staggering gait. It may cause liver, kidney and heart damage. The pupils are sometimes widely dilated and unreactive to light. The liquid can defat the skin, producing a dermatitis characterized by drying and fissuring. It rarely causes temporary blindness. Ingestion of this compound can enhance the effects of coumarin, anticoagulants, antihistamines, hypnotics, sedatives, tranquilizers, insulin, monoamine oxidase inhibitors, and antidepressants.*

5. ACETONE - Clear Colorless Liquid

SAX Toxicity Evaluation - THR: Moderately TOXIC by various routes. A skin and severe eye irritant. Human systemic effects by inhalation and ingestion. Narcotic in high concentrations. In industry, no injurious effects have been reported other that skin irritation resulting from its defatting action, or headache from prolonged inhalation. A common air contaminant. Dangerous disaster hazard due to fire and explosion hazard.

ACUTE/CHRONIC HAZARDS: This compound is TOXIC by ingestion and inhalation. It is an irritant of the eyes, mucous membranes, nose, throat and upper respiratory tract. It rapidly penetrates skin. It is absorbed through the lungs. It is narcotic in high concentrations. When heated to decomposition it emits TOXIC fumes of carbon monoxide, carbon dioxide and unidentified organic compounds in black smoke. If Tyvek-type disposable protective clothing is not worn during handling of this chemical, wear disposable Tyvek-type sleeves taped to your gloves.

When working with this chemical, wear a NIOSH-approved full face chemical cartridge respirator equipped with the appropriate organic vapor cartridges. If that is not available, a half face respirator similarly equipped plus airtight goggles can be substituted. However, please note that half face respirators provide a substantially lower level of protection than do full face respirators.

STORAGE PRECAUTIONS: You should store this chemical in an explosion-proof refrigerator and keep it away from oxidizing materials and acids. Protect from moisture and light. STORE AWAY FROM SOURCES OF IGNITION. If possible, it would be prudent to store this chemical under inert atmosphere.

SYMPTOMS: Symptoms of exposure to this compound may include headache, nausea, vomiting and dizziness. High concentrations cause narcosis. Irritation of the mucous membranes and upper respiratory tract may also occur. On prolonged contact, irritation of the skin may occur. Other symptoms include central nervous system effects, convulsions, kidney and liver injury, unconsciousness and death. Coma has been reported. Fatigue, excitement and bronchial irritation have also been reported. Exposure may cause restlessness, hematemesis, collapse and stupor. It may also cause slight intoxication, central nervous system depression, lassitude, drowsiness, loss of appetite, insomnia, somnolence, loss of strength, shallow respiration, hyperglycemia, weakness of the limbs, lightheadedness, general malaise and hepatorenal lesions. It can cause dryness of the mouth, uncoordinated movements, loss of coordinated speech, rapid and irregular respiration rate, fainting, coughing, inflammation of the stomach and duodenum and giddiness. It can also cause changes in EEG, changes in carbohydrate metabolism, nasal and respiratory system effects, muscle weakness and metabolic changes. Hypoglycemia may result.

Skin contact may result in drying of the skin. It may also result in mild edema and hyperemia. Prolonged skin contact may lead to defatting of the skin resulting in dermatitis. Erythema also occurs from prolonged contact.. Ingestion may cause gastric irritation. Eye contact may result in burns. Severe eye damage may occur. Stinging sensation of the eyes may also occur.

Use of alcoholic beverages enhances the TOXIC effect of this compound. Preexisting eye or skin disorders may be aggravated by exposure.

6. URETHANE - Colorless crystals or white granular powder

SAX Toxicity Evaluation - THR: Moderately TOXIC by ingestion, intraperitoneal, subcutaneous, intramuscular, parenteral, intravenous and possibly other routes. An experimental CARCINOGEN, neoplastigen and TUMORIGEN. A transplacental CARCINOGEN.

An initiator. Experimental reproductive effects. A powerful teratogen in mice. Human Mutagenic data. It has been found in over 1000 beverages sold in the United States. The most heavily contaminated liquors are bourbons, sherries and fruit brandies (some had 1000 to 12000 ppb). Many whiskeys, table and dessert wines, brandies and liqueurs contain potentially hazardous amounts. The allowable limit in alcoholic beverages is 125 ppb as of January 1, 1989. It is formed as a side product during processing.

ACUTE/CHRONIC HAZARDS: This compound is TOXIC by ingestion. It is harmful by inhalation or skin absorption. It may cause irritation. When heated to decomposition it emits TOXIC fumes of carbon monoxide, carbon dioxide and nitrogen oxides.

This chemical has not been tested for permeation by Radian Corporation; however, the Gloves+ expert system was used to extrapolate permeation test information from compounds in the same chemical class. The Gloves+ system uses permeation date from literature sources; therefore, extra safety margins should be used with the estimated protection time. If this chemical makes direct contact with your glove, or if a tear, puncture or hole develops, replace them at once.

Where the neat test chemical is weighed and diluted, wear a NIOSH-approved half face respirator equipped with a combination filter cartridge, i.e. organic vapor/acid gas/HEPA (specific for organic vapors, HCl, acid gas, SO2 and a high efficiency particulate filter).Since this chemical is a KNOWN or SUSPECTED CARCINOGEN you should contact a physician for advice regarding the possible long term health effects and potential recommendation for medical monitoring. Recommendations from the physician will depend upon the specific compound, its chemical, physical and TOXICITY properties, the exposure level, length of exposure, and the route of exposure.

STORAGE PRECAUTIONS: You should store this chemical under ambient temperatures.

SYMPTOMS: Symptoms of exposure to this compound include burning in the throat, watery to bloody diarrhea, abdominal pain, oliguria, fall in blood pressure, anuria, cardiovascular collapse, delirium, convulsions, muscular weakness with respiratory failure, coma, hemorrhages and kidney and liver injury. It may cause nausea, vomiting and bone marrow depression. Other symptoms may include central nervous system depression and focal degeneration in the brain. Exposure may lead to gastroenteric hemorrhages and drowsiness. It may also cause irritation. Anorexia and dizziness have been reported. Large doses make debilitated persons more prone to hepatitis or fatal hepatic necrosis.

7. POLYVINYL CHLORIDE (Liquid Vinyl) This ingredient was used in all medical devices made at Edward's Lab, from tubing to gel., so I heard) - Viscous white liquid (51% emulsion in water)

SAX Toxicity Evaluation - THR: Not available

ACUTE/ CHRONIC HAZARDS: This material may cause irritation on contact. When heated to decomposition it emits TOXIC fumes. Where the neat test chemical is weighed and diluted, wear a NIOSH-approved half face respirator equipped with an organic vapor/acid gas cartridge (specific for organic vapors, HC1, acid gas and SO2) with a dust/mist filter.

STORAGE PRECAUTIONS: You should protect this material from exposure to light, and store it in a refrigerator.

SYMPTOMS: Symptoms of exposure to this compound may include dermatitis. It may cause digestive system CANCERS, CANCERS of the BREASTS and URINARY ORGANS in WOMEN. Inhalation of dust or decomposition fumes leads to respiratory distress.

8. LACQUER THINNER - Clear, colorless to amber liquid

SAX Toxicity Evaluation - THR: POISON by intraperitoneal route. Moderately TOXIC by intravenous, subcutaneous and possibly other routes. Mildly TOXIC by inhalation. An experimental teratogen. Human SYSTEMIC effects by inhalation. EXPERIMENTAL REPRODUCTIVE effects. Mutagenic data. A human eye irritant. An EXPERIMENTAL skin and SEVERE eye *irritant. In the few cases of acute POISONING reported, the effect has been that of a narcotic, the workman passing through a stage of intoxication into one of a coma. Recovery following removal from exposure has been the rule. A common air contaminant.*

ACUTE/CHRONIC HAZARDS: This compound may cause irritation of the respiratory tract, mucous membranes and throat. It may also cause eye and skin irritation. It may be harmful by inhalation, ingestion or skin absorption. It is readily absorbed through the skin. When heated to decomposition it emits TOXIC fumes of carbon dioxide and carbon monoxide.

This chemical has not been tested for permeation by Radian Corporation; however, the Gloves+ expert system was used to extrapolate permeation test information from compounds in the same chemical class. The Gloves+ system uses permeation data from literature sources; therefore, extra safety margins should be used with the estimated protection time(s). If this chemical makes direct contact with your glove, or if a tear, puncture or hole develops, replace them at once.

Where the neat test chemical is weighed and diluted, wear a NIOSH-approved half face respirator equipped with and organic vapor/acid gas cartridge (specific for organic vapors, HCl, acid gas and SO2) with a dust/mist filter.

STORAGE PRECAUTIONS: You should store this chemical in an explosion-proof refrigerator and keep it away from moisture. If possible, it would be prudent to store this compound under inert atmosphere. STORE AWAY FROM SOURCES OF IGNITION.

SYMPTOMS: Symptoms of exposure to this compound include eye irritation, dilation of the pupils, impairment of reaction in association with fatigue, slight pallor of the fundi, inebriation, ocular disturbances and reddening of vision. It may cause dizziness, headache, nausea, mental confusion, blood disease and dermatitis. It may also cause giddiness. Other symptoms may include hallucinations or distorted perceptions, narcosis

47

in high concentrations, motor activity changes. An occasional report of CHRONIC POISONING describes an anemia and leucopenia. It causes loss of appetite, a bad taste, lassitude, impairment of coordination and reaction time and an enlarged liver. It may cause central nervous system depression, bone marrow depression, petechial hemorrhages, noncoagulated blood, CONGESTION OF ALL ORGANS, SEVERE bone marrow aplasia, necrosis or fatty degeneration of the HEART, LIVER and adrenals, weakness, euphoria, vomiting, tightness in the chest, blurred vision, tremors, shallow and rapid respiration, ventricular irregularities including fibrillation, paralysis, convulsions, violent excitement or delirium, unconsciousness, kidney or liver damage, skin irritation, scaling and cracking, drowsiness, nervousness, pallor, petechiae, abnormal bleeding, irreversible encephalopathy with ataxia, tremulousness, emotional lability, diffuse cerebral atrophy and DEATH. It may also cause abnormal tendon reflexes, reduced grasping power, decreased finger agility, metabolic acidosis, hepatomegaly, exhilaration, lightheadedness, cardiovascular collapse, cardiac arrhythmia's, bradycardia, mydrasis, insomnia, restlessness, staggering gait, lack of self control, stupor, increased irritability (personality changes), exaggerated mood swings, equilibrium disorders and vertigo. Symptoms of exposure may include skin sensation such as a pins and needles feeling or numbness and difficulty in seeing bright light. It may cause high urinary pH, nightmares, vertical nystagmus and status epilepticus. It may also cause loss of memory, anorexia, palpitation and aplastic anemia. Other symptoms include renal but also neural and especially cerebellar dystrophy, lacrimation, hilarity, nasal mucous secretion and metallic taste. High concentrations may result in paresthesia, collapse, cardiac sensitization and FATAL CARDIOTOXICITY. It may cause irritation to the nose and throat, respiratory arrest, coughing, gagging, distress, pulmonary edema, griping and diarrhea. It may also cause chemical pneumonitis, coma and conjunctivitis.

9. ETHYL ACETATE - Clear, colorless, mobile liquid

SAX Toxicity Evaluation - THR: Moderately irritating to the eyes, mucous membranes, gums and respiratory tract. Prolonged inhalation can cause renal or hepatic damage. Prolonged contact can cause conjunctival irritation and corneal clouding. POISON by inhalation. Moderately TOXIC by intraperitoneal route. Mildly TOXIC by ingestion. Mutagenic data.

ACUTE/CHRONIC HAZARDS: This chemical is TOXIC by inhalation, ingestion, or skin absorption. It is an irritant of the skin, eyes, mucous membranes and respiratory tract. The vapor is heavier than air and can travel a considerable distance to a source of ignition and flash back. When heated to decomposition it emits ACRID smoke, irritating fumes and TOXIC fumes of carbon monoxide and carbon dioxide.

When working with this chemical, wear a NIOSH-approved full face chemical cartridge respirator equipped with the appropriate organic vapor cartridges. If that is not available, a half face respirator similarly equipped plus airtight goggles can be substituted. However, please note that half face respirators provide a substantially lower level of protection than do full face respirators.

STORAGE PRECAUTIONS: You should keep this material in a tightly closed container under an inert atmosphere, and store it in an explosion-proof refrigerator. STORE AWAY FROM SOURCES OF IGNITION.

SYMPTOMS: Symptoms of exposure to this compound include irritation of the eyes, mucous membranes, gums and respiratory tract. Irritation of the nasal passages and throat may occur. Skin irritation may also occur. Prolonged contact may cause corneal clouding. Prolonged inhalation can cause renal or hepatic damage. Prolonged inhalation may also cause damage to the lungs and heart. Other symptoms include gastrointestinal disturbances, nausea, headache and vomiting. Exposure may cause narcosis and dermatitis. It may also cause drowsiness, unconsciousness and sleepiness. High concentrations can cause stupor. Repeated or prolonged contact can cause drying of the skin and cracking. Central nervous system depression may occur. Chronic exposure may lead to anemia, leukocytosis, cloudy swelling and fatty degeneration of the viscera.

10. EPOXY RESIN - Clear colorless liquid

SAX Toxicity Evaluation - THR: Moderate via oral, inhalation and dermal routes. An experimental CARCINOGEN and equivocal TUMORIGENIC agent.

ACUTE/CHRONIC HAZARDS: This compound is a STRONG SKIN and TISSUE irritant. This chemical has not been tested for permeation by Radian Corporation; however, the Gloves+ expert system was used to extrapolate permeation test information from compounds in the same chemical class. The Gloves+ system uses permeation data from literature sources; therefore, extra safety margins should be used with the estimated protection time(s). If this chemical makes direct contact with your glove, or if a tear, puncture or hole develops, replace then at once.

STORAGE PRECAUTIONS: You should store this chemical under refrigerated temperatures, and protect it from moisture.

SYMPTOMS: Symptoms of exposure to this compound include strong skin and tissue irritation. It may also cause central nervous system depression. Other symptoms include testicular atrophy, conjunctivitis, eye and skin inflammation, mucous membrane irritation, vesiculation, blistering, dyspnea, difficulty in breathing, dermatitis, respiratory failure and coughing.

Symptoms of exposure in animals include lung congestion, leukopenia and necrosis of the thymus. Other symptoms in animals include vasodilation, unstable gait and liver congestion. It has also caused chronic pulmonary edema. (Both Epoxy resin and Epoxy Hardener are chemically known as glycosides Ether of Bisphenol A)

11. Epoxy Hardener - Tan Flakes

SAX Toxicity Evaluation - THR: POISON by ingestion, subcutaneous and intraperitoneal routes.

An experimental CARCINOGEN and tumorigen. Human systemic effects by ingestion. An eye irritant. Mutagenic data. It is not rapidly absorbed through the skin.

ACUTE/CHRONIC HAZARDS: This compound is HARMFUL by inhalation, ingestion or skin contact. It may be absorbed through the skin. When heated to decomposition it emits TOXIC fumes of carbon monoxide, carbon dioxide, nitrogen oxides, HYDROGEN CYANIDE and aniline. This compound may cause irritation to the skin, eyes and respiratory tract.

This chemical has not been tested for permeation by Radian Corporation; however, the Gloves+ expert system was used to extrapolate permeation test information from compounds in the same chemical class.   The Gloves+ system uses permeation data from literature sources; therefore, extra safety margins should be used with the estimated protection time(s). If this chemical makes direct contact with your glove, or if a tear, puncture or hole develops, replace them at once.

STORAGE PRECAUTIONS: You should keep this material in a tightly closed container under an inert atmosphere, and store it at refrigerated temperatures. Keep it away from oxidizing materials and protect it from light.

SYMPTOMS: Exposure to this compound causes TOXIC HEPATITIS. It is the causative agent in "Epping Jaundice", a condition which includes severe right-upper-quadrant pain, and high fever and chills, with subsequent jaundice. This condition may also result in portal inflammation, eosinophil infiltration, cholangitis and cholestasis. Other symptoms of exposure to this compound include weakness, abdominal pain, nausea and/or vomiting and anorexia. Inhalation and/or ingestion of the dust leads to liver damage. Eye contact may cause burning, itching and tearing. It is painfully irritating to the eyes at 4 ppm. Skin contact can result in reddening and swelling, as well as skin sensitization causing allergic dermatitis with rash, itching, hives and swelling of the arms and legs. Myocardial damage has also been reported. It is suspect in the development of CHOROIDAL

MELANOMA. It may also cause kidney damage. Persons with pre-existing skin disorders or impaired pulmonary function may be more susceptible to the effects of this chemical. Other symptoms include corneal burns, irritation to the skin, eyes and respiratory tract, blood and spleen damage and conjunctivitis.

12. Amine - All the Author could find on this substance is a definition which follows:

    a. Any of the organic compounds produced when one or more hydrogen atoms of "ammonia" is replaced with organic groups.

b. When used as a suffix in a long name for an organic molecule (i.e. "amine" in glutamine"), it indicates the presence of an -NH2 group.

13. PRINTING INK - Viscous semi-solid suspension also very viscous black liquid

SAX Toxicity Evaluation - THR: Component 1: A human CARCINOGEN by inhalation which produces gastrointestinal TUMORS. A human teratogen by inhalation which causes testicular TUMORS in the FETUS. An eye irritant.

Component 2: Mildly TOXIC by ingestion, inhalation and skin contact. A nuisance dust in high concentrations. While it is true that the tiny particulates of carbon black contain some molecules of CARCINOGENIC materials, the CARCINOGENS are apparently help tightly and are not eluted by hot or cold water, gastric juices or blood plasma.

Avoid glove types which exhibit breakthrough times of less than the anticipated task time plus an adequate safety factor. If this chemical makes direct contact with your glove, or if a tear, puncture or hole develops, replace them at once.

Where the neat test chemical is weighed and diluted, wear a NIOSH-approved half face respirator equipped wit an organic vapor/acid gas cartridge (specific for organic vapors, HCl, acid gas and SO2) with a dust/mist filter.

ACUTE/CHRONIC HAZARDS: Component 1 is an irritant of the skin and eyes and is harmful by ingestion. When heated to decomposition this compound emits acrid smoke and fumes.

STORAGE AND PRECAUTIONS: You should protect this material from exposure to light, and store it under ambient temperatures.

SYMPTOMS: Symptoms of exposure to Component 1 may include mild irritation of the respiratory tract, severe lung irritation, pulmonary edema, central nervous system excitement followed by depression and irritation of the stomach. It may cause a mild laxative effect. It may also cause anal seepage and pneumonia, irritation, granuloma and skin reaction. It dissolves and prevents absorption of vitamin A from intestinal contents and aspiration may occur with subsequent pulmonary infiltration. Irritation to the skin and eyes may also occur. Symptoms of exposure to Component 2 may include black pigmentation of the palpebral conjunctiva.

14. TOLUENE - Clear, colorless to amber liquid

SAX Toxicity Evaluation - THR: POISON by intraperitoneal route. Moderately TOXIC by intravenous, subcutaneous and possibly OTHER routes. Mildly TOXIC by inhalation. An experimental teratogen. Human systemic effects by inhalation. Experimental reproductive effects. Mutagenic data. A human eye irritant. An experimental skin and severe eye irritant. In the few cases of acute POISONING reported, the effect has been that of a narcotic, the workman passing through a stage of intoxication into one of c COMA. Recovery following removal from exposure has been the rule. A common air contaminant.

Where the neat test chemical is weighed and diluted, wear a NIOSH-approved half face respirator equipped with an organic vapor/acid gas cartridge (specific for organic vapors, HCl, acid gas and SO2) with a dust/mist filter.

ACUTE/CHRONIC HAZARDS: This compound may cause irritation of the respiratory tract, mucous membranes and throat. It may also cause eye and skin irritation. It may be harmful by inhalation, ingestion or skin absorption. It is readily absorbed through the skin. When heated to decomposition it emits TOXIC fumes of carbon dioxide and carbon monoxide.

Where the neat test chemical is weighed and diluted, wear a NIOSH-approved half face respirator equipped with an organic vapor/acid gas cartridge (specific for organic vapors, HCl, acid gas and SO2) with a dust/mist filter.

STORAGE PRECAUTIONS: You should store this chemical in an explosion-proof refrigerator and keep it away from moisture. If possible, it would be prudent to store this compound under inert atmosphere. STORE AWAY FROM SOURCES OF IGNITION.

SYMPTOMS: Symptoms of exposure to this compound include eye irritation, dilation of the pupils, impairment of reaction in association with fatigue, slight pallor of the fundi, inebriation, ocular disturbances and reddening of vision. It may cause dizziness, headache, nausea, mental confusion, blood disease and dermatitis. It may also cause giddiness. Other symptoms may include hallucinations or distorted perceptions, narcosis in high concentrations, motor activity changes. An occasional report of CHRONIC POISONING describes an anemia and leucopenia. It causes loss of appetite, a bad taste, lassitude, impairment of coordination and reaction time and an enlarged liver.It may cause central nervous system depression, bone marrow depression, petechial hemorrhages, noncoagulated blood, congestion of ALL ORGANS, SEVERE bone marrow

61

aplasia, necrosis or fatty degeneration of the heart, liver, and adrenals, weakness, euphoria, vomiting, tightness in the chest, blurred vision, tremors, shallow and rapid respiration, ventricular irregularities including fibrillation, paralysis, convulsions, violent excitement or delirium, unconsciousness, kidney or liver damage, skin irritation, scaling and cracking, drowsiness, nervousness, pallor, petechiae, abnormal bleeding, irreversible encephalopathy with ataxia, tremulousness, emotional lability, diffuse cerebral atrophy and DEATH. It may also cause abnormal tendon reflexes, reduced grasping power, decreased finger agility, metabolic acidosis, hepatomegaly, exhilaration lightheadedness, cardiovascular collapse, cardiac arrhythmia's, bradycardia, mydrasis, insomnia, restlessness, staggering gait, lack of self control, stupor, increased irritability (personality changes), exaggerated mood swings, equilibrium disorders, and vertigo. Symptoms of exposure may include skin sensation such as pins and needles feeling or numbness and difficulty in seeing bright light. It may cause high urinary pH, nightmares, vertical nystagmus and status epilepticus. It may also cause loss of memory, anorexia, palpitation and aplastic anemia. Other symptoms includerenal but also neural and especially cerebellar DYSTROPHY, lacrimation, hilarity nasal mucous secretion, and metallic taste. High concentrations may result in paresthesia, collapse, cardiac sensitization and FATAL CARDIOTOXICITY. It may cause irritation to the nose and throat, respiratory arrest, coughing, gagging, distress,pulmonary edema, griping and diarrhea. It may also cause chemical pneumonitis,coma and conjunctivitis.

15. DICHLOROMETHAN (METHYLENE CHLORIDE) - Clear colorless liquid

SAX Toxicity Evaluation - THR: Poison by intravenous route. Moderately TOXIC by ingestion, subcutaneous and intraperitoneal routes. Mildly TOXIC by inhalation. An experimental CARCINOGEN and TUMORIGEN. An experimental teratogen. Experimental reproductive effects. An eye and SEVERE skin irritant. Human mutagenic data. There is CLEAR data stating this is via inhalation CARCINOGENIC to the Female Rat and to the Male and Female Mouse.

When working with this chemical avoid glove types which exhibit breakthrough times of less that the anticipated task time plus an adequate safety factor. If this chemical makes contact with your glove, or if a tear, puncture or hole develops, replace then at once. Wear a NIOSH-approved full face positive pressure supplied-air respirator or a self-contained breathing apparatus (SCBA). Since this chemical is a KNOWN or SUSPECTED

CARCINOGEN you should contact a physician for advice regarding the possible long term health effects and potential recommendation for medical monitoring. Recommendations from the physician will depend upon the specific compound, its chemical, physical and toxicity properties, the exposure level, length of exposure, and the route of exposure.

ACUTE/ CHRONIC HAZARDS: This compound is moderately TOXIC by all routes. It is an irritant of the skin, eyes and respiratory tract. It is readily absorbed through the skin. When heated to decomposition it emits TOXIC fumes of chlorine, hydrogen chloride gas, carbon monoxide, carbon dioxide and phosgene.

If Tyvek-type disposable protective clothing is not worn during handling of this chemical, wear disposable Tyvek-type sleeves taped to your gloves.

When working with this chemical, wear a NIOSH-approved full face positive pressure supplied-air respirator or a self-contained breathing apparatus (SCBA).

STORAGE PRECAUTIONS: You should store this chemical under refrigerated temperatures, and protect it from moisture. If possible, it would be prudent to store this compound under inert atmosphere.

SYMPTOMS: Symptoms of exposure to this compound may include headache, elevated blood concentrations of carboxyhemoglobin, nausea, and irritation of the skin and eyes. Central nervous system depression, pulmonary edema, hemolysis, chronic intoxication and paresthesia may also occur. Other symptoms include narcosis, temporary neurobehavioral effects, increase in serum bilirubin, increased urinary formic acid concentrations and increased risk of spontaneous abortion. In addition, intravascular hemolysis, unconsciousness, lack of response to painful stimuli, rapid followed by slowed respiration, erythema, blistering, TOXIC ENCEPHALOPATHY, painful joints, swelling of the extremities, mental impairment, diabetes, skin rash, aspiration pneumonia, gross hematuria, reduction of blood pH, gastrointestinal injury and narrowing of the intestinal lumen may also occur. Other symptoms may include upper respiratory tract irritation, giddiness, stupor, irritability, numbness, tingling in the limbs and hallucinations. A dry, scaly and fissured dermatitis, skin burns, coma and DEATH may also result. Other symptoms may include dizziness, sense of fullness in the head, sense of heat, dullness, lethargy and drunkenness. In addition, mental confusion, lightheadedness, vomiting, weakness, somnolence, lassitude, anorexia, depression, fatigue, vertigo, liver damage, nose and throat irritation, anesthetic effects, smarting and reddening of the skin, blood dyscrasias, acceleration of the pulse and congestion in the head may result. Staggering may also occur. Other symptoms of exposure to this compound may include neurasthenic disorders, digestive disturbances and acoustical and optical delusions.Arrhythmia's produced by catecholamines may also result. Additional symptoms include edema, faintness, loss of appetite and apathy. Hyporeflexia, gross hemoglobinuria, epiglottal edema, metabolic acidosis, gastrointestinal hemorrhage, ulceration of the duodenojejunal junction and diverticula may also occur. Other symptoms may include kidney damage, lung damage, corneal injury, abdominal pain and an increase in salivary gland tumors. Cyanosis may also occur. Exposure may also cause altered sleep time, convulsions, euphoria and a change in cardiac rate.

16. FREON - Clear, Colorless oily liquid

SAX Toxicity Evaluation - THR: A human POISON by ingestion. POISON experimentally by intravenous and subcutaneous routes. Moderately TOXIC by inhalation, skin contact andintraperitoneal routes. An experimental CARCINOGEN, neoplastigen,

TUMORIGEN and teratogen. Human systemic effects by ingestion and inhalation. An experimental transplacental CARCINOGEN. A strong narcotic. Experimental reproductive effects. A skin and eye irritant and a strong local irritant. Its smell and irritant effects warn of its presence at relatively safe concentrations. Human mutagenic date. A priority pollutant. Avoid glove types which exhibit breakthrough times of less than the anticipated task time plus an adequate safety factor. If this chemical makes direct contact with your glove, or if a tear, puncture or hole develops, replace them at once. When working with this chemical, wear a NIOSH-approved full face positive pressure supplied-air respirator or a self-contained breathing apparatus. (SCBA)

Since this chemical is a known or suspected CARCINOGEN you should contact a physician for advice regarding the possible long term health effects and potential recommendation for medical monitoring. Recommendations from the physician will depend upon the specific compound, its chemical, physical and toxicity properties, the exposure level, length of exposure, and the route of exposure.

ACUTE/CHRONIC HAZARDS: This compound is TOXIC by ingestion, inhalation, and skin contact.   It can be absorbed through the skin.   It is an irritant of the skin, eyes and respiratory tract.   The vapor is heavier than air and may travel a considerable distance to a source of ignition and flash back.   When heated to decomposition it emits TOXIC fumes of carbon monoxide, carbon dioxide, hydrogen chloride gas and phosgene.

If Tyvek-type disposable protective clothing is not worn during handling of this chemical, wear disposable Tyvek-type sleeves taped to your gloves.

When working with this chemical, wear a NIOSH-approved full face positive pressure supplied-air respirator or a self-contained breathing apparatus (SCBA).

STORAGE PRECAUTIONS: You should protect this chemical from exposure to light. Keep the container tightly closed under an inert atmosphere, and store it in an explosion-proof refrigerator. STORE AWAY FROM SOURCES OF IGNITION.

SYMPTOMS: Symptoms of exposure to this compound may include irritation of the skin, eyes and respiratory tract, corneal clouding and dermatitis. It may cause conjunctivitis, corneal ulceration, headache, mental confusion, depression, fatigue, albuminuria, central nervous system depression, convulsions, diarrhea, hepatomegaly, hypoglycemia, jaundice, narcosis and pulmonary edema. It may also cause flaccid paralysis without anesthesia, somnolence, cough, nausea, vomiting, hypermotility, ulceration, fatty liver degeneration, change in cardiac rate, cyanosis, coma, edema of the lungs and TOXIC effects on the kidneys. It may cause feeling of drunkenness, drowsiness, nconsciousness and DEATH from respiratory and CARDIAC FAILURE, defatting of the skin, swelling of the skin and chemical pneumonia. Other symptoms may include mental confusion, abdominal pains and liver and kidney damage. It can also cause watery stool, weak and rapid pulse and internal bleeding. It may cause corneal opacity. Other symptoms may include edema of the brain, vascular congestion in the lungs, heart and spleen, weight loss and oliguria. It may also cause dizziness, narcosis, intestinal hemorrhages, weakness, trembling and severe shock. Chronic exposure may result in loss of appetite, epigastric distress, tremors, nystagmus, leukocytosis and low blood sugar levels.

17. SILICONE - Colorless liquid

SAX Toxicity Evaluation - THR: POISON by intraperitoneal route. Moderately TOXIC by ingestion. It is corrosive to tissue.

Avoid glove types which exhibit breakthrough times of less than the anticipated task time plus an adequate safety factor. If this chemical makes direct contact with your gloves, or if a tear, puncture or hole develops, replace them at once.

When working with this chemical, wear a NIOSH-approved full face chemical cartride respirator equipped with the appropriate organic vapor cartridges. If that is not available, a half face respirator similarly equipped plus airtight goggles can be substituted. However, please note that half face respirators provide a substantially lower level of protection than do full face respirators.

ACUTE/ CHRONIC HAZARDS: This compound is harmful by ingestion, inhalation and skin absorption. It is highly corrosive and extremely destructive to tissue of the mucous membranes and upper respiratory tract, eyes and skin. It is a lacrimator. When heated to decomposition it emits TOXIC fumes of chlorine, carbon monoxide, carbon dioxide, hydrogen chloride gas and silicon oxide.

If Tyvek-type disposable protective clothing is not worn during handling of this chemical, wear disposable Tyvek-type sleeves taped to your gloves.

When working with this chemical, wear a NIOSH-approved full face chemical cartridge respirator equipped with the appropriate organic vapor cartridges.

If that is not available, a half face respirator similarly equipped plus airtight goggles can be substituted. However, please note that half face respirators provide a substantially lower lever of protection than do full face respirators.

STORAGE PRECAUTIONS: You should keep this material in a tightly closed container under an inert atmosphere, and store it at refrigerated temperatures.

SYMPTOMS: Symptoms of exposure to this compound include corrosion and extreme destruction of tissue of the mucous membranes and upper respiratory tract, eyes and skin; and lacrimation. Severe damage of the cornea and lids may occur. Inhalation may be fatal as a result of spasm, inflammation and edema of the larynx and bronchi, chemical pneumonitis and pulmonary edema. Other symptoms include burning sensation, coughing, wheezing, laryngitis, shortness of breath, headache, nausea and vomiting.

18. FLUX - Colorless cystalline solid

SAX Toxicity Evaluation - THR: An experimental teratogen and it has gastrointestinal effects. Mutation data. High via subcutaneous, unknown and oral routes. Moderate via oral and skin routes in infants, skin route in children, subcutaneous and intravenous routes and oral route in mice.

Avoid glove types which exhibit breakthrough times of less than the anticipated task time plus an adequate safety factor. If this chemical makes direct contact with your glove, or if a tear, puncture or hole develops, replace them at once.

Where the neat test chemical is weighed and diluted, wear a NIOSH-approved half face respirator equipped with an organic vapor/acid gas cartridge (specific for organic vapors, HCl, acid gas and SO2) with a dust/mist filter.

STORAGE PRECAUTIONS - You should store this material under ambient temperatures.

ACUTE/CHRONIC HAZARDS: This compound may cause eye and skin irritation. When heated to decomposition it forms boron oxide.

Avoid glove typed which exhibit breakthrough times of less than the anticipated task time plus an adequate safety factor. If this chemical makes direct contact with you glove, or if a tear, puncture or hole develops, replace them at once.

Where the neat test chemical is weighed and diluted, wear a NIOSH-approved half face respirator equipped with an organic vapor/acid gas cartridge (specific for organic vapors, HCl, acid gas and SO2) with a dust/mist filter.

SYMPTOMS: Symptoms of exposure to this compound include skin and eye irritation. It can cause nausea, vomiting, diarrhea and erythematous lesions on skin and mucous membranes. Central nervous system effects may occur. In addition, abdominal cramps, circulatory collapse, cyanosis and tachycardia *are possible. It can cause delirium and coma. Other symptoms include convulsions, collapse, tremors, meningismus and jaundice. Headache and peeling of the skin have been reported. Symptoms of acute exposure include erythroderma, followed by desquamation, excoriation's, blistering, bullae and sloughing of the epidermis, twitching of the facial muscles and extremities, lethargy, hyperpyrexia, kidney damage with oliguria and anuria, fall in blood pressure and collapse. Inhalation of high concentrations can cause upper respiratory irritation. Possible, although rare, disturbances of vision can occur including hallucinations, decrease in visual acuity to half normal, plus diplopia lasting more that two weeks. It can cause metabolic acidosis. DEATH nay occur in less than a day or after as much as a week. Illness usually begins about 8 hours after ingestion. Ingestion of large quantities can cause shock.*

Symptoms of chronic exposure include anorexia, vomiting, mild diarrhea, skin rash and alopecia. Weight loss, convulsions and anemia can occur. In addition, weakness, gastrointestinal irritation, disturbed digestion, nausea, dryness of the skin and membranes, reddening of the tongue, cracking of the lips, conjunctivitis, palpebral edema, kidney injury, atrophy changes in respiratory mucous membranes and joint pains have been reported. This compound can also cause dizziness, chronic dermatitis and depression.

19. SOLDER - Pale, straw-colored liquid

SAX Toxicity Evaluation - THR: Mutagenic data.

This compound is used in textile and paper processing compounds, in catalysts in urea-resin formation, as a polymerizing agent for resins and oils, in rust removers, as a soldering flux and as a chemical intermediate.

STORAGE PRECAUTIONS: You should store this material in a refrigerator.

ACUTE/ CHRONIC HAZARDS: When heated to decomposition this compound emits TOXIC fumes of phosphorous oxides.

If Tyvek-type disposable protective clothing is not worn during handling of this chemical, wear disposable Tyvek-type sleeves taped to your gloves.

If this chemical makes direct contact with your glove, or if a tear, puncture or hole develops, replace them at once.

Where the neat test chemical is weighed and diluted, wear a NIOSH-approved half face respirator equipped with an organic vapor/ acid gas cartridge (specific for organic vapors, HCl, acid gas and SO2) with a dust/ mist filter.

SYMPTOMS: Information concerning symptoms of exposure to this chemical is not available.

20. METAL CLEANING ACID - Clear colorless liquid

SAX Toxicity Evaluation - THR: POISON by intravenous route. Moderately TOXIC by ingestion, subcutaneous and intraperitoneal routes. Mildly TOXIC by inhalation. An experimental CARCINOGEN and TUMORIGEN. An experimental teratogen. Experimental reproductive effects. An eye and SEVERE skin irritant. Human mutagenic data.

STORAGE PRECAUTIONS: You should store this chemical under refrigerated temperatures, and protect it from moisture. If possible, it would be prudent to store this compound under inert atmosphere.

ACUTE/CHRONIC HAZARDS: This compound is moderately TOXIC by ALL routes. It is an irritant of the skin, eyes and respiratory tract. It is readily absorbed through the skin. When heated to decomposition it emits TOXIC fumes of chlorine, hydrogen chloride gas, carbon monoxide, carbon dioxide and phosgene.

Avoid glove types which exhibit breakthrough times of less than the anticipated task time plus an adequate safety factor. If this chemical makes direct contact with your glove, or if a tear, puncture or hole develops, replace them at once.

When working with this chemical, wear a NIOSH-approved full face positive pressure supplied-air respirator or a self-contained breathing apparatus (SCBA).

SYMPTOMS: Symptoms of exposure to this compound may include headache, elevated blood concentrations of carboxyhemoglobin, nausea and irritation of the skin and eyes. Central nervous system depression, pulmonary edema, hemolysis, chronic intoxication and paresthesia may also occur. Other symptoms include narcosis, temporary neurobehavioral effects, increase in serum bilirubin, increased urinary formic acid concentrations and increased risk of spontaneous abortion. In addition, intravascular hemolysis, unconsciousness, lack of response to painful stimuli, rapid followed by slowed respiration, erythema, blistering, TOXIC encephalopathy, painful joints, swelling of the extremities, mental impairment, diabetes, skin rash, aspiration pneumonia, gross hematuria, reduction of blood pH, gastrointestinal injury and narrowing of the intestinal lumen may also occur. Other symptoms may include upper respiratory tract irritation, giddiness, stupor, irritability, numbness, tingling in the limbs and hallucinations. A dry scaly and fissured dermatitis, skin burns, coma and DEATH may also result. Other symptoms may include dizziness, sense of fullness in the head, sense of heat, dullness, lethargy and drunkenness. In addition, mental confusion, lightheadedness, vomiting, weakness, somnolence, lassitude, anorexia, depression, fatigue, vertigo, liver damage, nose and throat irritation, anesthetic effects, smarting and reddening of the skin, blood dyscrasias acceleration of the pulse and congestion in the head may result. Staggering may also occur. Other symptoms of exposure to this compound may include neurasthenic disorders, digestive disturbances and acoustical and optical delusions. Arrhythmia's produced by catecholamines may also result, Additional symptoms include edema, faintness, loss of appetite and apathy. Hyporeflexia, gross hemoglobinuria, epiglottal edema, metabolic acidosis, gastrointestinal hemorrhage, ulceration of the duodenojejunal junction and diverticula may also occur. Other symptoms may include kidney damage, lung damage, corneal injury, abdominal pain and an increase in salivary gland TUMORS. Cyanosis may also occur. Exposure may also cause altered sleep time, convulsions, euphoria and a change in cardiac rate.

21. LOFOL (FORMALDEHYDE) - Clear colorless liquid

SAX Toxicity Evaluation - THR: Human POISON by ingestion. Experimental POISON by ingestion, skin contact, inhalation, intravenous, intraperitoneal and subcutaneous routes. A suspected human CARCINOGEN. An experimental CARCINOGEN, TUMORIGEN and teratogen. Human systemic effects by inhalation. Experimental reproductive effects. Human mutagenic date. A human skin and eye irritant. A SEVERE experimental eye and skin irritant. An air concentration of 20 ppm is quickly irritating to eyes. A

*common air contaminant. The gas is a more dangerous
fire hazard than the vapor.*

*STORAGE PRECAUTIONS: Store this material at
ambient temperatures, but not below about 15C (60F),
Keep under an inert atmosphere in a tightly closed
container. Protect from exposure to light.*

*ACUTE/CHRONIC HAZARDS: This liquid and
its vapors are irritants to the skin, eyes and mucous
membranes. It is also an irritant to all parts of the
respiratory system.   It can be absorbed through
the skin.   It can cause lachrymation.   Thermal
decomposition products may include carbon monoxide
and carbon dioxide.*

*If Tyvek-type disposable protective clothing
is not worn during handling of this chemical, wear
disposable Tyvek-type sleeves taped to your gloves.*

*Avoid glove types which exhibit breakthrough
times of less than the anticipated task time plus an
adequate safety factor. If this chemical makes direct*

contact with your glove, or if a tear, puncture of hole develops, replace them at once.

Where the neat test chemical is weighed and diluted, wear a NIOSH-approved half face respirator equipped with a combination filter cartridge, i.e. organic vapor/acid gas/HEPA (specific for organic vapors, HCl, acid gas, SO2 and a high efficiency particulate filter).Splash proof safety goggles should be worn while handling this chemical. Alternately, a full face respirator, equipped as above, may be used to provide simultaneous eye and respiratory protection.

Since this chemical is a KNOWN or SUSPECTED CARCINOGEN you should contact a physician for advice regarding the possible long term health effects and potential recommendation for medical monitoring. Recommendations from the physician will depend upon the specific compound, its chemical, physical and toxicity properties, the exposure level, length of exposure, and the route of exposure.

SYMPTOMS: Inhalation of this compound may cause irritation of the eyes, mucous membranes and upper respiratory tract. It may also cause irritation of the nose. Higher concentrations may cause bronchitis, pneumonia or laryngitis. Exposure may also cause headache, dizziness, difficult breathing and pulmonary edema. Coughing or dysphagia may also result. Contact with the vapor or solution causes skin to become white, rough, hard and anesthetic due to superficial coagulation necrosis. With long exposure, dermatitis and hypersensitivity frequently result. Prolonged exposure may also cause cracking of skin and ulceration, especially around the fingernails and may also cause conjunctivitis. Ingestion of this compound causes immediate intense pain in the mouth and pharynx. It may also cause abdominal pains with nausea, vomiting and possible loss of consciousness. Other symptoms following ingestion include proteinuria, acidosis, hematemesis, hematuria, anuria, vertigo, coma and even DEATH due to respiratory failure. Occasional diarrhea (possibly bloody), pale, clammy skin and other signs of shock, difficult micturition, convulsions and stupor may also occur. Ingestion also leads to inflammation, ulceration and/or coagulation necrosis of the gastrointestinal mucosa. Corrosive damage in the stomach and esophageal strictures sometimes occur and tissue destruction may extend as far as the jejunum. Circulatory collapse and kidney damage may also occur soon after ingestion. SEVERE lung changes may result from aspiration of the ingested compound in combination with stomach acid. Degenerative changes may be found in the liver, kidneys, heart and brain. Primary points of attack for this compound include the respiratory system, lungs, eyes and skin. Lachrymation may occur.

22. TALCUM POWDER - White to grayish-white, very fine crystalline powder (unctuous)

SAX Toxicity Evaluation - THR: Not available

ACUTE/CHRONIC HAZARDS: This compound can cause irritation of the eyes and lungs.

Recommendations based on permeation test results are made for handling the neat (undiluted) chemical. If this chemical makes direct contact with your glove, or if a tear, puncture or hole develops, replace them at once.

Where the neat test chemical is weighed and diluted, wear a NIOSH-approved half face respirator equipped with an organic vapor/acid gas cartridge (specific for organic vapors HCl, acid gas and SO2) with a dust/mist filter.

STORAGE PRECAUTIONS: You should store this material at ambient temperatures.

SYMPTOMS: Symptoms of exposure to this compound may include eye irritation, scarring of the lungs, shortness of breath and coughing. Massive inhalation can cause dyspnea, tachycardia, tachypnea, cyanosis and fever. Chronic exposure can cause heart failure.

23. COLOR PIGMENTS AS RELEASE AGENTS - Grayish-yellow, white or reddish-gray crystalline powder

SAX Toxicity Evaluation - THR: POISON by ingestion and intraperitoneal routes. A human

CARCINOGEN which produces bladder TUMORS and BLOOD in the urine. An experimental CARCINOGEN and TUMORIGEN. Human mutagenic data. Any exposure is considered EXTREMELY HAZARDOUS.

STORAGE PRECAUTIONS: You should protect this chemical from exposure to light. Keep the container tightly closed under an inert atmosphere, and store under refrigerated temperatures.

ACUTE/CHRONIC HAZARDS: This compound is TOXIC by ingestion, inhalation and skin contact. It is rapidly absorbed through the skin. It is a SEVERE IRRITANT of the skin and eyes. When heated to decomposition it emits HIGHLY TOXIC fumes of NOx

If Tyvek-type disposable protective clothing is not worn during handling of this chemical, wear disposable Tyvek-type sleeves taped to your gloves. If this chemical makes direct contact with your glove, or if a tear, puncture or hole develops, replace them at once.

Where the neat test chemical is weighed and diluted, wear a NIOSH-approved half face respirator equipped with a combination filter cartridge, i.e. organic vapor/acid gas/HEPA (specific for organic vapors, HCl, acid gas, SO2 and a high efficiency particulate filter).

Since this chemical is a KNOWN or SUSPECTED CARCINOGEN you should contact a physician for advice regarding the possible long term health effects and potential recommendation for medical monitoring. Recommendations from the physician will depend upon the specific compound, its chemical, physical and TOXICITY properties, the exposure level, length of exposure, and the route of exposure.

SYMPTOMS: Symptoms of exposure to this compound may include irritation of the skin and eyes. Other symptoms may include damage to the blood, including hemolysis and BONE MARROW DEPRESSION. If ingested, it can cause nausea and vomiting. This is sometimes followed by liver and kidney damage. It can cause skin sensitization and contact dermatitis. It can also cause bladder irritation. Long term exposure can result in an increase in urination, hematuria and urinary tract TUMORS. It can also cause pain on urination. Cystitis has been reported.

24. OAKITE - The best the author could do for this compound is from Eastman Chemical Company which describes it as being a liquid chemical that dissolves other chemicals. Important in formulating coatings such as: paints, varnishes, lacquers, inks and resins

25. EASTMAN 910 GLUE - (cyanoacyrylates) Clear colorless, syrupy liquid

SAX Toxicity Evaluation - THR: POISON by inhalation. Moderately TOXIC to humans by ingestion.

Moderately TOXIC experimentally by ingestion and intravenous routes. Mildly TOXIC by subcutaneous route. An experimental CARCINOGEN, TUMORIGEN and teratogen. An eye and human skin irritant.

STORAGE PRECAUTIONS: You should store this chemical under ambient temperatures, and protect it from moisture. Keep it away from oxidizing materials and bases. If possible, it would be prudent to store this compound under inert atmosphere.

ACUTE/CHRONIC HAZARDS: This compound is an irritant of the skin and eyes and may be readily absorbed through the skin. When heated to decomposition it emits acrid smoke, irritating fumes and TOXIC fumes of carbon monoxide and carbon dioxide. This chemical has not been tested by the Radian Corporation; however, the Gloves+ expert system was used to extrapolate permeation test information from compounds in the same chemical class. The Gloves+ system uses permeation date from literature sources; therefore, extra safety margins should be used with the estimated protection time(s). If this chemical makes *direct contact with your glove, or if a tear, puncture or hole develops, replace them at once.*

Where the neat test chemical is weighed and diluted, wear a NIOSH-approved half face respirator equipped with an organic, vapor/acid gas cartridge (specific for organic vapors, HCl, acid gas and SO2) with a dust/mist filter.

SYMPTOMS: Symptoms of exposure to this compound include nausea and vomiting. Other symptoms include headache, anuria, narcosis, cyanosis, tachypnea, tachycardia, hypotension, stupor, prostration, hypoglycemia and unconsciousness. Exposure can cause alcohol intoxication, muscle tenderness, pulmonary edema, convulsions and DEATH. It can also cause degenerative changes in the kidneys and liver, central nervous system depression, nephrotoxicity, abdominal pain, weakness, respiratory failure, cardiovascular collapse, hypocalcemic tetany (rare), metabolic acidosis (rare), acute renal failure and BRAIN DAMAGE. Somnolence has been reported in children.

26. ETHYLENE OXIDE - Colorless gas at room temperature

SAX Toxicity Evaluation - THR: POISON by ingestion, intraperitoneal, subcutaneous, intravenous and possibly other routes. Moderately TOXIC by inhalation. A suspected human CARCINOGEN. An experimental CARCINOGEN, TUMORIGEN, neoplastigen and teratogen. Experimental reproductive effects. Mutagenic data. A human skin irritant and experimental eye irritant. An irritant to the mucous membranes of the respiratory tract.

STORAGE PRECAUTIONS: You should store this chemical under ambient temperatures and away from mineral acids and bases. STORE AWAY FROM SOURCES OF IGNITION.

ACUTE/CHRONIC HAZARDS: This compound is VERY TOXIC by inhalation. It is highly irritating to the skin, eyes, mucous membranes and respiratory tract. When heated to decomposition it emits acrid smoke, irritating fumes and TOXIC FUMES of carbon monoxide and carbon dioxide. The vapor of this compound is readily initiated into EXPLOSIVE decomposition.

Avoid glove types which exhibit breakthrough times of less than the anticipated task time plus an adequate safety factor. If this chemical makes direct contact with your glove, or if a tear, puncture or hole develops, replace them at once.

When working with this chemical, wear a NIOSH-approved full face positive pressure supplied-air respirator or a self-contained breathing apparatus (SCBA).

Since this chemical is a KNOWN or SUSPECTED CARCINOGEN you should contact a physician for advice regarding the possible long term health effects and potential recommendation for medical monitoring. Recommendations from the physician will depend upon the specific compound, its chemical, physical and toxicity properties, the exposure level, length of exposure, and the route of exposure.

SYMPTOMS: Symptoms of exposure to this compound include irritation of the skin, eyes, mucous membranes and upper respiratory tract. Other symptoms include convulsions, nausea, vomiting, olfactory and pulmonary changes, and in high concentrations, pulmonary edema. It can cause bronchitis, coma, conjunctivitis, corneal damage and delayed burns and blistering. It can cause headache, TOXIC dermatitis with large bullae, and in high concentrations, unconsciousness and seizures. Anesthesia may occur. Drowsiness may also occur. Exposure may cause erythema, marked desquamation, formation of residual pigment, urticarial wheal, weakness, dullness of head, stupor, coughing and bradycardia. It may also cause loss of taste and smell, incoordination, dyspnea, cyanosis, hemolysis, sensitization, anaphylaxis, KIDNEY DAMAGE and DEATH. Chronic exposure may lead to lymphocytosis, peripheral neuropathy, CHROMOSOMAL DAMAGE to lymphocytes and LEUKEMIA. LIVER DAMAGE may occur. SEVERE dermatitis may also occur. Other symptoms include diarrhea, vertigo and central nervous system depression. This compound can cause frostbite, gastric irritation, lung injury, shortness of breath, reproductive effects and neurotoxicity. It can also cause redness, edema and ulceration of the skin, and encephalopathy (rare). Necrosis of the skin has been reported. Difficult breathing may occur. Exposure may also cause emphysema.

27. CARBON BLACK - Gray-black microcrystals

SAX Toxicity Evaluation - THR: An experimental TUMORIGEN and CARCINOGEN. Mutagenic data.

STORAGE PRECAUTIONS: You should store this chemical under ambient temperatures, and keep it away from oxidizing materials.

ACUTE/CHRONIC HAZARDS: This compound may be absorbed through the skin. When heated to decomposition it emits VERY TOXIC fumes of nitrogen oxides, disodium oxide and sulfur oxides.

If this chemical makes direct contact with your glove, or if a tear, puncture or hole develops, replace them at once.

Where the neat test chemical is weighed and diluted, wear a NIOSH-approved half face respirator equipped with a combination filter cartridge, i.e. organic vapor/acid gas/HEPA (specific for organic vapors, HCl, acid gas, SO2 and a high efficiency particulate filter).Since this chemical is a KNOWN or SUSPECTED CARCINOGEN you should contact a physician for advice regarding the possible long term health effects and potential recommendation for medical monitoring. Recommendations from the physician will depend upon the specific compound, its chemical, physical and toxicity properties, the exposure level, length of exposure, and the route of exposure.

SYMPTOMS: Information concerning symptoms of exposure to this chemical is not available.

28. XYLENE - Colorless liquid

SAX Toxicity Evaluation - THR: Moderate via inhalation and oral routes.

STORAGE PRECAUTIONS: You should store this chemical in an explosion-proof refrigerator and keep it away from oxidizing materials. STORE AWAY FROM SOURCES OF IGNITION.

ACUTE/CHRONIC HAZARDS: When heated to decomposition, this compound emits TOXIC fumes of CO and CO2. It can be narcotic in high concentrations. It causes eye, nose and throat irritation.

If this chemical makes direct contact with your glove, or if a tear, puncture or hole develops, replace them at once.

Where the neat test chemical is weighed and diluted, wear a NIOSH-approved half face respirator equipped with an organic vapor/acid gas cartridge (specific for organic vapors, HCl, acid gas and SO2) with a dust/mist filter.

SYMPTOMS: Symptoms of exposure to this material include irritation of the eyes, nose and throat; drying and defatting of the skin which may lead to dermatitis; chemical pneumonitis, pulmonary edema, hemorrhage, central nervous system depression, dizziness, staggering, drowsiness, unconsciousness, anorexia, nausea, vomiting and abdominal pain. It may be narcotic in high concentrations. It may also cause headache, fatigue, lassitude, irritability and gastrointestinal disturbances. It can also cause reversible eye damage, a burning sensation in the mucous membranes, salivation, bloody vomit, impaired motor coordination, slurred speech, ataxia, stupor, coma, tremors, shallow respiration, ventricular irregularities, paralysis and convulsions. It causes eye irritation and foggy vision.

29. HEXONE - Clear , colorless, mobile liquid

SAX Toxicity Evaluation - THR: A POISON by intraperitoneal route. Moderately TOXIC by ingestion. Mildly TOXIC by inhalation. It is very irritating to the skin, eyes and mucous membranes. A human systemic irritant by inhalation. It is narcotic in high concentrations.

STORAGE PRECAUTIONS: You should keep this material in a tightly closed container under an inert atmosphere, and store it in an explosion-proof refrigerator. STORE AWAY FROM SOURCES OF IGNITION.

ACUTE/CHRONIC HAZARDS: This compound is an irritant of the skin, eyes and mucous membranes. It is narcotic in high concentrations. It is readily absorbed by the skin. Flashback along the vapor trail may occur. When heated to decomposition it emits TOXIC fumes of carbon monoxide and carbon dioxide.

If this chemical makes direct contact with your glove, or if a tear, puncture or hole develops, replace them at once.

Where the neat test chemical is weighed and diluted, wear a NIOSH-approved half face respirator equipped with an organic vapor/acid gas cartridge (specific for organic vapors, HCl, acid gas and SO2) with a dust/mist filter.

SYMPTOMS: Symptoms of exposure to this compound include irritation of the skin, eyes and mucous membranes. Other symptoms may include irritation of the nasal passages and throat and mental sluggishness. Irritation of the respiratory tract may occur. Gastroenteritis may also occur. Exposure may cause dizziness and unconsciousness. It may also cause weakness, headache, nausea and vomiting. Lightheadedness, narcosis and incoordination have been reported. High concentrations may cause central nervous system depression. Prolonged skin contact may cause drying of the skin. Eye injury may also occur.

30. HEXANONE 2 - Clear colorless liquid

SAX Toxicity Evaluation - THR: Moderate via oral, inhalation and intraperitoneal routes.

MODERATE irritation in rabbits via skin and eye exposure.

STORAGE PRECAUTIONS: You should store this chemical in an explosion-proof refrigerator and keep it away from oxidizing materials. STORE AWAY FROM SOURCES OF IGNITION.

ACUTE/CHRONIC HAZARDS: This compound is TOXIC by inhalation and skin contact. It is also HARMFUL by ingestion. It is readily absorbed through the skin. It is an irritant of the mucous membranes and upper respiratory tract. It is also an irritant of the eyes. High concentrations may cause narcosis. When heated to decomposition it may emit TOXIC fumes of carbon monoxide and carbon dioxide.

If this chemical comes into direct contact with your glove, or if a tear, puncture or hole develops, remove them at once.

Where the neat test chemical is weighed and diluted, wear a NIOSH-approved half face respirator equipped with an organic vapor/acid gas cartridge (specific for organic vapors, HCl, acid gas and SO2) with a dust/mist filter.

SYMPTOMS: Symptoms of exposure to this compound include eye irritation. It may also be irritating to the mucous membranes and upper respiratory tract. It is narcotic in high concentrations. Ingestion may cause gastric irritation. Chronic exposure may result in loss of sensation in hands and feet, and possible risk of IRREVERSIBLE effects. PERIPHERAL NEUROPATHY is frequently reported. Inhalation of high vapor concentrations has caused lethargy. It may also cause SYMMETRICAL DISTAL POLYNEUROPATHY with both motor and sensory deficits. This may include muscle weakness in fingers and toes, and loss of deep sensory reflexes. A decrease in nerve conduction velocity precedes onset of symptoms, and the loss of vibration sense. Other symptoms include nausea, dizziness, headache, neurotoxic effects and dermatitis. It may have central nervous system effects. High vapor concentrations may cause ocular irritation followed by central nervous system depression. Chronic inhalation may result in degenerative axonal changes primarily in PERIPHERAL NERVES and long spinal cord tracts, atrophy of testicular germinal cell epithelium and depression of circulating white blood cells. It may also cause weight loss. Acute toxicity may result in coma and cardiorespiratory failure. It may also cause nasal irritation and may even result in DEATH.

31. THIXON-OSN-2 - I found this listed under Methyl Ethyl Ketone (MEK) with carbon (solids content 19 percent by weight)

USE: ADHESIVE CEMENT

The manufacturer is Morton International Incorporated Division: Specialty Chemical Group

Look under methyl ethyl ketone for information

32. ANTIOXIDANT (RUBBER) - Colorless liquid

SAX Toxicity Evaluation - THR: HIGH via intravenous route. MODERATE via oral route. LOW via inhalation route. A human irritant. A skin and eye irritant.

STORAGE PRECAUTIONS: You should keep this material in a tightly closed container under an inert atmosphere, and store it at refrigerated temperatures. STORE AWAY FROM SOURCES OF IGNITION.

ACUTE/CHRONIC HAZARDS: This chemical irritates the skin and eyes. It can be absorbed through the skin. When heated to decomposition it emits TOXIC fumes.

Where the neat test chemical is weighed and diluted, wear a NIOSH-approved half face respirator equipped with an organic vapor/acid gas cartridge (specific for organic vapors, HCl, acid gas and SO2) with a dust/mist filter. Glove materials are not available.

USES for this chemical are: Intermediate for dyes, pharmaceuticals, RUBBER accelerators and emulsifying agents; solvent for fats, fatty oils, dyes, resins and oils; catalyst in making polyurethane foams.

SYMPTOMS: Symptoms of exposure to this chemical may include irritation of the skin, eyes and mucous membranes and visual aberrations.

33. ACID STEARIC - White, shiny, flaky crystals or hard somewhat glassy solid

SAX Toxicity Evaluation - THR: POISON by intravenous route. An experimental TUMORIGEN by IMPLANTATION route. H human and experimental skin irritant.

STORAGE PRECAUTIONS: You should store this chemical under ambient temperatures, and keep it away from oxidizing materials.

ACUTE/CHRONIC HAZARDS: This compound may cause irritation of the skin, eyes, nose and throat. When heated to decomposition it emits acrid smoke, irritating fumes and TOXIC fumes of carbon monoxide and carbon dioxide.

If this chemical makes direct contact with your glove, or if a tear, puncture or hole develops, replace them at once.

Where the neat test chemical is weighed and diluted, wear a NIOSH-approved half face respirator equipped with an organic vapor/acid gas cartridge (specific for organic vapors, HCl, acid gas and SO2) with a dust/mist filter.

SYMPTOMS: Symptoms of exposure to this compound may include irritation of the skin, eyes, nose and throat. Ingestion of large doses may cause intestinal obstruction. Skin sensitization rarely occurs. Inhalation may cause chemical pneumonitis. Inhalation of large amounts may cause coughing, sneezing and labored breathing. Skin contact may result in surface inflammation.

34. ZINC OXIDE - "ziram" - White Powder

SAX Toxicity Evaluation - THR: POISON by ingestion, intraperitoneal and intravenous routes. Moderately TOXIC by inhalation. Mutagenic date. An experimental CARCINOGEN and TUMORIGEN.

STORAGE PRECAUTIONS: You should store this chemical under ambient conditions, and keep it away from all oxidizing materials.

ACUTE/CHRONIC HAZARDS: This compound is a skin and mucous membrane irritant. It may be absorbed through intact skin. When heated to decomposition it emits TOXIC fumes of carbon monoxide, carbon dioxide, sulfur oxides and nitrogen oxides.

Avoid glove types which exhibit breakthrough times of less than the anticipated task time plus an adequate safety factor. If this chemical makes direct contact with your glove, or if a tear, puncture or hole develops, replace them at once.

Where the neat test chemical is weighed and diluted, wear a NIOSH-approved half face respirator equipped with a combination filter cartridge, i.e. organic vapor/acid gas/HEPA (specific for organic vapors, HCl, acid gas, SO2 and a high efficiency particulate filter).

Since this chemical is a KNOWN or SUSPECTED CARCINOGEN you should contact a physician for advice regarding the possible long term health effects and potential recommendation for medical monitoring. Recommendations from the physician will depend upon the specific compound, its chemical, physical and toxicity properties, the exposure level, length of exposure, and the route of exposure.

SYMPTOMS: Symptoms of exposure to this compound include irritation of the skin, nose, throat and eyes. It may also cause gastritis, reduced hemoglobin and vegetodystonia. Other symptoms include BRAIN EDEMA and hemorrhage. In vivo, it may be corrosive to the eyes and cause hemolysis, DYSTROPHY OF THE MUSCLE, liver and kidney damage, emphysema, local necrosis of the intestine, neural and visual disturbances, irritation of the skin and mucous membranes and dermatitis. It can also cause headache, tightness of the chest and irritation of the respiratory tract.

35. NAPTHA - (RUBBER SOLVENT) - Colorless to pale purple crystals

SAX Toxicity Evaluation - THR: An experimental neoplastigen, CARCINOGEN and EQUIVOCAL TUMORIGENIC agent.

STORAGE PRECAUTIONS: You should keep this material in a tightly closed container under an inert atmosphere, and store it at refrigerated temperatures.

ACUTE/CHRONIC HAZARDS: There is CLEAR EVIDENCE that this compound is CARCINOGENIC in animals. When heated to decomposition it emits TOXIC fumes of CO, CO2, and NOx.

Avoid glove types which exhibit breakthrough times of less than the anticipated task time plus an adequate safety factor. If this chemical makes direct contact with your glove, or if a tear, puncture or hole develops, replace them at once.

Where the neat test chemical is weighed and diluted, wear a NIOSH-approved half face respirator equipped with a combination filter cartridge, i.e. organic vapor/acid gas/HEPA (specific for organic vapors, HCl, acid gas, SO2 and a high efficiency particulate filter).

Since this chemical is a KNOWN or suspected CARCINOGEN you should contact a physician for advice regarding the possible long term health effects and potential recommendation for medical monitoring. Recommendations from the physician will depend upon the specific compound, its chemical, physical and toxicity properties, the exposure level, length of exposure, and the route of exposure.

SYMPTOMS: This compound is an irritant.

36. PHENOL - White crystalline solid

SAX Toxicity Evaluation - THR: Human POISON by ingestion. An experimental POISON by ingestion, subcutaneous, intravenous, parenteral and intraperitoneal routes. Moderately TOXIC by skin contact. A severe eye and skin irritant. An experimental CARCINOGEN and neoplastigen. Human mutagenic data. Absorption of phenolic solutions through the skin may be very rapid, and can cause DEATH WITHIN 30 MINUTES to several hours by exposure of as little as 64 square inches of skin. A common air contaminant.

STORAGE PRECAUTIONS: You should protect this chemical from exposure to light. Keep the container tightly closed under an inert atmosphere, and store under refrigerated temperatures.

ACUTE/CHRONIC HAZARDS: This compound may be FATAL by ingestion, inhalation or skin absorption. It rapidly penetrates the skin. It is an irritant of the skin and eyes, and a severe irritant of the nose, throat and respiratory tract. It is corrosive to the skin and eyes. When heated to decomposition it emits TOXIC fumes of carbon monoxide, carbon dioxide and UNIDENTIFIED organic compounds.

If Tyvek-type disposable protective clothing is not worn during handling of this chemical, wear disposable Tyvek-type sleeves taped to your gloves.

Avoid glove types which exhibit breakthrough times of less that the anticipated task time plus an adequate safety factor. If this chemical makes direct contact with your glove, or if a tear, puncture or hole develops, replace them at once.

Where the neat test chemical is weighed and diluted, wear a NIOSH-approved half face respirator equipped with an organic vapor/acid gas cartridge *(specific for organic vapors, HCl, acid gas and SO2) with a dust/mist filter.*

SYMPTOMS: Symptoms of exposure to this compound include irritation of the skin, eyes, nose and throat, blindness, headache, dizziness, loss of appetite, abdominal pain, skin depigmentation, severe skin burns, vomiting, diarrhea, difficulty in swallowing, muscular weakness, unconsciousness, coma and DEATH. Other symptoms include HEART DAMAGE, central nervous system depression, respiratory arrest, irritation of the respiratory tract, mouth and stomach, giddiness, jaundice, shortness of breath, bladder damage, CARDIAC ARREST, severe burns of tissues and the eyes, burning pain in the mouth and throat, irregular breathing, corrosion of the skin and eyes and blurred vision. Liver and kidney damage may occur. Nausea may also occur. Exposure may result in circulatory collapse, tachypnea, paralysis, convulsions, greenish to smoky-colored urine, necrosis of the mouth and gastrointestinal tract and icterus. It may also result in respiratory alkalosis followed by acidosis, methemoglobinemia, necrosis of the mucous membranes, cerebral edema, bladder necrosis, erythema, pulmonary edema followed by pneumonia, profuse sweating, intense thirst, hyperactivity, stupor, blood pressure fall, hyperpnea, hemolysis, oliguria, anuria, central nervous system damage and muscle contractions. Eye effects include conjunctiva chemotic, white and hypesthetic cornea, edematous eyelids, iritis and carbolochronosis. Other symptoms may include necrosis of the skin, ulcerative esophagitis, laryngeal edema, white or brownish stains and areas of necrosis about the face, mouth and esophagus; NEUROLYSIS OF THE CERVICAL POSTERIOR ROOTS, hypersensitivity, idiosyncrasy, hypothermia, loss of vasoconstrictor tone, cardiac depression, stertorous breathing, mucous rales, frothing of the mouth and nose, ventricular arrhythmia's, hyperbilirubinemia in newborns, Heinz body hemolytic anemia, SORES and burning in the mouth, pallor, weakness, TINNITUS (ringing in the ears), weak and irregular pulse, hypotension, shallow respiration, cyanosis, fleeting excitement, confusion, rhonchi and fever. Exposure may cause antipyresis, tremors, digestive disturbances, ptyalism, anorexia, fainting, vertigo, mental disturbances, ochronosis and

GANGRENE. *It may also cause spasm, inflammation and edema of the larynx and bronchi; chemical pneumonitis, burning sensation, coughing, wheezing, laryngitis, dermatitis and central nervous system disturbances. Mucocutaneous and gastrointestinal corrosion may occur. Damage to the pancreas, spleen or lungs may also occur. Skin eruptions and rapid and difficult breathing have been reported. Other reported symptoms include SEVERE eye damage and SKIN RASH. Exposure may cause irritation of the mucous membranes, weight loss, MUSCLE ACHES AND PAINS and conjunctival swelling.*

37. BENZENE - Colorless to light yellow liquid, aromatic odor

SAX Toxicity Evaluation - THR: POISONING occurs most commonly through inhalation of the vapor, though benzene can penetrate the skin, and POISON in that way. Locally, benzene has a comparatively strong irritation effect, producing erthema and burning, and in more severe cases, edema and even blistering.

STORAGE PRECAUTIONS: You should keep this material in a tightly-closed container under an inert atmosphere, and store it at refrigerated temperatures.

ACUTE/ CHRONIC HAZARDS: TOXIC. Suspect CARCINOGEN, highly flammable. May travel considerable distance to a source of ignition and flash back. No spontaneous heating. Can vigorously react with oxidizing materials, such as BrF5, C12, OCr03, O2NCl04, O2, O3, perchlorates, (AlCl04 + FC104), (H2SO4 + permanganates), K202, AgC104 + aecti acid), and Na202.

Permeation data indicate that nitrile gloves may provide protection to contact with this compound. Nitrile over latex gloves is recommended. However, if this chemical makes contact with your gloves, or if a tear, hole or puncture develops, remove them at once. When working with this chemical, wear a NIOSH-approved full face chemical cartride respirator equipped with the appropriate organic vapor cartridges. If that is not available, a half face respirator similarly equipped plus airtight goggles can be substituted. However, please note that half face respirators provide a substantially lower level of protection than do full face respirators.

Since this chemical is and KNOWN or suspected CARCINOGEN you should contact a physician for advice regarding the possible long term health effects and potential recommendation for medical monitoring. Recommendations from the physician will depend upon the specific compound, its chemical, physical and toxicity properties, the exposure level, length of exposure, and the route of exposure.

SYMPTOMS: Exaggerated sense of well-being, excitement, headache, dizziness, incoherent speech, narcosis, stimulation of CNS, then depression. Blistering.

38. PLATINUM II - Deep yellow solid

SAX Toxicity Evaluation - THR: POISON by ingestion, intramuscular, subcutaneous, intravenous, and intraperitoneal routes. Human systemic effects by intravenous, intradermal and possible other routes. An experimental CARCINOGEN. Experimental teratogen and reproductive effects. Human mutagenic data.

STORAGE PRECAUTIONS: You should store this chemical under ambient temperatures, and keep it away from oxidizing materials.

ACUTE/CHRONIC HAZARDS: This compound is corrosive. When heated to decomposition it emits TOXIC fumes of chlorine and nitrogen oxide.

If Tyvek-type disposable protective clothing is not worn during handling of this chemical, wear disposable Tyvek-type sleeves taped to your gloves.

Avoid glove typed which exhibit breakthrough times of less than the anticipated task time plus an adequate safety factor. If this chemical makes direct contact with your glove, or if a tear, puncture or hole develops, replace them at once.

Where the neat test chemical is weighed and diluted, wear a NIOSH-approved half face respirator *equipped with an organic vapor/acid gas cartridge (specific for organic vapors, HCl, acid gas and SO2) with a dust/mist filter.*

Since this chemical is a KNOWN or SUSPECTED CARCINOGEN you should contact a physician for advice regarding the possible long term health effects and potential recommendation for medical monitoring. Recommendations from the physician will depend upon the specific compound, its chemical, physical and toxicity properties, the exposure level, length of exposure, and the route of exposure.

SYMPTOMS: Symptoms of exposure to this compound may include TINNITIS, HEARING LOSS, myelosuppression, hypomagnesemia, hypocalcemia, hypokalemia, hypophosphatemia and hyperuricemia. Other symptoms include nausea, vomiting, diarrhea, leukopenia and thrombocytopenia. Prolonged exposure can cause liver and kidney damage. It can also cause an allergic respiratory reaction. Exposure can cause papilledema and headache. Exposure may also cause hemolysis and tetany. This compound may cause a *change in auditory acuity, depressed renal function tests, CHANGES in BONE MARROW, changes in kidney tubules, hallucinations and corrosion to the skin. Distorted perceptions and primary irritation may occur. It may also cause blood changes, peripheral neurotoxicity, electrolyte disturbances, anaphylactic-like reaction, transient bronchial irritation, SKIN RASH, and conjunctivitis.*

THE ELEMENT SILICONE

The element silicone is ubiquitous, existing in many different products. It is found in shampoos, toothpaste, cleaners, beer (to reduce foaming) and is also known as silica or crystalline silicone dioxide; a major component of sand and is found in a large percentage of the earth's crust.

There are more than 100 medical devices which include silicone. Some of these include artificial joints such as; hips, fingers, and knees. Some other uses for this type of silicone are; dental surgery grafting, blood vessel grafts, and heart valves. Silicone, synthesized first in the late 1930's, has been used as a lubricant, insulator, sealant, and coolant. "Silly Putty", which was one of Dow Corning's first silicone products, was and still is marketed to children.

Most of the silicone produced commercially is done by reducing silica (sand) to the elemental silicon and allowing its reaction with methyl chloride and water to produce silozanes, an example is dimethhylsilozane or dimethicone. Octamethylcyclotetrasilozane is the most prevalent silozane of this process and is treated with silanoate catalysts to form polydimethylsiloxane, the silicone used in silicone gel implants

The actual silicone gel found in breast, chin, hiatal hernia and testicular implants is contained but not "attached" to the envelope or shell containing it. This component of fluid is capable of passing through or diffusing through this envelope or shell which contains the silicone and this is what is called "gel bleed".

Upon reading the list of chemicals and their toxicity's and hazard information, the storage precautions and the symptoms associated with these implants, it is difficult for the author to believe other than some or all of the illnesses' you are about to read in these stories could definitely be caused by the toxins in these implants.

Section Four - The True Breast Implant Stories

Toxic Silicone Poisoning - the TRUE Breast Implant Stories The TRUTH OF THE GREATEST TRAVESTY AGAINST WOMEN IN THE 20ᵀᴴ CENTURY

What you are about to read are the actual true stories uncut from many women out of the 440,000 who have been affected by the toxins in silicone implants. Included are also stories from women who had saline implants. If these implants contribute to or cause the diseases documented here, you, the reader will have to decide.

The incidence of Capsular Contracture, Connective Tissue Disease, Sjogren's Syndrome, Lupus, Multiple Sclerosis "Like" Syndrome, Sleep Disorders, Migraines, Gum and Teeth Problems, Sleep Disorders, Memory Loss, Repeated "Strange" Infections, Hair Loss, and Strange Rashes, seem to be the prevailing "connecting thread" uniting these women's' complaints. Dealing with the simplest of every day stresses can be overwhelming to their systems which are already "overloaded" from the chemical poisoning in their bodies.

Thank you to all of the women who contributed their stories, for their courage and conviction to inform the world about the injustices and pain that has befallen us all....................

1.   Diane, a young South Florida woman writes: "I am getting really scared. For the past three weeks I have symptoms I never had before.

Besides all the muscle spasm, chronic inflammation and infections, I had for years, I now have severe pains involving the complete left side of my upper body, also, pains in my hips and legs; dizziness and memory loss." "The plastic surgeon I consulted feels she is not qualified to remove my implants, so now I must find another one!" "Where do I go, What do I do?"

2.   Amy states "It is painful to write this: "I was implanted in 1977, with silicone gel breast implants. I had many tumors removed from my breast, my right one had five removed. I didn't just make the

127

decision overnight. The doctor who did my implants was a very reputable physician, known for his breast reconstruction on patients who had lost their breast(s) to cancer. (I believe and know that he would never have done anything to hurt anyone if he had known what was going to occur years later.

That was 1977. 1982, I had my first rupture, it was replaced and I didn't seem to have any problems. Around 1985, I can remember feeling tired all of the time, hurting all over; I broke out with a rash on my chest, it almost looked like a fungus. I would wake up during the night with my hands numb. Sometimes I would have areas of my body that were so sore for no apparent reason. My joints would hurt then I would have the most terrible tiredness. In 1986, another rupture. It was replaced. Strangely, at that time, I started getting better after the implant was replaced. Now I remember not knowing there was any connection at the time but looking back I remember the rash going away after the surgery. In my mind I thought that the sterilization solution they swab on the body before surgery probably killed the rash. Now I know it was the silicone implant being removed...

Beginning in 1986 through 1992, I had severe bouts of chronic fatigue, joint pain and in the late 1980's, the numbness in my face and lip started; then my right foot became numb and my hands became drawn. My husband would rub my back and legs and I would hurt so much that I couldn't sleep. By 1992, I had spent a fortune trying to find out what was wrong with me. In late 1993, I went to Houston, Texas.......I will finish later I am so tired....I have to go." (She never finished her story)

3. Chris, a recipient of polyurethane/silicone gel breast implants writes: "I am a friend of Judy....I met her during one of my hospital trips to Houston, while I was being treated by a physician there. On my first stay I met a woman who is since deceased...but she was this physicians first silicone patient...Through her determined efforts many of us have benefited, to say the least, and many of us are alive to tell her story.

When I first met Judy she was already paralyzed from her mid-torso down and I don't think she had use of her arms. She was accompanied by her mate who took on the majority of her special needs. This was in the early Spring of 1993....I was lucky enough to have my mother accompany me to the hospital where she met many of the victims of silicone breast implants and their caretakers; which she brought to my room as I was in denial about just how bad this silicone was and refused to consider the notion that my life was in jeopardy!

God bless Judy; she, in her wheelchair, came to my room to "enlighten" me to what my future might eventually be and she told me then that we had the "flip side" of HIV/Aids; with regards to how our immune systems were reacting. She was working on a book about laughter and the immune system as she knew she was in the final stages of her life. I don't know what happened to her notes, nor do I know what happened to the boxes and boxes of documents she had about the manufacturers. I do know that her case was settled with her at her deathbed…just days before she expired.

Her mate was in my room when the doctor called him about not cremating her body because many could benefit from research on her remains. I am sure many were his patients' eventually, if not I am sure he is well known and thought of because of his dedication to the silicone travesty……I personally believe I would have died without his intervention. I can attest to his thorough testing which almost maxed out my insurance policy, largely due to the fact that I was sick from day one.

This started with a collapsed lung that my plastic surgeon overlooked for 2 days, and continued to ignore my intense pain and inflammation locally, along with foul smelling urine. I had the gel implants out within seven months of implantation and was reimplanted by another plastic surgeon, in another state with saline, without my knowledge or consent. (The operative report states that the plastic surgeon removed polyurethane implants and scraped the foam *from the capsule). During this surgery the doctor sent my friend out to the bank to withdraw the $1600.00 for replacement of the implants while I was asleep. Later, I would find out that I did not have polyurethane but, according to another physician, a severe toxic reaction producing foamy white histieosites,*

How could the chief of plastic surgery at a teaching hospital mistake the allergic reaction with foam? These saline implants were removed in Houston, Texas.

This physician also told me that he was ruling out any other possibilities for my deteriorating health so all the tests were done to prove his theory about all silicone victims. He brought in a whole team of specialists and I am very grateful because I am alive to tell the story.

I asked this doctor to accompany me to a meeting where there were doctors speaking about their area of expertise regarding silicone breast implants. Tapes were made and each physician went into great detail using pictures and diagrams. I took these tapes back to the northwest and gave a set to my attorney, and also sent a set to my hired assistant. The tapes have now disappeared along with a photo album full of newspaper clippings from Houston newspapers during the years 1993 through 1995. This assistant is no longer in my employ and the attorney has lost the items as well."

4.   Sidney writes: *"My wife's silicone gel breast implant ruptured April, 1999. The doctor had to remove dead tissue and mounds of sticky, viscous silicone gel material. A call to Mentor customer service resulted only in a "too bad, don't bother us", response. It appears that her November, 1992, implant was covered under an earlier class action suit, of which we, were never notified. My wife's medical bills for emergency surgery, lost work, etc., are in the thousands. Mentor continues to make these devices and we can't bring suit against them. Is there something wrong here?*

She still has silicone crystals coming out of her feet, hands, and other parts of her body. There are still times that she cannot even move about...How much worse will it get?"

5.   Charlene writes: "I can only speak for one person, me. I know my body, my pain, my good times and bad. I had silicone gel breast implants in 1973 and sometime around 1985 things began to go wrong. I didn't have a clue. I applied for Social Security Disability and was turned down. Sometimes I would even get lost driving home! My knees hurt and they were Hot!

I always had a low grade fever. My neck was always red (like it was sunburned). I stayed in trouble at work because I forgot to call my numbers into the office or I couldn't remember how to fill out my paperwork! I was always late for work and fall asleep in sales meetings. My hands were continuously red and swollen. I had trouble breathing. I never felt like cleaning my home and really didn't give a darn! Sometimes I didn't even think I could get up to brush my teeth or take a shower! I do not care what anyone thinks, says, cares, or believes. I know something was making me sicker and sicker every single day. After I had my implants removed (which I really hated to do), I started to get better and better. In my heart, I don't think I'll ever really be well, but I do know, I feel a whole lot better than I did in 1997!"

6.   *Ziggy from Europe expresses her concern about the denial of problems with silicone gel breast implants. "I cannot understand when docktors are talking about International studies....What countries have been in these studies? Is it women from all over the world? We have not heard about any study here, so I wonder what country(s) are in this study? Are we maybe forgotten because we are a small island on the map? But the truth is, even if we are a small island, there are many hundred of women here implanted with silicone, and I know many of them are sick. If it is from the silicone, I do not know because it has not been studied here. Some of the docktors tell the women this is the safest implant and will last forever. Other docktors tell women to have the implants removed then they will not say anything more! So this is a hide and play, maybe they know something that they do not dare*

tell the women the truth about because we are such a small country? But anyway, we are women too, and have silicone implants that we think are causing us to be sick. There have been no studies here and we are not satisfied with that, we are not counted in any study that is going on all over the world! We have not heard a word about any studies. The silicone implant that many of us have is made in the USA. Why did they not inform us about the settlement and the studies they were doing? I wish I could get some answers."

7.   Darlene says: "I am an excellent source to attest to what can happen to a person with silicone gel implants. Having grown up being very flat chested and teased can be devastating. Men too, can be very cruel...at least back in those times. I say back in those times because I am now in my early 50's and at the age of 28 elected to have implants.

I didn't just jump into this, but was convinced by the plastic surgeon just how safe these silicone gel implants were so I had the surgery. As I had no breast at all, the surgery, in 1975, was very painful, but after the implantation, my body looked so much more normal. I was thrilled to buy a real bra (no foam padding) and clothes fit so much nicer! Not long after the surgery I began my downhill of health. First, it was my right shoulder freezing up. Then, I began having strange aches and pains in my joints. I found out after just 7 months' they ruptured! When I would go to the doctor he could never find anything; so, I began treating it like it was all in my head! I never had allergies, but today I have severe allergies. My eyes were sharp and now I wear "trifocals". My hearing was great, now, I have ringing in my ears constantly and am very hard of hearing. I have been told I am going deaf. My skin was moist and soft, now, it is dry, itchy and splotchy. My neck is stiff from arthritis; my back feels like it is going to break, I think because I have arthritis of the spine. The palms of my hands look like I've been scrubbing the floor with bleach and are red all of the time! To touch any part of the skin on my body is painful. It is even painful to sit or to lie down to try and sleep at night. Those breasts that I wanted so much are hard as rocks, especially the right one and there is no feeling in areas of both of them. However, I have shooting pains like someone is stabbing me with a knife and I have muscle spasms under them that makes me feel like I am having a heart attack. The list goes on and on."

"I was an attractive woman and now I fight every day to just get up and go on! I still work but I work in pain. There isn't a day I am free of the pain. Yes, I was stupid, but we were all lied to, deceived and are still lied to and deceived.

I think that after 23 years of having these implants I can be an expert spokesperson regarding what "I" personally am experiencing! Hopefully, after the last 5 years I will at least be allowed to have my "normal" body back by having them removed. If not, I am almost at the point of removing them myself before I go completely mad with pain! It's not the money with me, since I doubt I will ever see a dime! My plastic surgeon died over 17 years ago and with him went all of my medical records. But I will not be beaten by a manufacturer who has lied to me and all of those who are just like me. To toss out pennies while making billions is insulting to the human race and a pathetic ploy to get out of the issue and continue to make billions. If the manufacturers feel they are not at fault, then ask yourself this question, "Why are they willing to settle at all?" If you were accused falsely, wouldn't you fight to the end?

Money is power and it doesn't matter how many of us say different!" Darlene now has had her implants removed and states, "I have a home, a small child, my pets and my work which mean the world to me." "I will not give up." "The day I give up is the day they will bury me."

8.   René' writes: "I am in frail health and suffering great financial devastation as a result of silicone gel implants I received over 25 years ago, around 1975. I have Lupus and Chronic Fatigue Syndrome and have been unable to hold down a job for several years. I live basically hand to mouth, never knowing how I will scrape together enough money for food and rent, much less medical care!

I became part of the Global Implant Settlement back in 1993. I went through hell to meet the needed deadlines, so that I might have a chance to receive a settlement check (badly needed now that I have kidney disease, too). I waited 6 long years watching the lawyers "ratchet down" the benefit amounts to practically nothing, while making sure they took care of themselves, at the expense of a lot of desperately ill women. What little money I have received so far, has mainly been taken by the lawyers, who are refusing to abide by the fee rules of the settlement agreement.

Example: They were allowed under the agreement to take 10% of the first $10,000. I was paid $5,000. But only received $2,500. They took 50%!

They weren't supposed to receive anything on an explantation claim, they took 28%! They have added what they call Pro Rata Bilt costs, which they have tacked on the regular attorney's fees. These fees are not itemized and so far they have deducted almost $4,000. (I have already paid any liens and outside *vendor costs, so I know this is just another way of ripping me off).*

I contacted the local Bar Association, who arbitrates fee disputed between clients and attorney's. That was a dead-end because BOTH parties have to agree to arbitration, fat chance!

So, now I have a check in front of me that I cannot cash! I need the money desperately! The lawyers have already taken their money off the top. If I cash it, that means I cannot dispute their share. Where do I go for help?"

9.	Libby writes: *"I am 44 years old. I received my silicone gel breast implants in 1984. In April, 1998, I went to the doctor for a lump in my breast. It was discovered that both of my implants were "bleeding" (this was assessed by sonogram) at that time dated X-rays were taken and I was advised to have them removed immediately. It was discovered at the same time that I had thyroid cancer. After many months of treatment and bills I had not the energy of funds to have the implants removed. I have had joint and muscle pain for the past few years but had attributed that to age! I now have water retention in the lower part of my body that causes my legs to swell twice their size daily. I understand it may be possible to submit a late claim, I would like very much to have this poison removed from my body but would never have the funds to do so on our income."*

10.   Kinsley writes: "I had the polyurethane/ silicone gel breast implants in 1991 and the plastic surgeon collapsed my lung and did not catch it for 2 days so I had pneumonia by the time he admitted me through the back door of the hospital. First of all, the implants were 100 cc's over what we had agreed upon and I became sick right away. June 4ᵗʰ was the implant day and by October, I was practically bedridden. I went to Seattle to doctors then Oregon where a physician removed my implants. While I was on the operating table, without my knowledge, the doctor sent my ex-husband to the bank to get money for saline implants! The surgeon carefully described how I had polyurethane implants and how he "scraped the foam" from the capsule (I already had capsular contracture and was inflamed) he even stated that some of the foam was still attached to the implant; however, "He saw no problem with silicone". The doctor said he saw no problem with the silicone implants, but his secretary told me I was the second sickest patient he had ever seen. I was never offered the option to have reconstructive surgery and in fact, a plastic surgeon and internal medicine doctor told me that I was so inflamed he very likely would not be able to sew me up! The internal doctor found a severe urinary tract infection as well as inflammation in my blood stream sometime in early January, 1992. All of which the plastic surgeon tried to ignore, even writing me a letter telling me to go anywhere in the State of Washington to get "fixed" as I had a surgical procedure problem and certainly not anything to do with silicone.....that it was all a political scam, and that he would put implants in his wife or daughter!!!

Stay away from the media and take your pain medication exactly as prescribed. As for the foul smelling urine, I should drink more water and the lethargy was because I had my days and nights mixed up! The saline implants, once again, contributed to my health starting on another spiral down. In a couple of month's I was at my folks home in Texas flying back and forth to Oregon for treatment…..One of the residents there finally referred me to a neurologist in Plano, who arranged for me to go to Baylor. Since I became sick right away they ran every test imaginable to rule out any other cause, except silicone. The saline implants were removed; pictures were taken, nerve and muscle biopsies were taken, brain spects, MRI's etc…..

Four month's later I was back in the hospital being told to get my house in order as I was dying! My legs were paralyzed, bowels inactive and my bladder had shut down. I had received several steroid "cocktails" intravenously and then six rounds of plasmapheresis, which turned me around. I was in the hospital for over 2 months and started cytoxin by mouth for 1 year, along with gamma globulin for over 3 years.

When I ceased taking the gamma, I had chicken pox type blisters sparsely over my entire body and my lips were completely covered with fever blisters. These became so severe that I had necrosis."

11.   Michelle writes: "I settled early on with the manufacturers because I was not having problems and I was misguided about the women who were having problems. It was that group settlement years ago. What are my options now? Can a file another suite against the manufacturer?

I was recently diagnosed with silicone toxicity (poison in the tissue and the blood stream), and in the early stages of Lupus. After an MRI, the doctors discovered a rupture in my breast implants and unfortunately, the spill has gone beyond the implant and beyond the capsule that formed around the implant. (A previous mammogram and ultrasound did not pick this up).

I want to educate as many people as I can. This affects our mothers, sisters, girlfriends, and wives.

Also, remember breast cancer victims who look toward implants after losing their breasts.

My surgeon has me scheduled for removal of the implants and the tissue around them. The doctor said that all the "accidents" I have experienced with sutures and broken bones (causes disorientation), depression, emotional disorders, alcohol intolerance, severe sun reactions, drug reactions, fatigue, insomnia, skin disorders, weight struggles, muscle/joint aches, severe sinus problems and allergies, are all caused by neurological, auto-immune and rheumatologic diseases from being poisoned by the silicone. My symptoms didn't start right away....It was over a 5 year period, each woman is different."

12.   Carrie writes: "Today started out as most days do for me. I forced myself to get out of bed and go to my part time job. As I pulled into the drive-way after work, I decided to check the mail. Excitement filled my heart when I saw the large envelope with my attorney's return address printed in the left corner. I parked the car in the garage and ran into the house and tore open the envelope. It had been months since I had heard from my attorney. Our last conversation was about getting my breast implants removed. He strongly urged that I do this as soon as possible.

That conversation was November, 1998. The first week of December, I did as he suggested and had my implants removed. They were ruptured! The total expense for the explantation was just under $8,000.00. Today, as I stood in my kitchen and tore open the envelope I was thrust to the floor in tears from shock. Seven years of endurance and waiting were abruptly halted. My settlement offer had finally arrived. "We strongly recommend that you accept this offer before it is withdrawn, even though it is far less than anticipated only a short time ago." The offer is just about enough to pay the credit card bills that I used for my surgery. Today I sat on my kitchen floor and cried seven years worth of tears; today I sat there and felt as though someone had ripped my heart from my chest! Today I admit defeat!

After the attorneys receive their share, and after the judges receive their percentage...I won't have very much. The breast lift I had planned for someday will go into the trash along with the letter from the attorney. I want nothing more to remind me of the nightmare I have endured. What fight I have left inside of me will be spent in letter writing and label reading. I will do more research on products made by the breast implant manufacturers and I will buy no products made by them! I will write letters to any and all publications and advertisers who promote these products and tell them why I refuse to buy their publications and support their endeavors. I am just one small voice in the dark, but I will do this for me and for those of us women left on this earth who have been so adversely affected by silicone.

13. A "Parable": This parable was written by one of the women I have been blessed by knowing only a short time....She committed suicide during the summer of 2000 because she could no longer tolerate her pain and anguish. She felt so much guilt because her children became ill as a result of her silicone gel breast implants!......."One day a woman named Kelli went to the drug store to purchase a can of formula for her baby. As soon as she arrived at home she made a bottle and fed the infant. After she rocked her sweet baby to sleep she started to clean up from the mess she had made while preparing the bottle. (Kelli was a careful mom so she had sterilized the bottle and nipple before the feeding). To her horror she discovered that the can of formula had fungus in the bottom of it and it smelled metal-like, as if it had chemicals in it. She nervously called to her husband Bill, who happened to be a chemist. Upon further inspection Bill concluded that indeed, the can of formula was contaminated.

The next morning Kelli checked on the baby who was fussy and upset. She called the pediatrician who examined the baby and determined that the baby was sick. Kelli called the drug store where she had purchased the can of formula only to be advised that the company that had produced the product had never tested it as far as human consumption. She called her husband and he called the FDA. The FDA said that yes, they were aware of the fact that the company had not tested the product and that there had been other reports of sick children but they just wouldn't do anything about it. The doctor at the FDA said they had also had reports that some of the mothers who had handled the cans were also ill. Oh well, said the doctor at the FDA, no one really cares about babies and mothers anyway.Could this story be true? Call or write today and ask the FDA why they have not made a firm statement on the effects of breast-feeding on the mothers with silicone gel implants and saline implants.

Medical Term: Double Lumen Silicone Gel Implants Layperson's Term: Leaking bag of fungus infected (Aspergillus Niger in my implant), bacteria laden mix of salt water and chemicals that were virtually untested if exposed to the human body. The effects on the offspring of the implanted woman are "unknown"."

"I was never provided with a list of all the ingredients in my implants nor was I given the nutrition facts so that I could make an informed decision as far as

breast feeding. Do the ingredients (please refer to the layperson's term) meet the requirements of the National Academy of Pediatrics in terms of recommended daily allowance for nursing infants?"

14.   Donna writes: "I just got a call from my attorney today. The manufacturer of my implants made me the most obscene offer I can imagine! I can't stop crying long enough to even think. Help!! I don't know what to do. These S O B's have just about killed me and they want to give me some stupid amount! After my attorney gets his share I will end up with less than a years' wages.

I have had pre cancers removed, bone tumors and bone grafts done. I have silicone induced Multiple Sclerosis, Fibromyalgia, I pee myself and poo myself, the pain and the headaches are incredible, asthma, and the list goes on. I have had over $125,000.00 worth of medical expenses in just the last 5 years. My arms and legs don't work half the time! I have multiple cuts and bruises from falling down a lot. This is not the first crack the manufacturers have had at me. They almost *killed me with that damn Dalkon Shield, it did kill my daughter, and now this. They have taken my life and my rights, and my ability to make a living. Which is best, suicide or homicide? Either way they won…. Either way they killed me!*

15.   Emily writes about her Mom: "My mother just recently had the saline breast implant surgery to replace her silicone implants. She has the hardening of the breasts, the pain, and the constant squeaking sound in her head. I realized that although some of her symptoms have disappeared a lot of them such as her Chronic Fatigue and dry eyes and boils on her buttocks are still in place. I don't think that the silicone has ever left her body, for this I feel sad. I, myself, have had aches and pains and constant dry eyes. I also have a really severe case of asthma. I have a form of arthritis that has been with me since I was 12 years old. The thing that really hurts me is that the researchers that have completed the studies don't agree that silicones in the body do harm! Why didn't they study the extracted implants that have been in the bodies of these women for years? Maybe the reason for all of these illnesses doesn't lie in the freshly made silicone, but in the silicone that may have expired in a woman's body after many years of implantation? Maybe silicone becomes toxic after a certain time period? I, myself, have been thinking this is just another conspiracy against women! Do you know how many lawsuits the manufacturers have gotten out of? It is not just silicone implants, it's also various forms of contraceptives as well as heart valve replacements and asthma and allergy medicines. These companies are Fortune 500 businesses and no one can touch them! What this world all comes down to is MONEY! A life has no value! Currency matters, not people!"

16.   "My name is Jim and I am going to tell you a story on behalf of my wife, Lu Len. She is about to undergo her ninth surgery in the past year! All for the same problem.About 13 years ago when Lu Len was a young girl, she had silicone injected into her breasts. Her breast sizes were different, 36" right side and 34" left side. She was a dancer in a club in Korea trying to make money for her family.

We married and she became pregnant. 'During her pregnancy, her breast grew to a size 44". Lu Len is only 5'4" tall and weighs only 110 pounds, she gained up to 178 pounds. After delivery, she breast fed for 100 days, then went to the doctor to have her breast milk dried up because her breasts were so big. About 2 days later her breasts had dried "flat"!

Not only the milk but the silicone, and she has been in severe pain ever since.During September, 1998, she began what we thought was the end of her breast problem. She had surgery to remove the dry, hardened silicone from her chest and have saline implants put in. The procedure seemed to work but she had lots of pain and there was still hard lumps of silicone in her breasts.

Two weeks after this surgery she developed an infection in her left breast. The puss literally exploded out all over the place! We went back to the hospital for emergency surgery to remove the implant and clean the infection. They sent us back to Korea with a hole in her chest where her left breast used to be! I had to pack it with gauze and wash it out with saline solution. This was very difficult for me and caused severe pain for Lu Len.

After four months of having only one breast she went back to the hospital to have surgery once again for implantation of yet another saline implant. With a one day stay in the hospital it was back to Korea. One week later, her left breast began to swell, growing 5 to 10 times its normal size! It was up over her shoulder, around her arm to her back and down her arm. The pain was unbearable, she had trouble breathing and thought she was going to die. She was rushed to the hospital for emergency surgery. The surgeons found that internal bleeding caused the swelling and there was a hole in the implant. Lu Len has since had four more surgeries to remove the silicone which has spread throughout her body.....The doctors here are trying to remove as much of the silicone as they can, but they say they can never remove all of it.

Right now, she doesn't have the implants and is still in severe pain. This next surgery is already *scheduled to try to remove even more silicone and relieve as much of her pain as they can, but there are no guarantees. Lu Len wants her story told so that all of this doesn't happen to anyone else. She wants the world to know that they should live with the body that God gives them and not alter it with cosmetic surgery."*

17.   Linda writes: "I am a very ill woman who was implanted in 1976, with silicone gel breast implants. At that time I owned a real estate company, had a financial statement in excess of one million dollars and an annual income in excess of one hundred twenty thousand dollars. Since the toxicosis (disease resulting from poisoning) from silicone I have lost my company, been depleted of my financial resources and deprived of the pleasure of playing with my grandchildren. I now use narcotics every 4-6 hours due to chronic pain.

I have cornea erosion (double vision), loss of teeth due to connective tissue problems, compressed spinal cord with spurs, memory loss, Fibromyalgia, Chronic Fatigue Syndrome, Sjogren's, Raynauds,

Neurological problems and Sciatica, just to mention a few. Now multiply this by the tens of thousands of women in these United States and Globally who suffer from these same illnesses and more!

This can no longer be swept under the rug and the "mega corporations" will be held accountable for the products that maim and kill people. The corporations' irresponsibility by no scientific proof, and no testing with human subjects before these products were marketed, now are being forced to show proof after the fact. The proof is there! But now, this has all boiled down to a hard and dirty fight between large, seemingly "insensitive" corporations, and a relatively large group of terminally ill people who, along with their families and loved ones, are experiencing prolonged physical and financial hardships. For many years now the victims of implants have been treated like really dumb or "boob conscious" bimbos. The vast majority of us are not! Many who opted for implants had cancer surgery or deformities and were trying to restore a normal appearance. Others', like myself, had elective surgery. (All of the literature stated they were entirely SAFE). I

157

did not decide to have silicone implants, just an uplift, after having 5 daughters (the last being twins) to correct my fallen breasts. The plastic surgeon and his staff assured me these were not in any way like having the silicone injections and would "last a lifetime", I agreed for the small ones for curvature. I certainly did not need larger breasts. (D cup). My operative report shows an immediate problem. We women should never have been lied to or exposed to these kinds of illnesses we must live with every day.

I will now have to represent myself in court because the attorney who was representing me decided he would not go to court because of the lack of "scientific evidence" connecting silicone breast implants with disease. This was a 5 year waste of time for me and I am sure, others as well. I am still an American Citizen and due my day in court, even if I must do it myself!

We need someone who has the personal integrity to stand up and say NO MORE! We need some one to say there are funds for the "UNBIASED" research needed to uncover the cover-up that continues to go on!

18.   Cecilia writes: "I was the single parent, mother of two beautiful daughters, a full time student and a victim's advocate. It was challenging but I had the energy, health and skills to manage with a certain amount of personal fulfillment. I balanced the different areas of my life with skill even though that balancing act was, at times, tentative.

As a victim's advocate I rode with law enforcement on their domestic runs, lobbied the State Legislature, transported victims to shelters and wrote programs. I worked with victims and the men who battered them. I made videos, lectured and produced two major benefits.

I felt like I had it all . I owned my own home, had a beautiful family, a very high IQ, a career I enjoyed, an education, a sports car, never had been ill and was reasonably attractive. I had all the material things I would have ever expected in my mid-20's and more! I had life by the tail and, as is frequently human nature, I wanted more.

I was one of the many women in America who bought into the male ideal and media depiction of females. I was one of the many women who acted on that belief. At a time when there was no negative press on the subject I had silicone gel breast implants. My life was immediately and forever changed. Within days of implantation, my hair was falling out, my right arm was grossly swollen, my knees hurt and I had an infection. Only later did I find out that for a week one of the implants was literally exposed. Within days I was taken back into surgery to have one of the implants removed. Only one implant was removed because I had no health insurance and the other was not infected. Appearing normal was not a medical necessity.

After the removal of the implant, which left me with one breast size C and the other a size AA, my health continued to decline. I hurt all over and had no energy. I was diagnosed with arthritis and functioning was difficult. The media had done nothing yet on silicone

160

and all doctors denied any connection. Believing, as most people still do, that doctors were superior people of integrity - I believed them. I was now deformed with two different breast sizes and I could get one put back in for a lessor amount of money than having the other one removed; I waited for 6 months and then had the infected implant replaced. During that surgery I woke up! While my wrists were strapped down I pulled up and off of the table, cut my head on a lamp and found myself in the recovery room. My body shook violently and the pain was unbearable as the nurse informed me that she was given strict orders to give me nothing for the pain! As they wrapped me in hot blankets another nurse slipped me something that reduced the pain. The anesthesiologist came in and I told her I would have her license! She said, "No one will do anything." She obviously know something I didn't yet know.

Another implant only solved the aesthetic problem. At the age of 30 I could no longer get up and down stairs because of the pain and swelling in my knees. I remember thinking that it felt like someone had a voodoo doll sticking needles into it (doll was me);

I had shooting pains, aches, pulls and throbbing all over my body. It was frightening and confusing.

Lobbying was the first thing I had to give up, then I had to drop out of school and began raising my children from the bed. Family time was spent with two little girls romping and wrestling over the aching body of a mother who felt and acted 50 years her senior. The pain was so bad that I began drinking to numb the pain. I had to quit my paying job and any volunteer work, like the advocacy, was out. My home was in foreclosure, my rheumatoid factor and ANA were positive and my children were not being cared for. Then the media reported it......They made a connection between silicone and autoimmune diseases and there had been evidence of this long before I made the decision to "augment" my body through the "A BETTER YOU" Program.

Furious, I filed suit against the doctor that told me they were "perfectly safe", "that there was only a 2% chance of infection" and that I could take a hit during power volley ball and they would never break!

I filed suit against the doctor that said he would put them into his wife and there were no KNOWN side effects! How could they lie? I wondered.... This was a violation of the oath he took and I had always thought that was serious. He sold out my life and the mother of my children for what was probably no more than a month's worth of country club dues! To me he was an aberration - a medical whore! I just knew he could not get away with this and he would be held accountable. After all, he wasn't a batterer or sex offender; his peers would never overlook this! I hadn't yet realized that was exactly the point! I was no longer dealing with a batterer or a sex offender; like most medical malpractice victims, I was totally unaware of the power I had just challenged. I was totally unaware of the hell that was to come.

Suddenly, I couldn't get a doctor. They were rude, degrading, insulting and abusive. They seemed to take pleasure in humiliating me. A local rheumatologist lined six of his office workers against the wall of the examining room while he examined me! He introduced them as "his witnesses". Another time I

163

had been working with biofeedback to help control the pain. One night I had a temperature of over 104F. And had to go to the emergency room. I proudly bragged to the nurse about how I had raised the temperature of my hands during a session and she said,

"So that's how you got your body temp this high!" Shocked I turned my back to her and said "Get away from me". Because I had no health insurance I felt I had no choice but to go through this degradation..... I was afraid, and wanted this 4 pounds of toxic substance away from my heart and lungs! They no longer diagnosed me with arthritis or autoimmune disease. With the media reports came the diagnoses' of psychogenic, psychosomatic, and malingering. I thought I was the only one suffering this abuse! I thought it had something to do with me, I thought I had caused it to happen. I didn't know that hundreds of thousands of silicone infected women were getting the same reaction from those we had trusted.

Another doctor once left the examining room and told the nurse I had threatened suicide, to hold me and call for a psychological evaluation. He was lying but I just waited, totally irritated. I was starting to grasp the concept of unquestionable authority, and how people abuse that. When the psychologist arrived, it was a dear friend and colleague, he looked at me and said "I told you, medicine and justice don't mix". "You can't have both at once!" I nodded in disgust and he escorted me to my car. I knew I had just escaped something horrible and would later hear these stories from the victims who weren't lucky enough to have friends doing emergency psychological assessments.

Along with all of the other symptoms, my left breast was rock hard and purple! I was scared to death! I had sold my car to keep the house. My children cried for orange juice. I had no health insurance, which really didn't matter because according to the experts there was no problem and I was just suffering from an overactive imagination! It didn't help or matter that my blood work was positive before the media reports.

I was using alcohol to kill the pain in my joints and connective tissue. I was abusing alcohol to increase my energy and to numb my fear of the present and future. I never asked for drugs and didn't want them. After a few embarrassing and dangerous situations with alcohol, I realized that form of pain relief was costing me too much. I spent the night in jail for a DUI. In the probation office I ran into a judge whom I liked, respected and had even dined with. As much as I tried to hide the fact that my life was literally falling apart, I couldn't.

The purple breast was now a combination of shades of purple, black and yellow. It hurt so much and never moved. Without insurance and with doctors denying there was a problem, it couldn't be dealt with! One night a hospital worker, who identified herself as a plastic surgeon, did deal with it.

Later, as I gave my attorney more medical history, he told me that the procedure should never have been done. As he investigated further he found that three students had signed a surgeon's name and performed a surgical procedure on me while I was awake! They took turns squeezing the implant in an effort to break down the tissue around it. I had handprints from my neck to my waist and by the time the bruising disappeared the breast was again rock hard and even more discolored.

I got sicker and more vocal about what the medical community had allowed to happen to me. Our finances got worse and so did my health. I married a dear friend.

Life was looking up! For reasons I couldn't explain, I had found a doctor in the Yellow Pages who agreed to help me. To us, this was a miracle! No physician in town would see me because of the suit I had filed. There was also a surgeon in another town that was helping women affected by the toxins in silicone breast implants and they thought my insurance might pay, and my daughters occasionally had orange juice.

My health continued to get worse. My joints and connective tissue were inflamed. I had horrible rashes all over my body, two violent seizures, my hair was getting so thin, and my hips hurt so much that I frequently couldn't walk. I had ridiculously high heart rates that the doctor said was panic.

A microvascular surgeon in Cleveland said that she believed having the silicone removed could help me. She said that because the silicone had only been in me for a few years, I had a chance to recover. She said the autoimmune disease or my bloodwork would not turn around immediately, but she truly believed I could be helped. She said I would be deformed, my chest would be concave because I would lose my breast tissue. I agreed to undergo explant surgery and to become even more deformed in order to regain my health. Because of my paralyzing fear of doctors she demanded that I be released to a hotel adjoining the hospital on the condition that my husband and a friend take care of me and that I continue coming in for treatment. I had tubes running all through my chest and my husband drained the bags that hung from me. I don't remember anything about the week except the bandage removal and her discontent over a drug that my Yellow Pages doctor had given me -Dilaudid.

The surgeon removed the tubes and bandages and conversed about how good my breasts looked and got a mirror. She encouraged, even begged me to look. I wouldn't. When I got home I returned the Dilaudid to the other physician....It took weeks before I looked into the mirror. When I did, it was apparent that she not only did a good job but also cleaned up the scars left by the other surgeons.

My health had gotten worse. At 32 years old I spent much time in a walker and a wheelchair. My heart rate would go as high as 312 and I was on numerous drugs. My trusted Yellow Pages physician now had me on 60 mg. Of Restoril, 3 mg. Of Xanax, 12 Percocet, up to 30 mg. Of Prednisone, Verapamil 240 SR, .5 mg. Of Digitalis, Ultram, Wellbutrin, Paxil, Vicodin, Axid, just to name a few. I took these drugs in a single day, every day. My medical records reflect that when I met him I was on no drugs and that I was very concerned about what he was giving me.

I was not getting any better and my doctor literally said he had no hope for my recovery as he added more drugs! He told me that he wanted me to see one of his friends. He wanted this friend to put a port (a hole) in my spine to inject the drugs. I told him that would never happen, I had been mutilated enough. My doctor then went into his routine spew about how I had cancer cells on my cervix and needed a hysterectomy.

Earlier the doctor wanted to do a pelvic exam, I had refused but agreed to see one of his friends. These two had determined I needed a hysterectomy and even referred me to a gynecological oncologist. While they pressured me to have a hysterectomy, his other friend, the "port doctor", kept sending me stuff in the mail. He seemed absolutely determined to put a hole in my spine. This mail was pitched in the trash regularly. I decided to see a female gynecologist these men didn't know. Her response was that I didn't need a hysterectomy, I didn't have cancer and she didn't understand what was going on. I was too drugged to be suspicious. I was falling down, over sedated.

After a serious fall my husband took me to the emergency room, I had been on these drugs for years. He then took me to a neurologists' office. The neurologist looked at me and told my husband I was over sedated and that he wanted me to go into the hospital to get off the drugs. We then went to the internist who said he wanted me to go into the hospital to get off the drugs as well, and for testing; and the neurologist would do laser acupuncture and provide and tens unit for the undiagnosed hip and joint pain. The next day I was admitted to the hospital.

Much of my memory of this event is gone. The reconstruction of these events comes from my medical records, my family and what little memory I do have. The day I was admitted to the hospital an IV was put into my arm. I didn't realize I would be getting off drugs with an IV. My image of detoxing had always been people sitting around smoking cigarettes and drinking coffee. I remember asking about the drugs the nurse was giving me and she treated me like an idiot and refused to tell me.

It wasn't apparent to me that I was getting worse but my family was insisting the drugs be reduced. The nurses laughed when I said I was supposed to get a tens unit and laser acupuncture. According to their records on day 2, I pulled the IV out, it was replaced and the drugs were increased. On day 2, my oxygen saturation levels began to drop and I had gastroparesis due to the drugs. Which means that because of the drugs my bowels stopped working. I weighed approximately 89 pounds and was not getting rid of the drugs.

According to their records I was receiving: 20 mg. Of Methadone, up to 150 mg. Of Demerol every three hours, Percocet, Levopram, 60 mg. 3 mg. Of Klonapin, 3 mg. Of Xanax, Prednisone, Propulsid, .5 mg. Of Digitalis, Verpamil SR 240, Ultram, Wellbutrin, Paxil, Nicoderm ad nauseum......"

19. Brenda writes: "I have been trying since June, 1999, to get someone's attention and help for "Toxic Chemicals" that were omitted from the Global Settlement. We women were all told there was a lot of research being done on the breast implants. I found out there was nothing on Toxic Chemicals though, now or in the future! The only research is cancer and diseases that are in the Global Settlement.

I have called doctors, environmental clinics, medical universities, National Institute of Health, the CDC in Atlanta, the FDA, and Medicare....(Medicare won't pay for most of the tests we need as they are called experimental.

I wrote to President Clinton, Vice President Gore, Senators, Representatives, 20/20, 60 Minutes, Dateline, Today, Good Morning America, Oprah, and AARP. If I understand correctly, we need a Citizens Petition for the Environmental Adverse Reactions, which was omitted from the Global Settlement, and it needs to be addressed: For Environmental Adverse Reaction.

Most of the women don't know about the Toxic Chemicals; I didn't, until the seizures started, and I was fortunate enough to get a doctor that knew what to test for. 1984: Lived in Indiana, had the silicone gel breast implants The very next day I had a low grade fever and have had it ever since.

1985: I had a D&C for irregular bleeding, and went into menopause at this time. Slowly, I started putting on weight, and had arthritis and headaches all the time.

1986: Closed Capsulotomy's: I was having trouble with my memory, smell, taste, and a hematoma in the right breast. (A closed capsulotomy is when a physician physically manipulates the "hardened breast" with his hands in order to release the tissue that has become tight and make it more supple)

1987 or 1988: Closed Capsulotomy's again: My sense of smell was now gone and I had very little taste. I had to leave paper and pen in every room and vehicle; my memory was very bad.

1993: I didn't know what was wrong with me? Pain all over my body, from head to toe. The doctors did many tests; right lung aspiration, videopelviscopy,

Epstein Barr Virus, Spastic Bowel, and MRI-brain. I also went to the Taste and Smell Clinic in Chicago. The mammogram and ultrasound didn't look right so I had the silicone taken out and saline implants put in. The left implant was ruptured. Four months later I had to have open capsulectomy because of pain and swelling. Divorced after 38 years of marriage.

1994: Moved to Florida. Found out about the Global Settlement, and went through all of the tests with the results including: ANA speckled, Atypical Connective Tissue Disease, Organic Brain Syndrome with cognitive impairment, Atypical Neurological disease, Multiple Sclerosis like syndrome, Epstein Barr Virus-restricted, breast pain (burning and itching).

I went back to school but experienced problems retaining the new information. I had no computer training, and sometimes, I couldn't get into or out of the computer, even though I had the information right in front of me! What I can accomplish now, I may not be able to do in a few minutes from now! This happens with memory, reading, writing, speech, math, and even tying my shoes.

1995: I went back to school again. I filed for total disability because of illnesses: bronchitis, hair loss, dental problems, Chronic Fatigue Syndrome, and silicone antibody Toxicity. (Severe under the Social Security Act)

1996: Total disability retrograded to 1993. I was sleeping 18 to 20 hours a day three to five days at a time. I would have these episodes three of four times a month, I didn't know why?

I would have a reaction to about everything the doctor would give me; spasm of the esophagus (throat would almost close), endoscopy and dilation. This is when I was introduced to alternative medicines and vitamins etc.

1997: Emphysema testing

1998: Moved to Nevada. Had an MRI right shoulder, results were tearing of the Supraspinatus tendon, MRI of the left shoulder showed fluid in the joint. Allergy testing was done; I am allergic to about everything! By this time the sleeping spells were rare. I still have them when I am around pesticides, also my throat will begin to close.

1999: Went to a doctor in California as I was starting to have seizures often. Several tests were done; Spect scan was abnormal, ATOVA test was abnormal, Micro Cog - low average, elevated Thyroid antibodies, Pulmonary Function Test - low normal range,abnormal neurological examination, Tyrptase level - below normal, ANA titer - 8, Chemical sensitivity to small amounts of every day chemicals, toxic encephalopathy, dry eye syndrome in the right eye, chronic rhinitis, sinusitis, laryngitis, vestibular disorder - peripheral with vertigo,immune dysfunction and autoimmune disorder. Cholesterol high, 3m punch biopsy - viral exanthem, drug eruption - abnormal (T helper cells T4, Suppresser cell -T8, B-cell, CD3 & CD26T, IGG Benzene

Ring, Lipopolysaccharide, Staphylococcus Aureus, Apoptosis).

2000: I now have seizures every time I go out in public. I wear a mask, but I still have them. Different chemicals affect me in different ways; very bad headaches (some like migraines), hands and feet swell, sleeping spells, lungs won't expand so I can breathe, whole body jumping and jerking, one side of my body will become numb as if I am having a "stroke", real bad vertigo, slurred speech, blurred vision, throat swells almost shut, pulse racing or deminished, short term memory loss, loss of muscle control, chest pain (like I am having a heart attack and making the body immobile), feet flipping out of control. I am in pain 24 hours a day. Some seizures cause the pain to be almost unbearable.

Many of the doctors were disrespectful to me; saying I have an obsession about going to different doctors, and there is nothing wrong with me, it is all in my head and I need psychiatric help! They have told me there is no such disease as Epstein Barr Virus and there is no test for it! They say I need to stop taking vitamins, minerals and herbs; it is quackery to take gamma globulin, B-12, and B-Complex. It is impossible to have a low fever this many years and that I can't be allergic to so many things! They will not prescribe pain medications, and if there was something wrong with my memory, I wouldn't know it anyway, and none of these things that seem to be wrong with me have anything to do with the breast implants!

I could die from the mold, fungus, bacteria, and toxic chemicals in my body if the breast implants rupture.....I cannot have the implants taken out until I receive more testing and proof, so that the insurance company will pay for the procedure......Our illnesses are robbing all of us of our normal lives. It has cost some of us a spouse, children, careers, and family members. They don't understand our problems and illnesses and quite frankly we don't either!

20.   A POEM - "Gagged" by Order of the Court
I have a name but no one will ever know me.

No one will ever know my story.

As a young woman I touched the flame

Of the plastic surgeons' reach for glory

and bought his lie

That implants would last forever, even if I die.

He bought a yacht

And sent his kids to Harvard.

He went to the Himalayas

To do good for the sick and affirmed.

While at home we languished in untold pain

And mortgaged our homes for medical care

To support the greed that put us there.

My implants ruptured and spread their deadly toxin

Throughout my body until my bones were on fire.

My lungs hurt from the constant cough

That racked my body to the soul.......

And I did not know

That a judge had sealed many documents

That would have proved this deadly deed

Had been practiced knowingly upon the innocent.

I did not know they were not FDA approved

I did not know that contaminated foreign implants were sold to the unknowing

And used by the unethical in their reach for a fatter wallet.

I believed my government would protect me

From those who sought to increase their bank accounts

At the expense of my health.

My doctor I had placed upon a pedestal

And believed that he too would not lead me astray.

But, I was wrong, I was wrong about it all.

The implants ruptured and I grew daily sicker

My doctor not only didn't know what was wrong

He didn't want to search for answers.

Soon I couldn't walk with this unknown disorder

My bowels lost control.

My breath felt as if it were being choked from my body

And my eyes were growing dim.

Does anyone really think THIS is my choice?

Does anyone really believe I would choose to sit at home

And never climb the mountains again....?

And never walk on the sandy beach again.....?

And never sit in the sun again....?

And never sing in the choir again...?

And never hold the grandchildren for fear of dropping them......?

And wear adult diapers every day...?

While using a cane to get around...?

Is this the life you THINK I deserve...?

What if it were your daughter or mother or child.....

Someone you know and love?

Would they deserve it then?

My house I mortgaged for medical care.

Insurance I was denied.

It will someday be on the public dole

And the perpetrators of the pain of thousands will be free....

Free of accountability

Free of responsibility

For I gave up the battle yesterday

I signed many papers

To keep the deep dark secret.

And they gave me money to pay the doctors,

And so I wouldn't lose my house.

My future is dark and grim.

My health is gone and will never return again.

But the secrets are kept in the courthouse files.

And breast implant manufacturers get away with murder.

If I speak the truth or participate in any activities,

They will take my all away.

And it really wasn't much.

Just a pittance from their golden coffers

And when I die, who will know, who will care?

Who will my story share?

They have legally silenced me forever.

They have removed my right to freedom of speech.

They will constantly observe my every move and word…. All to protect THEIR evil deeds"

"A GAGGED VICTIM OF AN UNHOLY CIRCUMSTANCE"

21.   A Letter sent to someone who wanted implants: "I am so glad you are reaching out to find answers. You are right to be concerned when you saw

the red flags waving at the doctor's insistence of their safety.

a. *No implant has ever been approved by the FDA*

b. *No human testing was ever done on implants. (except the thousands of uninformed women)*

c. *Animal testing was discontinued when the manufacturers began to find answers they did not want to find....migration of silicone to vital organs*

d. *According to Congressional documents of December 1992, the manufacturers and the ASPRS (American Society of Plastic and Reconstructive Surgeons) fought hard to keep the word CANCER OUT of the "Informed Consent" the women would be given to read and sign*

e. *The FDA is collecting statistics on complaints of saline implants, too....That number is growing*

f. Dr. Pierre Blais, an implant expert from Canada, has documented bacteria and fungus in saline breast implants.

g. Saline implants are housed in a silicone shell. The shell may break open and the fluid disperse through the body. (Dr. Blais)

h. The silicone shell is a fine mesh that allows implant fluids and body fluids to intermingle, causing bacteria and fungus to breed. (Dr. Blais)

i. A plastic surgeon's main concern is the health of is wallet. How else could he drive a Mercedes, have a winter home in a ski resort, a summer home at the beach, and send his kids to Harvard so they can learn to run studies that make sick women look like nuts!

j. You don't say if you intend to have other children. Children who nurse implanted mothers end up *with the same health problems that are now apparent in the implanted women.*

k. *The average latency for health problems is 7.8 years. If you speak with women who have fairly new implants, you will get answers, most likely that don't reflect poor health. There are exceptions to that; however.*

The plastic surgeon has much to gain with the sale of the implants. You have your health to lose... .Your children will not have a mother who feels like doing all the Mom type activities, and your husband will not have the vibrant woman he married."

22. *Penny writes: "On July 5th, this year, I will be celebrating the 21st anniversary of my mastectomy! I just celebrated my 46th birthday.....*

I was diagnosed with breast cancer and had a radical mastectomy in 1978; just 25 years old at the time. I waited 5 years before deciding to have silicone reconstruction. I like to think of myself as a well-educated woman and I did my "homework" prior to choosing the plastic surgeon to do my reconstruction. At no time during my consultation visits was I advised of any health risks associated with the implants. I was told that silicone implants would last a lifetime.

Within 3 months of the reconstruction I was back in the operating room...my body had formed a hard capsule around the implant and the implant had moved up under my collar bone.

My symptoms of physical illness began slowly.....joint pain being the first noticeable sign. I first went to a doctor in fall, 1991. Since 1992, my symptoms have continually gotten worse. I have been diagnosed with "atypical autoimmune disease".... Autoimmune Connective Tissue Disease, Fibromyalgia, Myofacial Pain Syndrome, Chronic Fatigue Syndrome, Raynauds Disease, Irritable Bowel Syndrome, TMJ, and Osteoporosis.

In 1994, I had the implant removed. That surgery was the 5th operation at the breast implantation sight.

To date my out of pocket expenses total almost $35,000. You see, in 1991, the insurance policy that I had, had an exclusion, "They would not pay for any expenses related to my silicone reconstructive surgery." Gee, what did the insurance company know, that I did not know?

Twenty years ago breast cancer was the number one killer of women. I FOUGHT that battle and won. Today I am more ill and suffering with more pain than I was when I was fighting my cancer!

It maybe too late to save those of us that are already silicone victims, but it is NOT too late to save our future generations of unsuspecting ladies. The manufacturers' have set aside a $30 million dollar public relations fund to DISCREDIT silicone implant survivors. We have no resources to fight that; however, we do have our voices. We can contact the news media and our elected officials to be our voice. LET OUR STORIES BE TOLD"!

23.   "In 1969," Karen states, "I was a 23 year old cocktail waitress in Las Vegas, Nevada when the national media blitz about a woman in San Francisco and the wonders of silicone injections! My injections were done by a surgeon who had trained at the Mayo Clinic. I was told the same lies about their safety as we were all later told about the silicone gel implants. Very rapidly after surgery, I developed painful lumps in my breasts, and in 1970, consulted another physician about these lumps.   He diagnosed me as having severe fibrocystic disease which was impossible to treat because of the "free silicone" in my breasts and at this time he suggested a complete subcutaneous mastectomy to remove the silicone and fibrotic tissue; to follow with a later reconstruction with breast implants. In 1971, I underwent the first mastectomy. That was the beginning of a nearly two year nightmare which included several surgeries, another mastectomy and repeated implant removals and replacements.   My physician consulted with the manufacturers at the time and had them analyze the silicone that was removed from my breast tissue and found it to be their PURE MEDICAL GRADE 360 fluid!

During this time period I developed hematomas, infections, incisions that would not heal, migration of implants, and on one occasion, nearly two quarts of fluid was removed from my left breast! I think now, that my body was already sensitized to silicone, and that it was fighting the implants and trying to reject them. But as I went through complication after complication, I was accused of being a difficult patient and one who must have done something to injure herself!

This nightmare period ended when I finally healed up but all this left me with one normal looking breast except for the scarring underneath it where the incisions were, and one deformed left breast which I named "Twirpy".....I refused to have any more surgery to try to correct this. (By this time a healed, uninfected breast was fine with me no matter how deformed it might be).

"Twirpy" and I got on with my life without further complication although Twirpy hardened like a rock and twisted ever more sideways!

In 1984, I began to develop severe fatigue, a chronic white blood cell count, began having trouble with my eyes, pain in my left breast and difficulty using my left wrist. My GP could not find out what was causing my fatigue and elevated white blood count so I continued to try and live with it as I felt myself transform from high energy superwoman into a "draggy slug". The plastic surgeon said my breast, wrist, and arm pain was from scar tissue wrapping around my muscles and I had to have the left implant and the scar tissue removed. This was done in 1984. The eye doctor sent me to a world renowned eye specialist, who along with two other well known specialists operated on my left eye twice, leaving me legally blind! Meanwhile, I began to lose all control of my bowels and gained over 100 pounds, and a grossly distended abdomen, all within a years' time.

I kept trying to somehow get on with my life and started a business with my daughter since I could no longer see well enough to drive or work my former job.

During the next couple of years, I watched my teeth rot out, one by one; my hair thin and develop bald spots, my walk became what I called my "Quasimodo lurch" as my aching joints became unsteady. By 1991, I added breast pain, discoloration, and lumps to my ever increasing list of ailments and my GP sent me to a special clinic in California for breast and other consultations. The results from these consultations were: wear diapers, go to church more, and "Oh Yes," Another mastectomy, due to necrosis. (Dead and dying tissue that leads to gangrene, in both breasts)....They also inserted a tissue expander because at this stage, I had no breasts, very little pectoral muscle, skin or tissue in my chest anymore! I think my ribs are intact but they have been scraped, they tell me.

In 1992, the national news about silicone broke and I quickly deduced that silicone gel, just COULD be the cause of my problems!

Today I know I have Lupus, lesions in my brain that affect my short term memory and name recall, ANA positive and I live on strong anti inflammatories, in large doses. I am legally blind, have heart, kidney, liver, and colon problems. Grow more skin cancers than normal, wear full dentures, and am totally disabled since about 1990.

Now about my son. He was born in 1978, when I had silicone in my body for about 9 years. His delivery was by Cesarean section, and during this surgery the physician had to remove my uterus as it was adhered to my abdominal wall with inflammation. He weighed 8 ½ pounds and a delight as soon as I got out of intensive care and could see him. Although he appeared strong and healthy, he seemed to have a cold chronically, or pneumonia, or ear infections. At age 1 ½ he was in the hospital in intensive care in isolation with a coma. The final diagnosis? Immune system shutdown! He grew up with chronic aches and pains in his joints (undiagnosed), sniffles and was prone to any cold turning very severe if we didn't watch him closely. In 1993, he was diagnosed with Lupus, at the age of 15. He is a mentally gifted child and won a nomination to the Air Force Academy, which had always been his dream.....to be a pilot and to explore space!

At age 17, his shoulder started hurting more than his usual aches although there had been no trauma. It turned out to be a dislocated shoulder, which the doctor said he's never seen in any one with out trauma! My son came up one chin short of his physical for the Academy; and forget baseball now, even though he was an all-star player for many years. He's in college now, training his mind and each day I pray for a cure for him."

24. Bobbie writes: "My mom said I could write and tell you what I think. I am almost 14 years old. My mother had breast cancer when she was 27. She had breast implants put in before I was born.

Mom is sick most of the time. Sometimes she can barely walk. Sometimes she forgets words she wants to say. I make a list for her so she won't forget things when she goes to the store.

The doctor did not tell her that implants break open in the body. She had four of the same kind.

Three of them broke. Doctors lie because they want your money.

My dad doesn't know what to do. The doctors don't care and won't run tests on her. They say it isn't necessary because they believe the research studies. Neither of these told the TRUTH. They were paid by the companies who made the implants, to do the studies. The plastic surgeons paid for them too.

I tell everyone about my mom's implants. I don't want other women to get sick like my mom. I wouldn't let my mom do this kind of surgery again. The doctors lied to her once, they will again. They just want the money.

Tell your mom, your wife, your friends not to use the implants. They will only make them sick. Even the saline ones do. They need you. I am serious, Implants are dangerous!"

25. Gail writes: "As a breast cancer survivor since 1975, I can honestly say I was never sick prior

to undergoing a radical mastectomy. I did not have chemotherapy or radiation. Breast cancer did not run in my family. I climbed mountains, rode motorbikes, and walked anywhere I wanted to go...and I survived a divorce after 9 years of marriage....one year after the mastectomy.

One day I spoke with a friend who had undergone implant surgery. She told me I did not have to worry with prostheses' that were hot and sweaty, and seldom stayed in place. (They even fell out at inconvenient times). She said I did not have to worry when I went on a camping trip with a group of people, sleeping in the outdoors, wondering "What to do with IT?" Worrying if the packrats might think it was a juicy treat left for them if I laid it with my clothes.

I went to see the happy plastic surgeon who smiled at me and offered me a return to some resemblance to my former self. "Let me show you what I CAN DO FOR YOU". The first implant failed within 60 days. Four implants of the same manufacturer and they all ruptured! Was I ever told these implants had a high failure rate? NO! Yet the plastic surgeon still used them at least 3 years after my first ones. I talked to another one of his victims. She had five of the same brand....ALL RUPTURED...her first were 6 years before my first! Angry? Yes, I am. By the time that group of doctors got to me they must have known that product was totally faulty. Yet they persisted, no one telling the victims of the dangers of broken implants and poisoning by silicone.

Shortly, after the first implant ruptured, I began to experience burning sensations in my back and legs. I grew more tired each day. My skin, at times, had open sores. My ears rang and my vision has gone bad. My kidneys embarrassed me and my bowels became unpredictable.

During this time I was trying to live a normal life. I was a community volunteer for many causes. I served on the local city council and was chairman of the regional public transportation committee. Yet, I was getting sicker.

Doctors took my money and gave me no answers. Politicians have taxed me for the privilege of representing the very corporations who have poisoned me and do not even have a plant in our state. Some lawyers joined the bandwagon for whatever they could gain and then dumped the "low paying" diagnoses'.

I have been pushed for pills, herbs, potions, vitamins, clay, bark, saliva tests, electro-magnetic field testing, juice therapy, and enemas. All with the promise to cure what ails. Others have insisted that I become involved in multi-level marketing plans to sell phone service, vitamins, herbs, clothes and household goods. Meanwhile, I knew one thing, I was sick and getting sicker. No diagnosis....but sicker. Some doctors have found it easier to give the victims a sack full of anti-depressants, a prescription for more, and a patronizing smile, all without finding the base of the problem.

Do I believe the manufacturers are guilty of a massive cover-up? Yes. Do I believe they have been aided and abetted by elected officials who cannot see beyond their wallets? Yes. Do I believe women should sue for their rights to good health? A health which was robbed from us by the manufacturers? Yes, If they are sick and disabled. Do I believe the manufacturers' CEO's should be behind bars for the deliberate poisoning of over 500,000 women? Make that a YES. YES. YES. Do I believe every breast implant victim is entitled to a disability based on silicone poisoning? Why not? The government did not hold the manufacturers accountable. After all, we should be afforded the same disability rights as the drug addict on the street who collects a monthly check.

Any other product with a high failure rate, such as implants have, would have been pulled from the market never to be seen again!

I have worked hard to with-hold judgment on my fellow silicone sisters who had implants for reasons other than reconstruction. Why or how we all got the implants is not important to the issue. What is important is that we were all victims of corporate greed.

And corporate America is not being held accountable for its actions. Like a spoiled child, they have manipulated their way into the halls of congress to get their way. And like an over-indulgent parent, congress has smiled and given them the smoking gun to point right at the very victims the manufacturers have lied to and cheated.

I will survive. I refuse to be silenced, for through my silence others will be harmed!"

26. Carrie writes: "I will contribute my story and thoughts as soon as I feel able. Briefly, I can tell you about a few symptoms I have experienced. One in particular, I haven't heard too much about is that I felt like my "blood would boil", and at other times I felt like I had no blood at all! My nose becomes blotchy, red and/or swollen at times when it feels like there is sulfuric acid running through my veins. Other times, my nose and other extremities are like blocks of ice. I either feel like I am burning up from the inside out or have deep, deep freeze states. People unaffected by silicone would think I am crazy." (She never was able to feel well enough to add more.)

27.   Marlene   writes: "I   have   Chronic *Inflammatory Demylating Polyneuropathy, which there is no cure.   I also have as well as most of the other women, "crystallized saliva" and records to show that I lost over 360cc's of gel through gel bleed!"*

28.   Joanne, a "Judges" wife writes: "On *the recommendation of a well-known rheumatologist, I had my implants taken out only to find they were both ruptured.   At the time the plastic surgeon wanted to replace then with saline and I told him, NO, NO, NO! From the beginning: This same physician testified in my husband's court as an expert witness.   When I began feeling sick, we called him and asked his advice; he said, "If you were my wife I would have them removed". I did. The plastic surgeon spent hours trying to scrape all the silicone goo from my tissues, it was then followed by reconstruction.   For 6 months following the surgery, I had an open wound, where the*

incision was, on the left breast, about the size of a half dollar.

A couple of years later, I was diagnosed with breast cancer, in the same spot where I had the open wound for 6 months! Is there a connection between silicone poisoning and breast cancer? Who knows? I have my own suspicions that I cannot prove. After a lumpectomy, clean lymph nodes, and 8 weeks of radiation, I am cancer free. Who knows what might have happened to me had I not had my explantation?

My anger rests with the blatant disregard the medical community has for her harm they have done! They further compound their mistakes by refusing to acknowledge the women are sick and treat them for the presenting illnesses. All this because they fear losing money, being sued and admitting they made a mistake! The doctors have profited by implanting women and now, by explanting. The FDA should be ashamed of themselves for the neglectful way they have handled the breast implant situation. As for the manufacturers, the judges should close them down and divide the money between all the women! Unfortunately, this will not help the women who are very very sick, even dead. My heart goes out to them."

29.   Mary writes: "I was 24 years old and worked in the entertainment industry in Las Vegas, Nevada, when I got my silicone gel breast implants. By the age of 27, I had a complete radical hysterectomy, my hair started to fall out by the brush full. My breasts got so hard and so painful I almost lost my mind! At that same time my boyfriend left me, so I left my job and moved to California where my sisters lived and I stayed with them for a while. I thought I had the flu, or a virus that would pass but I was wrong. I got worse each day and year!

I am now on my own, totally disabled, and receive a small amount of money from the government per month to live on. I am not old enough to collect my full Social Security, so I get a little amount from SSI.

In 1996, I had my breast implants removed and had open heart surgery in 1997. When I had the silicone implants removed, they were replaced with saline implants as I was told they were very safe!

Just since August of 1999, I have had seven surgeries on my right breast, the most recent being January, 2000, and scheduled for another one in March, 2000. There is no implant in that breast but there is still infection, it's hard and very sore....The nipple has even disappeared! I have no feeling it at all; it feels like a piece of leather and has an odor. I have asked the doctor about that, he says it will pass with time and the breast will get softer!!!!!!! I don't think so...He offered to do the surgery again at no charge to "fix" it but I am very frightened to do that right now!

I have Fibromyalgia, cognitive dysfunction, memory loss, abnormal fatigue, diarrhea, numbness in my hands and feet, also extreme pain in my neck and shoulders. Do not trust the lies about the safety of any breast implants!"

30.   Anita writes: "*All began in the early 1980's, I believe at the ripe age of 32, I decided to do it!*

I had always hated being so small chested. I had recently been separated from my husband and was at home with two small children. I had a new boyfriend who was always looking at women with larger chests! I interviewed a plastic surgeon at a well known hospital here in Massachusetts...it was all so "heady" back then. Everything went real well, I finally had the chest I had always dreamed of. The hospital and staff were great, no complaints. In the late 1980's, I developed a thyroid condition known as Graves Disease, really strange to me and my family because I was always so healthy! I was treated with medicines for a while and got the condition under control. A few years later I developed some other problems; fatigue, muscle aches, mental confusion, foggy brain, and so forth. At this time the media was focused on the "Breast Implant Controversy". At this same time I developed an anxiety disorder separate from these new illnesses! So I began to be afraid of things.

I called the plastic surgeon and he assured me that everything was O K, that one could not rupture unless sustaining trauma to the breast! This plastic surgeon told me that these implants would last a lifetime! I asked if my illnesses could be related to the implants, by now calling my problem Chronic Fatigue Syndrome. He told me NO! He did question a mammogram on the left breast as it showed some sort of bulge, he did more testing but decided he did not think it was a rupture!

Time went on and a friend told me about a support group in the area for people who had silicone gel breast implants....I was afraid to attend but I went anyway. There, I learned there were other women who had Chronic Fatigue Syndrome. These women told me about a radiologist in the area who checked me and detected that I did, in fact, have a ruptured left implant! Now, I had to remove these things! I couldn't bear the idea that I would be flat chested again! I called everyone I could think of in my town and spoke with doctors, women and others, who said there was no problem with the saline breast implants! One woman said she was very sick with the silicone implants but after replacing them with saline she was better! So this is the route I chose.

I still have the saline implants that I received in the early 1990's, and I believe I am even sicker now than I was before having them! I have new symptoms now; neuropathy. The anxiety disorder I have seems to get in the way, but I know I must have these things taken out! I feel as though I am living my life in Limbo because of the illnesses."

31.   Rhonda's reply to a woman: "You can believe doctors are refusing to treat breast implant women. You see, doctors only know what the sales people of the manufacturers or the distributor tell them about a medicine or a product. Do we ever stop to think that doctors don't mix medicines any more?

Also, they see and hear the controversy going on and want no part of it as they are afraid they might be asked to testify to something they know nothing about!

Now a doctor would need to learn about silicone to properly treat it! A lot of doctors do not know where to get this information as it is pulled off the pages of scientific journals as soon as it is written. MANY REPORTS NEVER GET PUBLISHED!

The FDA has encouraged doctors to believe silicone does not hurt anyone and they do not do anything except voice a concern. FDA will say they use the "honor system" with the manufacturers as they do not have a lab either. If someone does not "go along" they are gotten rid of in the FDA. Even the head of the FDA was changed when some of the silicone implants were taken off the market!

Each time we report a problem, our manufacturers' come back with a "look you in the eye", "FREON" that what we use is not dangerous and will disperse in the body answer! A doctor would need to look and read what is going on as well as learn how to treat a breast implant recipient. Without the papers being published and the FDA standing out and saying there is a real problem here. It will not happen! The spin the ASPRS have put on this is working with most doctors that feel respect for their peers.

I personally have been to many doctors who have told me that they do not know how to treat me. The also have apologized for this! Most medical students that are in schools now are learning about silicone implants and will not put them in when they graduate and start practicing medicine....Now as soon as they learn the silicones in other medical products are just as bad we will be making progress!

The reason there are no "safe medical products" to replace the unsafe silicone medical products is because the world has not learned the products out there now using silicone are truly unsafe! No companies that I know of personally are looking to make a "safe" product as the silicone manufacturers are big companies, too big to compete with! They have *spent many years lying to people about the safety of their products."*

32.   Shirley writes: "I had a mastectomy and reconstruction with a silicone breast implant in 1980. I did not want the implant after the surgery, but my doctors reassured me the implant was safe, would not rupture, and would be the best thing for my physical and mental recovery. My fear was so great regarding a rupture, that the doctor and I performed sit and squash and pull tests on an implant to prove to me that the implant would not rupture! I wasn't exactly convinced at that point, but was overwhelmed by family and medical team pressure to agree to allow the implant into my body. I was 23 years old at that time.....Within 6 months after the surgery, I began to experience severe shooting pains, rashes and shoulder pain. I felt fatigue and started to develop allergies. I discussed my concerns with my doctors, they were concerned as well, and performed two exploratory surgeries to check on the status of my implant. The doctors were unable to find the source of my problems so I learned to live with the shooting pains, the shoulder and chest aches and limited movement, rashes, fatigue and allergies. I figured as long as I didn't have cancer I could learn to live with the discomfort I felt from the implant. Several years passed and I began to develop numerous autoimmune diseases: arthritis, severe allergies to food and pollens, asthma, Meniere's Disease, unusual bone fractures, memory and cognitive problems, Epstein Barr Virus, Chronic Fatigue Syndrome, rashes, and chronic pain. I began to think this may all be related to my implant and about that time there were news reports regarding problems that women were experiencing who had silicone gel breast implants. I discussed my concerns with my doctors again and they assured me that in no way could my implant be impacting my health negatively. I felt that it had to be the implant and insisted that they remove it! I had a battle on my hands, the doctors insisted that the implant was not the culprit and one doctor on the team, ever aware of the growing news about implants, joined a research team on the issue.

Eventually, in 1989, my doctors finally agreed to remove my implant. I insisted that the implant be returned to my possession after the explant surgery. Although my implant did not rupture, I was surprised to see how small it was. It was very apparent to me that somehow it had "leaked". The implant appeared to be a full cup size smaller.

Within just a few months after removal, I began to feel better! It seemed my health problems were getting better, I returned to work and had a few relatively good health years....I still had the unusual aches and pains, arthritis, allergies and fatigue, but somehow I managed to maintain a flexible work schedule to get through the health flare ups! Slowly the chronic problems developed and one after another began to overwhelm my body and Spirit; with each bout being of longer duration and severity. In the passage of 7 years my health had deteriorated to the point where I was forced to medically retire. My doctors did many tests and found silicone in my system and suspected a link to my former implant. I have been fortunate that the majority of the doctors that I consulted had an open mind and the awareness to research any and all of my illnesses and possible causative agents. By the year 2000, I had developed severe chronic fatigue, arthritis, severe cognitive and memory problems, severe allergies, sleep apnea, neuropathy in my hands and feet, unusual rashes and bumps on my hands and feet, hair loss, severe asthma, depression, dry eyes and mouth, connective tissue disease, Raynauds and severe chronic pain, trigger thumbs, Fibromyalgia, Meniere's Disease, stomach problems and numerous cysts.

I was, and still am overwhelmed with my continuing loss of vitality and numerous medical issues. Getting through each day and any activity almost seems beyond the struggle.

Just as I felt it couldn't get any worse, it did. I was diagnosed with a very rare autoimmune disease named SAPHO Syndrome. There is very little known regarding this syndrome but my doctors suspect that again the implant is the culprit. Seems this SAPHO can be caused by a viral infection or autoimmune disease. Needless to report, I am feeling very distressed about this new diagnosis. I wonder what is next? The SAPHO was discovered by a routine bone scan .It apparently affects the bone and causes severe inflammation, growth changes, the synovial fluids, ligaments, rashes on the hands and feet and of all other things, acne! I also have Silicone Toxicity Syndrome."

33.   Kahla, a 36 year old mother and wife writes. "Five years ago after having a baby, I decided to have saline breast implants put in. The doctor assured me they were 100% safe, and would last a lifetime! Over the years I started to have many symptoms that I did not even think were related to my implants. Memory loss, hair loss, very dry eyes, extremely tired all of the time. Then my joints started to swell, I ached so much I could hardly move. I had very hot skin (literally to the touch) and sharp, jabbing pains through my breasts that became so severe, I knew this was more than PMS! I started to do my own research, the second doctor I went to did many tests. My diagnoses' came back elevated ANA, Lupus, etc., I ended up finding a rheumatologist who specialized in silicone poisoning. He diagnosed me 100% disabled and advised me to have my implants removed immediately. I did. Within a week after explantation my right breast swelled 3 times its' size!   I went back to the surgeon and he drained about a cupful of blood, put a tube in me for a week so it could drain into maxi pads! A week after the tube was removed, it happened all over again! He did the same exact thing; and I quote him, "I've never seen anything like this, it is very bizarre". I left with another tube in me draining. I decided to go to another surgeon for a second opinion because I was feeling so sick. Up until this point I was on cephalexin. The second doctor performed a culture, bloodwork, and put me on cipro and penicillin. Got results back and I have two terrible infections in the right breast.

(Organism 1 Heavy growth, "Enterococcus species")

(Organism 2 Heavy growth, "Stenotrophomonas maltophilia")

I am on my 3rd prescription of cipro, and now a 2nd prescription of penicillin, to kill everything. Before he can do an ultrasound mammogram, I also have a cyst in there I have had for a year, but nothing could be done because of the saline implants.

I'm so disgusted, I paid in cash, $4,500. For cosmetic reasons, to be completely lied to!!!

Then when I finally got to the TRUTH and needed them out, I paid in cash, $4,700. And that does not include medications. We had to sell our business, because I just got too sick to work; so luckily we had the money to pay for the explantation. What on earth can be done about this particular problem? I was so healthy before the implants, (gave birth 7 years ago to a beautiful 10 pound 9 ounce baby girl, 24 hours of hard labor!) and two years later, because I thought they were FDA approved and completely safe, I had to go and have implants put in, that has changed my life drastically!! I hardly have the strength to care for my family, get out of bed, it's crazy! I pray to God they ban all implants!!!!!"

34.   René' writes: "I received a saline implant after the rupture of a silicone one. Having said that, I must tell you that if I had been given any information about cause and effect I would never have had either one! The silicone implant caused necrosis of the chest muscles to the point that they had to remove about a pound and a half of dead tissue. By putting in a saline implant with a silicone bag, all I did was compound the problems. I now have, tendonitis of the remaining chest muscles, bursitis, adhesive capsulitis, and rotator cuff tear. They are not sure if it's a complete tear, so I now have surgery scheduled again in a month which, I might add, is the 4th time in that general area...I am really getting tired of: A. Surgeries; B. People telling me how safe these implants are; C. People telling me I deserve what I get; D. Getting tired of having lymph glands rupture; Add nauseum.

I hope that safety can be proven. If not, the FDA is contributing to the wholesale destruction of peoples' lives. By the way, not one manufacturer, or any investigator has ever called or contacted me about my problems."

35. Marie writes: "I have silicone related issues...I have a collapsed spine...I am 43 years old and trying to obtain an appropriate procedure to take care of this. I have spinal stenosis, disc disease, degenerative arthritis, 3 herniated discs, and the doctors want to insert rods in my back and make me wear a body cast for 4 months....all from Lumbar L-2,3,4,5. I don't think I can bear the procedure!

I have been diagnosed with Lupus, had an abnormal ANA, which , by the way, returned to normal when I had the implant removed.

I want to be able to return to work as a rehabilitation counselor I have bone spurs in my shoulder sockets, and my doctors don't know what to do. My blood shows droplets of silicone everywhere! I have the pictures showing this.

My implant was removed 5 years ago, but I am still sick!"

36. *Irene writes: 'I suffered for years being told my disease was psychosomatic and the doctors did nothing while the disease got much worse and is much harder to treat! I am fighting to stay out of a wheelchair and off of an oxygen tank due to their neglect. One of the most basic things they could have done was run a Herpes I/II blood test which, by itself shows a host of diseases if present; any kind of blood test would have been fine. When all of this started happening I asked a primary doctor if there were any arthritis type tests he could run which would show an immune reaction? I didn't know what was happening to my body and I had all these weird things going on! He said maybe a rheumatoid panel but he DIDN'T KNOW WHAT THE RESULTS WOULD MEAN!!! Perhaps some people have tons of money to run from doctor to doctor looking for answers but I didn't; I was also trying to keep my job at the time. Each doctor visit meant more time off the job and each visit would mean being judged as a "hysteric" or whatever the doctor wanted to label me. One doctor literally started screaming he wouldn't help me because he didn't want to be involved in any legal cases! My attorney would recommend no one as he*

might be considered biasing the doctor. I was left to my own resources. I was fortunate in one respect...I found doctors who would run the tests but they never explained what the results meant! I had difficulty even getting my medical records. When I did I often found they had not even noted the most important reasons why I was seeing them! "One other doctor lost all my most important medical records"! I nearly lost my Social Security because he didn't have the most important ones. I was the one who asked for and ordered the EMG's, spinal tap, bloodwork, neuropsyche tests, MRI, eye exams, and Spect Scan. I didn't have more time to waste waiting for a diagnosis. Worse case scenario, I'd be out money but at least I'd know what was wrong with me and if it was truly psychosomatic, which it turned out wasn't in the slightest. I didn't find one single doctor who was interested in any diagnosis that included some so-called "silicone related problems"!

I don't usually recommend resorting to such drastic measures as this but when it comes to my health, I'm going to do it! Each woman has to decide what is right for her but in my case the long wait before the proper diagnosis was made and after spending $300,000. dollars looking for it, meant the disease had progressed much farther than it should have. Now that all of the doctors agree that I have this disease, what difference does it make? I am still miserably sick! Many still are saying that it is psychosomatic! A brand new doctor out of a well known teaching facility stood smiling at me while I suffered, and I mean suffered! I could barely walk, see, or stand up. She tried to negate objective medical tests, refused to prescribe anything which would help my medical condition, tried to insinuate that the neurologist who made the diagnosis after five years of suffering was a quack! And the only thing she prescribed for me was an expensive antidepressant, "So I could handle all of this anxiety better". We wouldn't have to resort to such drastic measures if anybody bothered to read our medical records, BUT THE DOCTORS DON'T, they don't have time, aren't interested, don't believe other doctors, WHATEVER....I've heard it over and over again, how they will not read other doctors' diagnostic notes, medical tests, etc., they want to make their own diagnosis.

If we aren't being diagnosed properly, can't get medication or sufficient help, what are we to do?

If it is up to me I'm going to educate myself as much as possible, they can call me crazy, say whatever, but I'm not going to die because of some doctor's laziness or ego!   If the tests don't show anything then call me hysteric, crazy, but if they do I am taking control of my health. If I pay their bills since they are supposedly rendering a service, then I should be treated accordingly!"

37.   Priscilla wants to tell of her experiences with saline implants.   "They were 450 cc, overfilled to 500 cc, under the muscle, put in on May 23, 1997. I want others contemplating surgery to understand what can and does happen with the so called "safe" saline implant!

Only a little more than two and a half years ago, my life was completely normal. I was completely healthy, now I am living with health that was destroyed.

After a career in management and the birth of my last two children, I had the fortune to become a stay-at-home mom, which was very important to me.

I was not happy with my figure after breast feeding 4 children, so I started saving money in 1996, to get implants. I worked for a year as a waitress saving the money I needed to get the implants, a sacrifice to my family. I had wanted them for years, did my research, watching the 20/20 shows, reading any news article I could find about the implants, (all positive) and I went to the library and checked out all of the books I could find (there weren't many at that time). I waited until my last baby was finally done with breast feeding, and then I made an appointment with a very highly regarded plastic surgeon in town.

I had a girlfriend who had implants for 8 years and she was very satisfied with them. Seeing her happiness made me want to go ahead and get the implants. My husband went with me to the doctors' office, we asked about the risks, and we were told they

223

were very safe, that the chance of having any problems was very very small (like 1 or 2 percent)).

This is what he said but where did he get his information?   There are no registries...? And he also said that my implants would go with me to the grave. We were looking forward to a very good outcome...We joked about how good I would look even when I was old and in a nursing home.

I had the surgery May 23, 1997, and did very well. I had no complications from the surgery. I went from an A cup to a D cup. My husband loved my new figure, as did I, of course! We went shopping for bras together, new clothes, we had a wonderful new sex life, I was the happiest I had ever been in my life. I felt that my life was now finally what I had always dreamed it would be. I was extremely healthy, active, financially secure, I felt beautiful and was told I was, I felt totally blessed in my life.

Then my world crashed!   January, 1998, I became frighteningly and alarmingly ill.   I thought I was getting Multiple Sclerosis or something, because my vision became disturbed. My head felt funny. I couldn't concentrate on simple things; like paying bills, watching TV or reading. I was extremely tired. Mentally, I was laboring, my head was in a fog all of the time. I couldn't care for the kids or the house. I had night sweats and sleep disturbances. My husband asked, "Do you think it is the implants?" I blew that off NO! It wasn't the implants! I went to three doctors, had blood work done and they found nothing. I was told that I was suffering from clinical depression and anxiety! This made absolutely no sense to me. I was happier than I had ever been! Of course my plastic surgeon reassured me that the implants were the safest on the market.

We got a computer and on the Internet, and found that other women with implants were experiencing the same things as I was. Of course, I didn't want to believe it. I fought it. I wanted to keep my lovely implants! I cried so many tears, I soaked my pillows.

I went to another highly regarded, ethical plastic surgeon in a larger city two and a half hours away from my home, and there I was told that I should get the implants removed and that I should see a rheumatologist. He believed, through his experiences with patients, that "IMPLANTS DEFINITELY ARE CAUSING SOME SERIOUS PROBLEMS".

The TRUTH was, the implants were hurting me, and I had only had them 8 months. I could not believe this was happening to me. I knew if I wanted to get better I had to have them taken out. This was the most heart-wrenching experience of my life...my joy since having the implants had turned to my worst nightmare in only a matter of months.

The implants were removed on February 27, 1998, and blood tests from a rheumatologist showed that I had an elevated rheumatoid factor, as well as a lowered C3 Complement, and macrocytosis. The rheumatologist told me that I was a very smart woman for having the implants taken out. He ordered a brain MRI, which he told me was normal but upon reading the radiologists' report myself, found it to say the following:

"Mild prominence of superior cerebellar sulci, significance uncertain. Suggest clinical correlation." "There is mild prominence of sulci over the superior cerebellar hemispheres bilaterally, of uncertain significance. This may indicate a mild degree of cerebellar atrophy considering the patient's age."

There is no doubt that the implants were harming me in a terrible way. It has now been almost 2 years since explant, and I have no more fatigue, my mind is much more clear, I am active and feel good most of the time. I still suffer from occasional brain fog and pray that I don't have permanent neurological damage. The rheumatologist claims the rheumatoid factor (elevated to 117 in April, 1998, and 159 in August, 1998) will return to normal over time. I have not been retested but feel certain that it has improved, as has my health. I have been working so hard to regain my health.

227

I was led to believe by my implanting plastic surgeon my implants would "fix" my post childbearing figure, that the chance of them causing disease was minuscule, that they would go with me to the grave! The cost has been too great. I got 8 months of pleasure, and then destroyed health, more surgery, huge medical bills, pain and loss to my children and husband, loss of work, and loss of future health coverage. There was no mention of these risks!

I do not consider the little he told me about implants to indicate "informed consent" in any way. If he had told me that neurologically I was at risk, there would have been no way I would have gotten implants! Would any woman risk the integrity of her brain or central nervous system function for a larger bust???? No!!!!! If he had told me that insurance companies deny women with implants, coverage, I would not have done this. But no where in my research about implants was any of this indicated.

The fact is; getting implants is a Russian Roulette, and the so-called "safe" saline implant is not safe. There is no such thing as a safe breast implant. These are inferior products, and need to be removed from the market. I know that the medical option for breast reconstruction exists and is desired. That women everywhere want to enlarge their breasts for self-esteem, but breast implants are not life saving devices, they are totally unnecessary and dangerous to health and well-being. They are costly to our society!'

38.   Mary Ann says,: "Since writing this I have had surgery for Barret's Disease and was just diagnosed with ovarian cancer.....This hell is never ending!"

In the early 1970's, I was having pain in my breasts with my periods. My mother did not speak to me about female problems as she did not know anything about them, and sex of any kind was never discussed!

I went to a doctor, who referred me to another one who told me I had a few lumps and that I needed a mammogram. I told him there was no cancer in my *family on either side. I had the test done and was told there was a lump on the right breast. My boyfriend, who was a policeman, wanted me to look into having silicone gel implants as his friends' wife had them and said they were wonderful! He went with me to the doctor's office and we discussed having implants put in at the time of the biopsy for the lump. I also requested that the other physician be present for the biopsy part of the surgery. I was told if there was no cancer that the implants would be inserted.*

Surgery was scheduled for May 5, 1975. I woke up to terrible indescribable pain. I was kept drugged for the next three days. I don't remember anything during that time. When I was "undrugged" I was told that both of my breasts had been removed and implants put in a couple of days later, and there was NO cancer! Many years later my mother told me the doctor told her there had been NO biopsy, but that it was his decision to remove both my breasts because of fibrocystic masses. (Please remember that only one small cyst was found on the right breast).

At this point, I want to say that NEVER was I told that this might even be done. I had a great-aunt who had her right breast removed 30 years earlier for fibrocystic disease and she did not have cancer either. I had told the doctor this and after I got my reports, which I had to call the medical board of Ohio to get for me, because this doctor refused to give them to me, I found that he described me as being" cancerphobic" in his reports! I was not, I was only concerned as anyone my age would be!

Six weeks after being sent home, my left breast was on fire! It also looked like the implant was coming through the incision! I returned to the doctors' office and he started me on Keflex 500mg. He inserted a needle into my left breast and made me hold the tray that the tube attached to the needle drained into. I turned my head away from the smell and sight of the pus and blood draining into the tray….I almost vomited on the floor…He ignored my discomfort and finished then sent me home!

A couple of weeks later I returned for a follow-up visit and he told me that the implant needed to be removed because the infection was not going away! I went in for that surgery and was sent home with an open incision to clean several times everyday, until the infection cleared. Several months later he put a new one in.

By August, 1977, there was enough space in the sides of both implants that you could lay 2 fingers in. They also looked like small round hard balls sitting up way too high on my chest and most definitely did NOT look anything like breasts. I discussed this with the doctor and he said he would remove them and put in a larger size that would match my body size better.

September, 1977, I had the surgery under general anesthesia. I started crying during the surgery because I could feel him and the other doctor cutting me! He asked me why I was crying and I told him I could feel him cutting me and he said No I couldn't! "Tell me, he said, "who's cutting?" and I told him the left one is being cut then the right one, then the left one and so on.   Then I was sent home where I passed out getting out of the car, and was carried to bed where I stayed for one week.

December, 1977, I felt something scratching my bra...when I took it off and noticed a small red spot under the left nipple and to the right a little, I touched something hard and small and saw something light blue sticking out of my skin. I pulled on it and a stitch that had several knots in it came out followed by a long string of sticky stuff. I took a picture of myself and sent it to the doctor, who wrote me back and said to see another doctor as I had moved to Oregon in November.

Several months later I was able to obtain an appointment with this physician and he did a slide of the sticky substance and told me it was silicone, and that I had been exposed to it and needed immediate surgery.   Two days later he removed the left implant. Six months later he put in a saline implant. He stated saline was a much better implant because it would not get hard from scar tissue like the right silicone implant was.   Within 2 months it was hard as a rock!! He told

233

me he could compress it and try to break up the scar tissue or inject me with something that would make the scar tissue dissolve. He also told me that compressing it would be very painful and I told him I had been through enough pain! He did not do the compressing. On my next visit to his office I was worried because the incision did not look like it was healing right. I started to cry and asked him to refer me to someone who could help me handle some of the depression that I was beginning to experience. He locked the doors and pinned me up against the examination table and slid his hands down the inside of my half slip and panty hose and kissed me on the mouth and told me that I was beautiful and that I didn't need any help like that. I cried harder and put both my hands on his chest and pushed him away. He backed up, unlocked the door and apologized for his unprofessional behavior and left the room! I got dressed and never returned for anymore follow-up visits!

I moved again, to Washington State in 1983. Found a good job and had good insurance coverage so I looked for the best plastic surgeon I could find to help me get rid of the two hard balls that were causing me so much pain in my chest. If I tried to lift anything heavy it felt like I was ripping apart and my chest would burn for days.

A doctor in Seattle examined me, laughed, took pictures of my chest and told me he was sending them to the doctor who put them into me...because the one who had implanted them had written a thesis on saline implants being so much better than silicone, because they didn't harden like silicone! And I was PROOF that his theory was all washed up! He said there were new implants out now that would not get hard, would bond with my own tissue and that I would never need to have another surgery for as long as I lived! They were POLYURETHANE "FOAM" coated implants.

I had the surgery in a center called a "day surgery", and was in the recovery room for hours. I could not wake up! I remember looking at the clock and thinking I had to wake up and get out of there, they were closing up and I had to go home. I vomited all the way home and into the next morning. On my first visit back to the doctor I pointed out to him that my left breast was lower than the right one. He said he could tuck it up and take a tuck in the skin and do it in his office. I decided NOT to do that.

In Seattle, I started developing back and head pain...I had several treatments for this: electric shock, and was given anti-depressants...The pain was in my head according to the doctors, Nothing seemed to help.

In 1986, I moved back to Ohio to be close to my mother who had suffered several heart attacks. I found work managing a clothing store and I loved the work. Then things started going terribly wrong for me. I had always been proud of my memory, now, I was forgetting things that I had just done. I could not concentrate for any period of time. I was late for work for the first time in my life because I couldn't remember when I was supposed to be there, or even what day it was. I left that job 6 weeks later.

I then found a job driving a "bookmobile" for the library, and loved this job too. I had developed a cough that made me vomit mucous, my bladder voided when I coughed as well; my back pain was unbearable and I was fatigued all of the time. I had to leave this job after about a year as I didn't have access to a bathroom when I needed it. I obtained another job, in sales, but with more flexibility. Then I started falling asleep in the middle of the day while driving. I saw an ear, nose and throat specialist because I thought maybe I had sinus infections that were causing the nausea and fatigue.... He stated I had silicone poisoning.....He said that one of my implants was broken...I argued with him telling him there was no way this was true because of the type of implants I had.

He said I would have to be on antibiotics for several weeks to clear up the infection before he could even take the implants out. Several months later he put silicone implants back in me and there was no way I was ever going to have another surgery! I was wishing I could die because of all the pain that I was going through.... The loss of memory, the vomiting every night (3 or 4 times), falling asleep on the couch at six in the evening only to wake up every 3 or 4 hours *feeling like I had no sleep at all! This goes on even to today! Nothing seems to help the nausea.*

I started having heart problems, the medicine I was given for the pain in my back and muscles would upset my stomach. I had scopes put down my throat, ate a radioactive egg to look at my digestive system, injected with dyes, had barium swallow tests, and the results were a hietal hernia!

Finally someone told me about a wonderful doctor whom I made an appointment with and she removed my implants, leaving some skin and my nipples as I thought I might have the "tram-flap" surgery someday when I was healed, physically, emotionally and mentally.

Six years later my skin has adhered to my ribs and causes severe pain when I do any work involving my arms. I have only been diagnosed with pleurisy, but this lasts months at a time. After explantation I prayed to feel better...I have not....I have tried all of the medications to try and stop coughing and vomiting but if I do go a few days without being sick I feel like I am suffocating and then I eventually upchuck again then I can breathe. I have been diagnosed with Chronic Fatigue Syndrome, Fibromyalgia, a 60% restricted main artery in my heart (this is mysterious because I don't have high cholesterol or any other blocks in my arteries), and very low blood pressure.

I finally found out about my stomach problems... I was diagnosed with Barret's Disease, the stomach lining crawls up into the esophagus, and was causing cancer. The doctor did a "Nisson Flap", removed the bottom one quarter of my esophagus and the top half of my stomach, then sewed me back together. I also had surgery on my neck twice. I had vertebrae rupture and instead of protruding outward they protruded inward toward and into my spinal cord causing me to be a quadriplegic, had I not had the surgery. I have degeneration of the bone and had another surgery to remove the titanium plate that broke in half

I have to find out how to free the tissue that has grown to and in and around my ribs. It could attach

239

itself to my lungs and I could suffocate and die.Please do more research, don't allow this to happen to any one else."

39. Jeannie writes on the "tram flap": I had a TRAM about 2 years ago and it was the BIGGEST MISTAKE of my life. My abdomen muscle was not cut from the opposite side like illustrated in the books, but was taken from the same side as the mastectomy. Within 3 months, I had a hernia, but the doctor said it was a bowel problem. It kept bothering me and I was having pain and my bowels were pushing out, so I called another doctor who told me it was a hernia and could be operated on. I went back for the hernia operation, was cut open again in the same place that was healing, and more mesh was added. Three months later, I developed severe pain in the groin below the incision, and the plastic surgeon said I needed a nerve block. I had to go to another doctor who stuck needles in my groin area to block any feeling sensations. This was only partially successful. In short, my life has been ruined, I spend my time in bed, I lost my job and career, I have to file for bankruptcy, my marriage is permanently damaged, and I don't seem to have any recourse.

I am PERMANENTLY CRIPPLED from the TRAM operation. I can no longer ride my bike, or take walks, or sweep the sidewalk with a broom. My life is over. I was butchered like a cow by plastic surgeons who never told me of the consequences, but they took all of my insurance money. I have pain under my arm every night along with the agony of my twisted and distorted guts which I can't bear to look at, especially my belly button that is off center! The left side of my abdomen is pushed out and the plastic surgeon said it will always look a little "fuller", and if I don't lose weight I will have another hernia!!!!! I only wish I had never had the reconstruction, but then I read that women who had the invasive cancer that I did only live 5 years after treatment (for only 70-80% of patients).......I only wish to die, after being butchered!!!!

*40.	Glenna writes about the "tram flap": I would love to know just how many Trams have been done in the United States.	Then I would give about* *anything to know everything that happened to these women and how many problems they have to date! I had surgery in 1990, for ruptured disks in my lumbar spine, it did not help for very long at all. Within less than a year, I had pain again and it just kept increasing. I think it was a couple of years ago and I had an MRI, only to find out that they were ruptured again, and more of them (4). I have had many blocks for pain, but will not let anyone operate again until I can't stand up! Funny, I guess I can't stand for very long periods of time now. My point is: This was done 3 years before the Tram and they knew of my back history and problems but never mentioned a word about what the Tram would do to it. Actually, I was not told that the rectus abdominal muscle was going to be cut in two. I wasn't told much at all...except that, It is a big surgery, well what the hell does that mean?*

Geez, when I had my breast removed and the implants put in that was a big surgery...so I guess I was stupid to not ask what's a big surgery.

I asked what I thought were good questions before the Tram but they were not good enough, or enough! What do you say? Are you going to tear me from limb to limb and back again? Is this mesh a possible problem? (It is out already....staph in it). Oh, by the way,am I going to herniate, lose blood, get staph and pneumonia, develop a huge hematoma or be in the operating room for 2 ½ hours????? And am I going to be in so much pain that I pray for 3 days to die????? When I didn't die, I was mad I hadn't, because I felt like someone had tried to kill me and my whole body was in spasm and I felt like a beach towel that had been twisted over and over in order to get the water out. It took over a month to stand up straight and then it was not normal, still slumped a little. Now, I have a navel that looks awful and is as big as a nickel. I could keep going......the mesh got infected and had to be removed, then I herniated and the doctors tried to fix it with muscle and not use any more mesh for fear of anther infection and or rejection.

I heard sometime after mine that there was a different type of "flap", can't remember....or poor memories. *If I remember correctly it was not so involved...maybe I dreamed it, but if I am right I would love to hear of it....BUT NOT HAVE IT! This is almost as close to a crime as the implants are; at least it is sounding like it, the more I read!*

41. "TRAM FLAP" - This is an excerpt from "The Truth About Breast Implants" by Randolph Guthrie, MD, FACS, a graduate of Harvard Medical School, a Professor of Surgery at Cornell University Medical School, and Chief of Plastic Surgery at New York Downtown Hospital and author of a leading medical text on all aspects of breast surgery.

"TRAM FLAP" (pages 55-58) "And now we come again to the infamous TRAM flap; the triumph of the plastic surgeon's mania for proving it's possible to move anything anywhere even if it flies in the face of common sense. I am spending so much time talking about this operation simply because it makes me quite angry to hear that it is being done.

The TRAM flap requires the full or near-full length of the rectus muscle that extends from the chest to the pubic bone and a far larger flap of attached skin and fat, from the belly. (For that reason it is sometimes called the long-rectus flap procedure).

Many doctors try to sell the operation to patients by telling them that a side benefit of the technique is a tummy tuck, though in fact because of the bulging of the ends of the hip-to hip scar that is left - what some plastic surgeons refer to as "dog ears" - the waist paradoxically grows in size

What's more, the operation usually produces an ugly, scarred misshapen blob of wide-pored, hairy, abdominal flab that sits bunched up on the chest like it had just come out a crenellated Jell-O® mold. Afterward, many women bitterly regret that they opted for this procedure instead of a simple implant or even instead of doing nothing."

"There's more". "People have died from blood vessel obstructions and blockages to the lungs caused *by fiddling around with all the abdominal fat. In up to ten percent of the patients, part of the TRAM flap turns black and dies within a few days as a result of poor circulation and must be removed."*

"For one in ten patients, problems don't surface for three months. Then it becomes apparent that the amount of flesh and fat transplanted isn't quite right, and the patient must go through another operation to reduce or enlarge the breast size. And that becomes more risky because the blood supply is being tinkered with, which is very tenuous in TRAM flaps. And even if the whole flap does not die, the part that was fat may melt away. And if it does, the result will be a breast that's too small.

I have read reports in medical journals by people who've performed a TRAM flap where the breast ended up too small, and they just blithely state, "So we went back in a couple of months later and put in a small implant".

42.   *Judge Spector hears from Sarah:: "I am one of 400,000 women who registered in the original breast implant global settlement in the early 1990's. I speak to you on behalf of the untold numbers of diverse women with breast implants who are too ill, or afraid or ashamed to go public. I appreciate your patience reading my four page letter. Please realize I've been ill for ten years because of the manufacturers' silicone gel implants."*

"It is very important to me to tell you my personal story. In 1994, I was promised $1.2 million to join the original class action rather than go to trial. My doctors had clearly documented my level of illness. Even if I received less than the projected $1.2 million, I felt I would be able to survive my remaining years on this earth. At that time, it was stipulated that attorney fees would be paid by the manufacturers, separate from monetary awards. I was told I would receive compensation from two manufacturers as there were two manufacturers involved with the production of my implants. Very ill, I joined this class action suit under

duress, like so many others, fearing the rigors of a jury trial.

I trust by now you have seen or read the TRUE life stories of women whose bodies are indelibly scarred, whose illnesses have ruined their careers, their relationships, their lives! I understand that no one wants to talk about or hear about how implants cause tremendous scarring as they move up to the shoulder or under the armpit, requiring 2nd or 3rd operations. Or how silicone gel has oozed out of nipples after implant ruptures. Or how silicone deposits are carved out of women's bodies, increasing scarring and disfigurement. Or how plastic surgeons replaced pair after pair of ruptured implants, without documenting this or even informing women of the rupturing. Or how young women with implants can never breast feed, because their nipples have been surgically removed, cut and pasted to fit on top of the large implants. Or that in the 1980's carcinogenic TDA's from 200,000 POLYURETHANE FOAM implants damaged women, fetuses, and entered breast milk. Or that women run support groups because innocent children have been harmed by their mom's breast implants. I wonder if the hearings have enabled you to personalize our daily reality????? Our feelings of profound fury and helplessness!

My next question to you is: Why is the public still not aware of these extant dangers? Why were breast implant sales up last year? Why are teen breast implants up 89% since 1992, when the FDA imposed a voluntary moratorium? Why are parents buying implants for their daughters upon graduation from high school? Why do mastectomy patients (and others) insist upon and receive silicone gel implants? The answer is an insidious and deadly combination of ignorance, corporate cover-up and plastic surgeons' collective greed!

I join countless women in silicone implant support groups in the United States and around the world in imploring you, a representative of the United States Government, to intercede and put a stop to this 30 year silicone implant fraud and cover-up by the manufacturers!

In 1978 I had breast cancer. I was told I would die in six months. I survived a mastectomy, chemotherapy and radiation treatments. My daughter and son-in-law cared for me. I opted for reconstruction. A silicone gel implant was placed in my right breast area, a dormant health disaster. In 1982, it was replaced. After six tortuous years, I returned to work in 1984. By 1989, I was ill with many strange symptoms, unable to focus on my work. In 1990, I had to stop working in the real estate business, I loved, where I had become a top saleswoman making $70,000. dollars a year! Since that time, I have coped with increasingly painful bouts of Lupus, auto-immune and connective tissue disease, with joint pain, respiratory and intestinal involvement, memory and concentration loss, mouth ulcers, losing my hair; I have so little hair left, I now wear a wig.

When I had the implant removed in 1992, my chest tissue was embedded with silicone, revealing that silicone gel had leaked from my implant into my surrounding breast tissue. This silicone has traveled throughout my body for many years, into my bloodstream and organs. I have all my medical records the implant itself and my chest biopsy intact, the evidence to prove my long term diseases are silicone related. Do you understand the full implication of this health crises for so many women like myself? I will never be well again! Today my illnesses are more advanced. No one can remove this silicone from my body tissue, bloodstream or organs!

I lived on Social Security Disability from 1993 until 1998. Government health care paid for my costly medications and numerous doctor visits to specialists (I still require $400./month in medications alone). In 1998, my attorney urged me to settle with the manufacturer for $150,000. Attorney fees by this time were not covered in the settlement, so my attorney received $50,000. dollars, 1/3rd of the settlement. I am told there will be $50,000. for me if I go on dialysis. This is little consolation to me. My attorney would receive 1/3 of this amount! She and I still believed I would receive additional compensation from another manufacturers' bankruptcy settlement. In January, 1999, she told me I would soon receive a settlement *from them, yet in June, she informed me I will receive nothing! Evidently, one manufacturer reimbursed the other manufacturer for their payment to me, and in this way my silicone gel claim against the manufacturer (#2) was nullified!*

I write to tell you, sir, that I feel violated! In 1998, when I received the settlement, I lost my disability and medical coverage. I pay all my living expenses, including private health insurance to cover ongoing doctor and specialist visits and $400. dollars per month for medications. My settlement will not last long! It does not compensate for lost wages, attorney fees, or medical care! Yet, I am told I am one of the lucky ones to get any money at all!

My attorney's assistant works with 200 women who enrolled in the global settlement. She stated 2/3rds of her clients will not go public. Many fear having the implants removed. They literally cling to implants that daily leak deadly silicone gel into their bodies. I have met and attended support groups with thousands of women. I testify to you their stories are all the same.

For years, plastic surgeons ignored our complaints. They advised women they would hate their bodies after explantation. They refused to remove implants unless they could replace them with a new pair! Each week my attorney's office receives phone calls from women with breast implants who are only now becoming ill! Across the country, women desperately seek help from silicone support groups! Who will help them?

During this global litigation, my attorney advised me not to speak about my case. I was effectively silenced and disempowered for many years. I, and hundreds of thousands of women in the United States and more worldwide are very ill. Many like myself are disabled forever. The federal and state governments have picked up the tab for a great portion of the manufacturers' negligence over a 30 year period. While the manufacturers pay millions or billions to attorneys, it is the common taxpayer who is paying for the ongoing health crisis caused by their TOXIC products! We feel outraged!

I feel like a prophet of old, howling, "How long, how long, O LORD, will the manufacturers be allowed to deceive the public and deny we exist? The business of breast implantation is pernicious, in my strong opinion, created by men to entrap women. To me it is akin to crime when I read studies by Dr., Jenny and Dr. Smahel in the 1970's, proving the migration of silicone gel from implants into tissue, bloodstream and organs!

The companies' manufactured and marketed breast implants for women. Breast implants rupture and leak silicone gel into women's' bodies. This is no different than being injected with liquid silicone, a practice carried out in the 1940's, through the 1960's, and banned in the 1970's. During that time, it is believed 50,000 people may have been injected with liquid silicone. For example, in 1963, Harvey D. Kagan, Osteopath, publicly announced that between 1946 and 1963, he injected patients with liquid silicone 200 Fluid, a non sterile, industrial version, on an experimental basis. The manufacturer was fined $5,000. In 1971, for carelessly shipping this drug to him and others, without adequate controls over an "unapproved drug".

The implant is simply a DELIVERY SYSTEM for silicone to enter the human body!

Any casual researcher can discover scientific literature, published by ethical researchers, in the 1970's, confirming the adverse action of silicone on the human body. The FDA failed to heed testimony in 1978, by Dr. Henry Jenny and Dr. Smahel, and ignored testimony by other prestigious scientists and doctors. Is it censorship? Are we victims of negligence and fraud? I say YES! The manufacturers' attorneys perpetuated a 30 year cover-up. Millions of women bought TOXIC BREASTS!

In June, 1999, the Institute of Medicine's report came out. Our claims of long term illness from breast implants were called fraudulent by Brian Williams on NBC, and Gene Burns, on KGO Talk Radio. Their taunts were echoed by every major network. As I lay sick in bed, I clearly saw the abusive tone, reflecting the low estate of our country's mentality and spirit.

I have no tolerance for injustice of this nature and scope! Please take a stand Judge Spector. You are the only one holding the line for us at this time. I pray you will stand up to the vast responsibility before you. We are ill, many have already died, waging campaigns from their sick beds, as I am. Now I hear the statute of limitations is run out! Another clever orchestration, by the manufacturers, another hurdle placed in front of sick women!

This personal campaign may be one of the last things I do on this earth. I would like to go out knowing I tried to stand up to a great injustice! I hope you will too, Judge Spector."

43. Deana writes: "I was modeling for Stanley of London in Beverly Hills, California, in 1969. My left breast was smaller than the right one so I was sent to a doctor on Wilshire Blvd., not far from UCLA, who told me that he could fix that and that the implant would be with me for the rest of my life....even when I am in the ground! I believed him and received the implant.

Within a years' time I was having trouble; I was crying a lot, and then my back teeth all fell out!

The dentists didn't know why, the teeth were perfect! The bone was deteriorating! Then my left ribs, then my left hip and then my left foot and then came the pain all over and lots of doctors, and now I am disabled and stay in bed much of the time!

I have no life! There is calcification everywhere. I am taking Prednisone, Vicodin, and many more medications. I was told I have lung cancer; it was silicone moving through, the same thing happened with my liver and kidneys.

Everyday I pray that GOD will never let this pain happen to anyone else. I live in doctors offices and in my bed. They all say there is no fix! They just say, "Make her comfortable."

If I could say one thing, be glad the way you look, we are all beautiful in GOD's eyes!"

44.   *"This is my labor of love,"* Catherine writes,. *"I want every woman to know the hazards of breast implants. The benefits are temporary. Even if you are not sick now, it's only a matter of time!*

In the early 1970's, I developed fibrocystic disease. The surgeon I went to felt that if I had silicone gel breast implants put in they would "protect me" from cancer! In 1974, I was augmented with silicone implants. The first month or so was very painful, and I could do very little. My breasts became very hard and my left nipple was very painful from day one. My suffering had just begun! I went back to the plastic surgeon, where he did a closed capsulotomy. (Squeezing the breast with his hands to break the capsule around the implants). That worked for a while, then it happened again, resulting in more open and closed capsulotomies. (An open capsulotomy is where the surgeon opens the old incision and actually cuts the capsule).

I was having symptoms but never associated them with my implants. I had black lumps in my mouth and went to a dental surgeon where he removed the lumps and wired my bottom teeth to save them. I was having gastrointestinal problems, severe nausea, headaches, sleep problems, chronic fatigue and depression. At one point they put me in the hospital and gave me nine enemas...They thought I had cancer of the bowel, but I didn't. I was having problems coping with all of this!

I finally went back to the plastic surgeon and he said that my first implants had failed and that he had to remove them and put new silicone breast implants in. This was done in 1976. Would you believe he removed the old silicone and left the old capsules in me, and put the new silicone breast implants into this mess????? I did not know he had done this. I knew nothing about breast implants, except what I had been told: They were safe and would last a lifetime!

I seemed fine for a while, although the left nipple was still painful, and I could never lie on my stomach to sleep. After a month or so my breasts had become hard again, so I went to my plastic surgeon again. He once again did open and closed capsulotomies, which only lasted for a short time. I decided to forget it, and get on with my life...I was having more symptoms now: severe flu like symptoms, joint pain, chills in my head, bladder and kidney infections. Many tests were done. I was constantly on antibiotics. Then I developed external cysts on several areas of my body. In 1985, a CT-scan showed cysts on my liver, but three months later they were gone; although my liver remained swollen. My right leg is still numb, my feet were painful and swollen as well. In 1990, large cysts were found on my ovaries. Soon after this my ovaries were removed. During this surgery a mass of slimy yellow substance was found in the ovarian cavity...silicone, I assume, as we now know that silicone migrates throughout the body. Somehow my tailbone was broken during this surgery and that was so painful I could not sit for over 3 years! It is still sore! I had sores in my mouth, my nose, and on my bottom. I lost most of my hair, periodically, I would lose my vision, and would often experience flashing, jagged lines in front of my eyes;

but with no pain. My eyes would become bloodshot for no apparent reason at all, and my headaches were now getting worse, I had gained 50 pounds! I developed hypothyroidism, numbness and swelling in my hands and severe numbness and burning in my right leg, foot and hip, sometimes in my left foot as well. I had this rotten smell in my nose all the time... My rib cage seemed to be bruised and was painful. No specialist ever check to see if my breast implants were the problem! I was having severe flushing on my face, terrible nightsweats, chronic fatigue, severe low back pain and brain fog. I would literally run into things! I was frightened. There was greasy film in my urine and phlegm in my stool. I also had ringing in my ears and whenever I would get overly tired I would have loud vibrations in my head.

In December, 1991, I went to my dentist for a checkup. When he had taken x-rays, he said my teeth were fine but something was wrong with me. I had a strange gait and my neck was a mess! He thought the breast implants were the problem! He ordered bloodwork, and put me on mycostatin for the sores in my mouth, and ordered physical therapy for my neck. I never went for the PT as I was too sick. When my dentist got the results from the bloodwork, he said I had tested positive for Lupus (SLE), that explained some of my symptoms. He then referred me to a neurologist who agreed that my breast implants were the problem. He put me on vitamin therapy to cleanse my system, and sent me to an orthopedic surgeon, who took x-rays and said that I was a mess! Again , physical therapy was ordered but I was too sick to go.

In 1992, I made an appointment with another plastic surgeon as mine had moved to the United States. I had no records at this point. The new plastic surgeon agreed to remove my breast implants, one week later. The day of the surgery I gave the nurse a letter requesting that the plastic surgeon keep my breast implants after removal if they were not ruptured. That phrase, "if they were not ruptured", got him of the hook! They were ruptured, so he threw them out! Also, he left the capsules inside of me! These capsules were contaminated with silicone, and my former surgeon had left the old ones in as well, back in

1976.......I was home later that same day as this was day surgery. I now had two sets of capsules...the shell from the implants, and the Dacron patches all meshed together left inside of me. My tongue started to burn after this surgery, it felt like it had been scalded with boiling water. There were lesions on the right side of my tongue. My tongue didn't burn before this surgery, and it still burns today. Was it a release of poisons? It has been almost three years! We feel that it is a fungal infection. I feel that I have a systemic fungal infection because of silicone poison and all of the antibiotics.

We understand that if the capsules are left inside the body there is no chance that we can get well! Even then some of us don't get well because of the TOXINS in silicone breast implants.

Finally my infectious disease specialist referred me to a plastic surgeon whom he knew, in 1996. He agreed to remove these capsules, and I gave him a letter also asking that all material removed during surgery was to be kept for research purposes. On the day of surgery I asked to see the capsules, seromas,

263

tissue, etc., He stated "he forgot" and threw everything out except for some select tissue.

After this surgery I was flushing badly, they put me on oxygen and kept me overnight in the hospital and the next day I was sent home with drains attached to my breasts. I lost most of my left breast in this surgery. This was the worst pain I had experienced! I could not roll over, it was hell. I was so disoriented I thought I had died. I kept asking my husband if I was really alive? For days it felt like my bed was drifting through space.

Since this surgery I spend most of my time in bed. I seem to be on antibiotics most of the time because of kidney and bladder infections. I continue to have throat infections, flushing, neck pain, aching teeth and chronic fatigue; sometimes the right side of my face becomes numb. I still have insomnia, and if I try to walk my feet burn, swell and ache. I still have small cysts erupt occasionally on my body, I still have a fungal infection they cannot seem to eradicate, or is it periprosthetic bacteria? I have positives for osteoarthritis, rheumatoidarthritis and fibromyalgia, as well as "bumps" on my bottom.

I have learned to live with all of this. My greatest fear is that I will not get well. My number one wish is to be me again! To have lots of energy, and to regain my lust for life. In short, my quality of life is gone, but I have no intention of giving up! I'm going to fight to get well. Also, I'm just too angry to give up!

I said my quality of life is gone, I cannot drive a car anymore, or go shopping alone. I have lost my confidence. I used to love to cook, bake, entertain and go grocery shopping. Now when I shop for groceries I don't desire anything, and I am worn out in minutes! Flowers were my passion. I still love them but I don't get the pleasure from them that I used to. I want all of this back! I am no longer independent! I'm dependent on my husband for most things! I'm like a prisoner in my own home! I hate this!

It's now November, 1997, and I am still sick! My potpourri of diagnoses' and symptoms? How could

265

I have all of this?   Systemic Lupus Erythematosus (positive), Atypical Multiple Sclerosis, Mitral Valve Prolapse, Vascular Disease, Rheumatoid arthritis, Steoarthritis, osteopenia, scarring of the esophagus, atherosclerosis, scleroderma, body does not absorb food causing weakness, hypothyroidism, Chronic Fatigue, Fibromyalgia, incontinence, Chronic recurring hepatitis, loss of vision at times, numbness in my hands and arms, painful chest wall, severe low back pain, burning feet and tongue, severe flushing, tremors, memory loss, nightsweats, sores and blood in my nose, cysts on my bottom, severe gastrointestinal attacks, loss of all pubic, armpit and leg hair, loss of libido, mass in the lymph node in the left side of my neck, and now they want to check for diabetes?

One of my dreams is to dance again!   Perhaps we will have the Last Dance with the Manufacturers!! !!!!!!!!!!!!!

I do take responsibility for having these deadly devices inserted into my body, but I was told they were SAFE! (They lied)!!!!!! I will pay for this mistake the rest

266

of my life, because I was taught to trust people in high places. The manufacturers must be holding hands with some very powerful people to have been able to escape the responsibility for what they have done and to avoid having to admit they made a big mistake!"

*45.   Sabrina writes: When I was 4 months into my 21*st *birthday, I was admitted in to the hospital for a bilateral mastectomy.   I was diagnosed with precancerous fibroid tumors, and was advised by 3 different doctors that the only safe thing to do was a preventive mastectomy.   I was admitted, January, 1978, during the worst blizzard this state has ever seen! My surgery went well, but I was in the operating room for almost 9 hours.   When I woke, in the recovery room, I immediately felt my chest for bandages, to my confusion, I felt breasts under the bandages.   I knew they were both removed, so I was very confused.   When the doctor came in to see me, he told me that since I was only 21 years old, he decided for psychological reasons he implanted me with silicone gel breast implants.   At the time, I was ecstatic, thinking I would never have to worry about breast cancer, and yet still have my*

267

breasts. What a mistake that was! Two weeks later, both implants ruptured, and my surgeon was no where to be found! He had gone on vacation.

He returned a few days later, and when my mother called him (I was still living at home) he came to the house to see me. He only lived a few blocks away so I thought that was a very sweet gesture on his part. Little did I know, at the time, what was in store for me. He took one look at me and immediately carried me to the car, had me admitted to the hospital and told me he had to take me back to surgery to cut out the infected scar tissue and the dead (necrotic) tissue. I agreed, and when I woke up again I had heavy bandages, but my breasts were intact, so I thought that all was well. This happened to me several times and each time the surgeon told me the same thing. What the doctor did not tell me was that each time he took me back to surgery it was to remove a ruptured implant! He would take out the ruptured implant, put in a new one, and no one was the wiser! I certainly had no idea! This went on for almost 4 straight years! I had by this time been to surgery 25 times for "infections". What I did not know at the time was that I had at least 8 different implants that had ruptured, and he had removed each one and put in a new one without cleaning out the silicone that had leaked out, or even taken out the necrotic tissue! Gangrene set in and I spent 3 and ½ months in the hospital with incisions wide open, and every 6 hours I had to have treatment where iced antibiotics were injected into the open wounds. The pain was so intense that at times I would literally pass out. On one occasion the infection had gotten so bad that the surgeon called for an operating room suite, none were available, so he had 2 nurses tie my hands to the bedrails, one held my legs down, as the surgeon climbed on the bed, straddled me, and took 2 hemostats clamped to the edge of the implants and pulled as hard as he could. He took the implants, along with the tissue that had grown to them. I screamed in pain, he told me to shut-up! That if a woman could bear a child with no pain medications then I could handle this!

I remember looking up at the nurse next to me and she was crying almost as hard as I was! She asked him if she could give me some pain medication and he yelled at her and said, NO! he was the doctor, not her! He took the implants out, but they already had ruptured, and I remember the silicone oozing all over me and the bed, and all over his hands. As soon as he walked out of the room, the nurse told me to fire him and call in an infectious disease doctor, which is what I did. The new doctor was in my room and had morphine started within 10 minutes! What a nightmare that was.

In the fifth year of having implants, I had them removed permanently, but I started to develop strange symptoms. Rashes appeared, my joints started to swell and hurt, I would forget things, the simplest of tasks I could not do, and the fatigue was so bad that sometimes I would sleep 20 out of 24 hours a day and still wake up feeling tired.

I was still seeing the infectious disease doctor, so he ran some tests, and found out I had Epstein Barr Virus. That was the beginning of diseases I had never heard of before. I developed an infection at one point that only 4 or 5 people in the United States had, and

I was only one still alive, so the doctor really didn't know how to treat me. He sent my blood work off to the CDC in Atlanta and found out that I had this infection (atypical bacterial fortuitum strain #4). I was placed on IV antibiotics for the next four years. However, I was still not getting any better. When I would get a cold, it would take 6 weeks to get over, when I would cut myself, it would take hours to get the bleeding to stop, if I should break a bone, it would take 2 to 3 months to heal. Nothing seemed to be going right. By now, I was working and had met a man who was to become my husband.

He insisted that I go to another doctor so I did. I went from doctor to doctor, but no one could tell me what was wrong! Still the rashes continued, the fatigue, and then the migraine headaches started, and I knew I was dying! I found a woman who had started a support group for silicone survivors, so I called her.

I could not believe what she told me. Everything that was wrong with me, she had as well. She said I had silicone poisoning and that I should see a special doctor for it. In 1994, I finally found one! He was in Houston, Texas, and specialized in silicone poisoning. I went to see him and he immediately put me in the hospital in Houston. I was to be there for 1 week of testing. Unfortunately, I snowballed, ending up in the hospital for 3 months. I had 2 major strokes, a couple of surgeries, and then ended up with blood clots in my legs. The clots broke loose, and hit my lungs. I just had one problem after another, and finally the specialist came to my room and told me the only thing left to do was chemotherapy. I was in shock after that statement. I did not have cancer anymore, I had silicone TOXICITY. He explained the chemotherapy was to kill off the silicone antibodies in my system, and hopefully my immune system would then take over and I would be fine again. Again, to my dismay, all the chemo. did was make me sick as a dog, and destroyed my immune system instead of destroying the silicone antibodies. I spent the next year on chemo. But it did not help.

The doctor told me to go home, make myself comfortable, and wait to die! There was nothing more he could do for me. That is what I did; I came back home went from doctor to doctor again, and no one knew what to do with me. I was given every experimental medicine that one could think of, but nothing helped. I just kept getting worse and worse. Then one day we found out what had really happened. All the surgeries being done, the ruptured implants, the old capsules being left in with the necrotic tissue, the old silicone being left inside of me! All of it!!!!!!

While I was in the hospital in Houston, I found out that I had silicone in my brain, lungs, liver, spleen, and reproductive organs. A neurologist diagnosed me with Multiple Sclerosis "like" syndrome. A rheumatologist did a bone density test and discovered that my bones were so brittle from all the chemotherapy, and the steroids that I had taken; my bones were that of a 75 year old woman! I was only 37 at the time! An eye doctor actually saw silicone leaking from my tear ducts! He sent me to our University Hospital for some specialized eye testing and found that the silicone had dissolved the myelin sheath of my optic nerve. Now, the news was that I would eventually be going blind! There was nothing that could be done for that. When I went back to the neurologist with that information she decided to do an EMG. Not surprising, the pain I was having in my legs was due to demylinating neuropathy. The lining of the myelin sheath was gone from my legs too! After this the rheumatologist started doing his testing. He discovered I had Connective Tissue Disease and Lupus! What this meant was that my body was beginning to destroy itself! There was no way to remove the silicone, so we dealt with the symptoms. The pain was getting worse, and now I was having all kinds of "female problems" too. So on to the OB/Gyn doctor who said I needed a hysterectomy, after several months of severe pain and cysts. I had the hysterectomy, but in the middle of the night, began to hemorrhage. The doctor on call was notified, off to surgery I went again to try to stop the bleeding. I was packed but the bleeding continued... The next day when my surgeon returned I ended up back in surgery again to cauterize the bleeding blood vessels. Because of insurance limitations, I had to leave the hospital that day. After this several other ugly problems began to rear their ugly heads, and I had an MRI done for my migraines, well, that showed I had a tumor on my thyroid, so off to surgery again for removal of most of my thyroid! That went pretty well, but I had to have routine chest x-rays and spots showed up on my lungs, so back to surgery for biopsies of the spots. The first biopsy showed inconclusive, but my lung collapsed, after having a chest tube shoved into my lung, I was sent home to recuperate. I went back a few days later, only to be told that I had to have another lung biopsy, again, inconclusive, but another collapse to the lung! We tried this for the third time but this time I was admitted to the hospital, went to surgery for the lung biopsy and woke up with another chest tube in me where the lung had collapsed again! Third time charm! Cultures were taken of my lungs, never did get the cultures back, but the doctors decided that I had developed hystoplasmosis, so 6 months of anti-fungal medication was given to me. Never did find out what the culture showed, but I bet it was silicone!

When I developed blood clots again, I was put on blood thinners to break up the clots, well that was fine, except that no one checked first to see if my stomach could handle all these hard medicines. What they found out was that when they started giving me blood thinners for my clots, I had stomach ulcers that began to bleed. Now we had to deal with GI problems. I was taken back to surgery: colonoscopies, sigmoidoscopies, upper and lower GI tests were done and diverticulitis, mega colon, and bleeding ulcers were diagnosed! Medications for those were given to me and I was sent home. My husband was happy I was home and gave me a hug....Back to the hospital for x-rays because the pain was so intense when he hugged me!!!! Well, that was because he cracked 3 of my ribs with that hug!!!! Osteoporosis was decided the reason for the fractured ribs!

It has been 23 years since the first implant was put in me, and since then I have had 40 surgeries, endured more painful tests that I would not wish on my worst enemy, and I continue to get worse. I started out running, then walking, then a cane, a walker, and now on bad days a wheelchair. The reason for all this???? SILICONE!!!! Want to know what it is like to wake up in the morning and have all your hair left on your pillow? Have silicone implants put in! Want to know what it is like to go blind? Have silicone implants put in! Want to know what it is like to lose everything because insurance denies 3 months of hospitalization? Have implants put in! Want to know what it is like to watch your family self-destruct? Have implants put in! Want to know how it is to lose all of your friends because you are too sick to join them in social activities? Have implants put in! Want to know what it is like to be dying slowly from chemical poisoning? Have implants put in! If you want someone to take responsibility for your illnesses, want compensation for all the pain and suffering, want someone to accept what chemical poisoning will do to the body? Have implants put in! When you become so ill that you can't feed yourself, or go to the bathroom by yourself, or dress yourself....Don't turn to the manufacturers of silicone because they will deny it!!!!!! They have the financial means to deny it!!!!! Don't turn to our government that we elected into office, because the manufacturers have already bought them off!!!! If you want help don't go to the FDA, because they never approved silicone for implants, yet they still allow them to be put into people!!!! I don't even suggest that you go to the media, because those same manufacturers have bought the media rights. You see, if you want to know what it is like to die a very slow, painful lonely death, then get implants! That is the end fate of what silicone implants will do for you and your body! If self esteem is what you are looking for, breast augmentation is not the answer, try GOD.

Well, this is just a shortened condensed version of what silicone has done to my life! I pray that this will never happen to you. Remember they are poison… it doesn't matter what the package looks like, it is still poison and the end result is always the same… .DEATH! May you never have the worry of being poisoned, or someone you love being poisoned to death by our medical community, for the sake of the almighty dollar! That is what it boils down to, Money!! From the manufacturers, to the doctors, to the lawyers, even to the family members who get sick and tired of you being sick and tired. Money is the reason for it all!

I pray that anyone who reads this; male or female, grasps the importance of keeping these poisonous bags out of the human body."

46.   Marie writes a letter to Judge Pointer: "I am but a simple woman living in Montana. I do not write elegantly, nor do I have any degree letters after my name. I am; however, a wife, a mother, and a grandmother.

My story is the same as thousands of other wives, mothers, and grandmothers, "women", who have been poisoned by silicone, so I will not take up your time repeating what you must have heard thousands of times over. I will not bore you with my details of disability at a young age, nor express the "gloomy" outlook for my future, as again you have heard it many times. After hearing it over and over again, it becomes "old hat" and the "same ole thing", that eventually one "tunes out" if one is to be able to get through yet another day, and be able to "focus" on matters at hand. So rather than putting you through all that yet again, I write for different reasons, and will hope that you see fit to read my words, thoughts, and feelings, although I would be greatly surprised if you even see this, for I am sure you have a "filtering system" for all the letters you must get that takes up valuable time. I will write this anyway and send it along to you.

Since I am but a simple woman, and "old fashion" kind of gal, I was raised in the belief of helping your neighbor when and should they need; not to meddle in others' affairs unless invited to do so, and to love my country, (to respect her and to honor "her" as my forefathers did before me, and who fought for the rights of mankind, so that I might live in peace) to believe in, and uphold her laws, (that my ancestors and others' ancestors wrote and defended through their own blood, for the descendants after them), to put in an honest days work, be a law abiding citizen, to stand for what is right, and not coward down to the evils that at times crowd around, but rather stand and defend our rights and the rights of others. To have good morals, to live and act toward others, as I want to be treated.

If I could cry, I know that I would, for all that I have been taught and what I have experienced, seen opposite of each other. My America that I love, believe in, has been defaced, she has fallen into the hands of, and is being bought by Corporations. I, and the thousands of other women who were poisoned, are living (and dead) proof of that .I have already witnessed the legal system that is supposed to be "for us", does not seem, or feel, or show itself to exist, but rather has been bought and purchased by the Corporations. A few dollars passed under the table by the good ole boys and laws are conveniently changed, rules are rewritten, proof is ignored or withheld, and justice is blindfolded. Women (wives, mothers, and grandmothers) die painful deaths, leaving their families in debt, the core of the family is ripped apart. And for what? For the protection of the corporations , who are waiting and hoping we just die and go away, and the money they pass on to those they can and do buy for their "favors". The American Dream is no longer "an honest days work brings an honest days pay", but rather "if you have money, you can get away with anything," including "murder", which is what has taken place with us women.

These breast implant cases have, or perhaps always were, "on a need to know bases"'(you only need *to know, if you can afford it). Knowledge has been kept from us, the women, and the people of America as to the REAL TRUTH of what the corporations, manufacturers, have knowingly done to women, and are getting away with. I am aware of the CD disks and the information that is on them, which is being kept from us women and the rest of America, I speak of the CD's that have information regarding the manufacturers, their products, in silicone breast implant litigation. The documentation on those disks is being kept from us. Millions of pages of helpful, informative knowledge being kept from us and the people! Why is our Freedom of Information being denied by using the judicial exclusions?*

What in God's name have we women done to deserve this? We are not even given information to help us at least feel we have a fighting chance.

Why is it, those women who are going into the court rooms, are being treated like they are the guilty ones?

Why is it allowed, they be torn to shreds, stripped of all dignity?

Why are judges over ruling the Peoples' Choice, should they rule in favor of the women?

Why, since the TRUTH is documented on the CD's should the women even have to go through the torture of going to court?

Why aren't the documented results from research done on the rats, dogs, rabbits and other animals being given out to the medical professionals so at least they will know the TRUTH and can treat us accordingly?

Why are the manufacturers being protected and not the women???????

Why is no information being released? A GAG Order? This is certainly not to protect the women or to uphold the law!"

47.   *Tamara says,: "I got tired of having very small breasts and wanted to look more shapely. I chose to get SALINE breast implants then and even after 22 years they never ruptured of even got hard. I even quit massaging after 1 month! I had them removed 1 ½ years ago.*

The first few years I had my implants, I looked great, felt sexy, and health-wise felt wonderful, (except I lost ALL sensation in one breast and about half in the other [forever] but it was worth it when I looked in the mirror or turned men's heads).

I used to play tennis and jog three miles a day, until knee/ hip joint problems made me quit, at age 27, 4 years after getting implants.

I used to be able to go anywhere without giving it a thought.   Then I began gradually developing sensitivities to breathing any type of exhaust or gas fuel, perfumes, tobacco smoke, cleaning products, new carpet, building products, or pesticides. I learned that this is Multiple Chemical Sensitivity (MCS). Breathing these substances would give me migraine headaches and make me nauseated. My first migraine was at age 28, 5 years after getting implants.

I would bicycle 15 to 20 miles a day until neck joint and muscle problems made me quit, at age 30, 7 years after getting implants. That was when I first saw stories about silicone-gel breast implant recipients getting scleroderma, fibromyalgia, Multiple Sclerosis and other horrible diseases, but never thought that my silicone shells might be causing my problems…..

Then I started walking for exercise, until any kind of semi-vigorous exercise started causing me to get even more migraine headaches, age 34, 11 years after getting implants. And yet, until the day the implants were removed after 21 years, my breasts never hardened like those "sick" women I'd read about. Unfortunately this gave me a false sense of security; I assumed that if I didn't have that obvious "negative" symptom, the implants couldn't be harming me……WRONG!

Yes, my implants made me sick, just not as quickly and as severely as those bitter women you hear about who have ruptured gel implants. From the silicone shell, I developed symptoms of rheumatoid arthritis and fibromyalgia and suffered from progressively debilitating chronic fatigue or at least 15 years. This fatigue has kept me from having children, I wouldn't and still don't have the energy to care for them. And at least one piece of the silicone shell (that we know about) broke off and migrated to my underarm area, causing a silicone-center lump that had to be surgically removed. (I have three siblings and two parents who share NONE of my health problems described herein). If I could choose one disease to rid myself of it would be the chronic systemic candida infection, I have had this for 20 years. I have fungus, yeast, growing in my intestines and elsewhere (outer ear) that I cannot get rid of. No matter what antifungal drugs I take and yeast avoidance diets I follow, I cannot eat any form of sugar, including honey, any type of fruit, or any dairy product. No starches; bread, potatoes, corn, dried nuts/seeds, alcohol, mushrooms, yeast, vinegar, or caffeine. I subsist on green vegetables, fish, meats and eggs.

The saline implants (soy oil too) serve as mini-terrariums in your body. They are initially filled with sterile saline solution, which has an expiration date; it's not made for use in breast implants, and even has a statement on the saline package stating this, and that it should be kept at a temperature well below the body's 98.6 degrees. The silicone shell is semi-permeable, and osmosis (movement of fluids through it) is really accelerated if you fly or scuba dive. Watch what happens to a half full bottle of water during plane landing.....Imagine what that same rapidly increasing pressure does to implants! I've read articles about women visiting very high altitudes winding up in emergency rooms because their saline-implant breasts were making bubbling noises! That's caused by depressurization!

Even if the initial saline was sterile, it is soon contaminated with organisms that normally live in any healthy body. That's how I got fungus growing in mine, and throughout my body! And my implants never even ruptured! When I saw how cloudy the saline in them *was after explant, I thanked God that mess had not ruptured inside of me!*

When I signed the release form before surgery 22 years ago, it said that infection was one of the risks. I thought they meant my stitches might get infected and I'd have to use Neosporin ointment. I had no idea that I would come down with this fungal infection for decades, maybe forever!

48. Beverly spoke at the Institute of Medicine July 24, 1998, this is her disease process which she spoke about: "The following is the documented disease process and the symptomatology caused by my breast implants which began almost three decades ago: I have been diagnosed as having atypical connective tissue disease; atypical neurological disease; two abnormal bone scans, showing systemic disease in my sinuses, neck sternum, shoulders, spine, elbows, hips, hands, knees, and ankles; Sicca Complex; Shirmer's Test in April, 1998, showing a grossly abnormal "0" in both eyes and comparable dry mouth; Raynauds phenomenon; arthralgia, myalgia and fibromyalgia with frozen shoulders and reduced range of motion of extremities because of pain and stiffness; Osteopenia of the lumbar spine; debilitating chronic fatigue with recurrent flu-like illness; low grade fever, night sweats, and severe hair loss; abnormal brain MRI; abnormal Spect scan showing decreased flow to my brain; an abnormal PET scan, and a grossly abnormal QEEG with constant ringing in my ears and hearing loss and cognitive dysfunction; coordination-Romberg and coordination are abnormal; abnormal T-cells to silicone antibodies; tested positive for silicone in my urine; abnormal anti-polymer antibody test; elevated and abnormal IGG, IGE, and IGM antibodies to Isocynate (TDA) which is a by-product of the polyurethane which is a known carcinogenic that was removed from hair dyes in the 1970's. I had grossly decreased natural killer cell activity (less than 5) at the time of my explantation; confirmed histological findings of granulomas and siliconomas; foreign pigment with giant cell response; sclerosing adenosis, apocrine metaplasia, fibrocollagenous tissue; hyalinized cyst, lobulated adiose tissue, dense stroma focally hyalinized; chronic inflammatory cells; intraductal hyperplasia; intracanalicular fibroadenoma;

289

left pectoralis muscle biopsy and skeletal muscle shows degenerative changes and brownish-black foreign material (believed to be polyurethane);abnormal silicone autoimmune blood panels showing striated and smooth muscle antibodies; parental cell antibodies, and elevated C3; abnormal ANA's; and rheumatoid factors; abnormal platelet, red and white blood cell counts, and abnormal liver enzymes; two abnormal adrenal steroid profiles; documented esophageal reflex disease; dysphasia; irritable bowel syndrome, butterfly rashes; photosensitive dermatitis and livido reticularis.

Documented silicone adenopathy bilaterally to include intercostal spaces, the internal mammary lymph chain supraclavicularly and retrospectorally, and silicone adenopathy in my left axilla; a painful bone lesion below my left shoulder, which is the sight of "an old failed implant"; local complications of burning pain that runs down my left arm through my chest wall. A board-certified neurologist has documented weakness and peripheral neuropathies; two abnormal EMG's; musculoskeletal pain with burning in my arms and legs and paresthesia (loss of sensation to pinprick);

atypical chest pain syndrome; and I have a mitra-valve prolapse that I believe was caused by bacteria from my breast implants.

I FEEL FORTUNATE TO BE STANDING AND ALIVE AND FEEL ENCOURAGED THAT A PERSON CAN SURVIVE BREAST IMPLANTS.

49.   Carson writes: "I got silicone gel implants in 1976, at Mayo Clinic. I had many surgeries on my common bile duct and was looking for a way to feel like I would live through all of it and after all was done the idea that breasts would give me a lift in the self-esteem area, cause I was going through a divorce too....It's so sad, I had problems from the beginning!

I had an open and closed capsulotomy in 1978. In 1988, I developed giant hives all over my body, for a year no one could find the reason for the daily hive mess. In 1985, I had been diagnosed with Chronic Fatigue Syndrome for lack of a better name for all the many symptoms that drove me to the Emergency Room hundreds of times every year.

Finally in 1989, I went to Mayo and had my breasts checked as they seemed smaller and hurt. The doctors were very interested when I explained I had been diagnosed with CFS and they said they would check the implants. They were degraded, infact, with free silicone running in the capsules. They took the mess out and cleaned me up "as best they could" and put in another set of implants. When I woke up they told me they FIXED everything and to go home and I wouldn't have any more problems. THEY DID NOT TELL ME ABOUT THE FREE RUNNING SILICONE OR THE DEGRADATION OF THE IMPLANTS OR THE MESS THEY TRIED TO CLEAN UP.

I moved to California with my fiancé', who knew nothing about implants....I tried to get a new life but the symptoms and illnesses would not go away. I have thousands of ER visits and take injectible pain medications for 10 years now! The second set of implants gave me trouble from the start. I was in a study for Dr. Middleton in San Diego and he did an MRI that showed extreme folds on my implants. In 1997, I had them *explanted and one was ruptured. Twenty days after the explantation I broke out in lesions on my chest, arms and legs and a red rash on my face and extreme fatigue and pain. I still have the rash on my cheeks and if I get ill the rash gets worse. I was diagnosed with General Connective Tissue Disease and Sjogren's Syndrome in 1995, by a board certified rheumatologist. Now in the last 3 years I have developed a Scleroderma problem with my hands and feet. My regular doctor says I am the worst case of silicone neuropathy he has seen. I have developed an ANA of <1:80, and take neurontin for the myelin problems, the nerves that make me feel like things are crawling on my skin. I live on a low income and Supplemental Security Income and have had a case filed since 1992, but after being dropped by 2 attorney firms I still have had no day in Court.*

That is my story....25 years of my life gone and 10 years of justice delayed! THE TRUTH OF THE COVER-UP AND MONEY AND POWER THAT HAVE BEEN SPENT TO KEEP THE CASH-COW GOING FOR THE PLASTIC SURGEONS AND THE MANUFACTURERS

FROM FACING THE RESPONSIBILITY THEY REFUSE TO ACCEPT!"

50. Darlene's letter to the FDA: "I was implanted with" Mentor" saline implants for cosmetic purposes in September, 1987. I was assured they would last a lifetime by the doctor and his nurse, who had implants at the time, unless I was run over by a Mack truck! The only complications I was told about that could possibly occur were: the possibility of infection from surgery, about and a one percent chance (1%) that they could get hard, in which case the doctor would just remove them and replace them. I played tennis 3 times a week, plus tennis matches, did aerobics 3 to 5 times a week and took dance class one night a week, but practiced dancing everyday. I took care of a home, husband and three kids! I was 40 years old and healthy!

At the Sugar Bowl, in January, 1989, (a little over a year later) I awoke to find that the right implant had ruptured totally flat! After having me write a letter to the manufacturer so that they wouldn't charge the doctor or me again, the doctor replaced both implants on January 24, 1989. This was after the ruptured silicone floated around in my breast for 3 weeks!

About 5 years later I began getting sick with muscle pain and fatigue. I had joint stiffness, muscle weakness, a few sun-related rashes, painful mouth, sores and swallowing problems. I began testing positive for the ANA factor. I have had to have my esophagus dilated two times, I have polyneuropathies, severe sleep problems and constant pain. I have had trigger point injections, chiropractic care, and physical therapy for pain. I developed high blood pressure. April, 1995, I had more surgery to remove a breast lump from the right side that had ruptured earlier. The doctor said it might be something that migrated from the implant. It was benign; however, we didn't know to test for silicone then. I also have extremely dry eyes and can barely stand to wear my contacts any more. I have Raynauds in my hands and feet. I have recurring bronchitis and broke 7 ribs in one year from coughing, 3 ribs last year. In the last few years I have tested positive for anti-ds-DNA and have been formally diagnosed with Lupus by my rheumatologist. I remain in constant pain in my muscles and joints, especially back and neck areas. I had to buy a TENS unit for the pain. I have nerve problems in my feet and cannot walk barefoot. I sometimes feel like I am in a fog mentally. My implants are 11 years old and due for another rupture as we all know by now. I am scared of what will happen to me when they do. They are much smaller now, so I know they leak over time. If mold and fungus or bacteria is growing inside, I could die from TOXIC shock when they rupture.

I do not have the $6,000. dollars to have them removed. Blue Cross Insurance does not cover it. I am appalled that the manufacturers were able to get off with paying such a small sum to us women. (Some haven't gotten anything) Especially those with ruptured implants and illnesses and they don't even have to pay for the explants!

Women must be told of the horrible risks related to saline implants! They must be told they have a high rupture rate, a high repeat surgery risk, capsular contracture risk, and autoimmune illnesses are possible."

51.   Mandy writes: "In 1974 I was a young model and was adamantly advised to have breast augmentation by a physician. I'd nursed my baby for about a year and he said I was much too young to have such ptotic breasts, I also had cysts periodically in my breasts.   The doctor told me that the solution to my problem was to have my breasts replaced with silicone implants, which would last a lifetime and permanently end my pain and discomfort. I had no idea that this was the beginning of a long period of pain, suffering and decline.

I ended up having not one surgery, but eight surgeries; specifically attempting to remedy severe capsular contracture and deformity. I started with silicone gel implants, and later replaced these with several sets of saline implants. I had one emergency surgery to deal with a hematoma where blood was literally spurting out of my breast! I had two more *emergency surgeries to deal with a near deadly staph infection.*

In 1987, 13 years after my first surgery, I consulted specialists at a university medical center where they assured me that they could solve my problems once and for all. They didn't! I had several other surgeries, including getting my first set of saline implants in 1992. They told me the saline implants were the safest kind, but my worst problems started after that surgery.

On July 18, 1995, I had my third set of saline implants put in, which were described as a new, greatly improved type of saline implant. I still had a great deal of deformity from all of the previous surgeries and the infection of 1986. That was my most recent invasion and reconstruction. There needs to be another. My doctor tells me I have to have these implants taken out now because my health has severely declined since 1992.

I am now living on Social Security disability. I was granted this in 1997, when I could no longer hold down a full time job, or work to support myself. I had been a successful free lance writer, a highly promising student in sculpting, working also as a crisis intervention counselor for a substance abuse facility. I lost my jobs because I kept getting sick! I had to quit college. In order to survive, I had to sit in a courtroom with the Social Security Judge and listen to people talk about me as though I were one of the most inept human beings, an incapable member of society. This was a most significantly tragic day for me.

There is not a single insurance company who will insure me. I'm considered high risk because of my saline implants. This entire mess has cost well over a quarter of a million dollars. Why??? Because I, like many others believed saline solution encased in silicone shells did not cause problems.

I have to get up every day and face chronic fatigue, Raynauds syndrome, and moments of excruciating chest pain that has had doctors sending me to the emergency room. My immune system has been compromised. I've developed what is known as chemically induced asthma. I have hematuria or blood in the urine, and no one knows why. My muscles weakened. I get sores on my skin that don't readily heal. I have episodes of severe depression. I've been told to limit the use of my arms to avoid the very real possibility of capsules forming again. I can't even pick up my grandchildren!

My current doctor ran some tests and thinks all my health problems are implant-related. I am afraid of another surgery but I am afraid not to have the saline implants removed for fear of additional medical complications. I can't afford to have these implants taken out but will when I can! Medicaid won't pay for it until they POP, and when they do come out Medicaid will no pay for reconstruction of the flaps of skin I will have hanging from my chest! I have no breast tissue of my own left! It's all disappeared, all been removed. Waiting for them to POP or form a so-called significant leak is also very scary, because no one knows what will happen.

I was once a very strong and healthy woman. I raised three children alone, without the benefit of child support. Illness was not even a consideration. Now, I pray every day for God to help me keep my Spirits up; for I know full well it is only that, plus the blessed love of my family and friends that keeps me going!"

52.   Amelia writes: "In this letter I am trying to express the physical pain that I have experienced daily from breast implants and the emotional pain caused by the doctors who were in such denial.

In December, 1972, I was implanted with Dow Corning 225 cc. volume silicone gel breast implants. Just 60 days before the surgery, I had divorced a very abusive alcoholic man after 23 years of marriage. Before I had my two children (both were breastfed), I had an average bust line, and this caused my bustline to increase.

When my husband grew angry, he would sometimes beat me and fouly curse me and make fun of my breasts. He had me totally convinced that if I ever left him, all men would find me ugly. I was in a dreadful emotional state. I believed that the only way I could rescue myself was to change my appearance.

By 1976, I had developed indigestion problems and my stone impacted gall bladder was removed. I developed water retention in my legs and body, followed by easy bruising, tenderness of my skin and muscles. And in 1978, numbness and tingling, burning of my hands and feet, (especially my feet) this kept me awake at night. Joint swelling and pain began in 1979.

In 1983, my stomach pain was severe. My stomach burned with acid and at night my throat often burned; my abdomen became distended as well. At this same time, I began to notice difficulty remembering what I had read and was sometimes confused. By 1985, I developed arthritis, especially in my hands and neck. and I experienced a lot of weakness. In 1986, I began getting easily disoriented.

Today I find it difficult to drive my car and operating the seat belt buckle is excruciating. I cannot press a pen hard enough when writing contracts with carbon paper. And it is impossible to turn keys to operate locks, or even work a keypad. I find it impossible to do my housework. The pain is so severe that I have to hire help. I cannot push buttons on photocopiers, elevators, or some banking machines because of the pain. I fear that someday I will lock myself in a bathroom that uses a turn button or key. I must leave the door or cubicle unlocked. There is no doubt in my mind the silicone implants have caused my hands this extra pain, twisting and weakness, especially in the last 5 years.

In 1985, I began to notice that my energy level was declining and some days work was impossible. By 1988, insomnia, incontinence, and very severe fatigue came. I also started stuttering and reversing words, letters, and numbers. I seemed to be sleeping more and more, but still feeling tired when I had just gotten up! Many times messages and instructions are hard to follow for me. During the last 4 years, I get lost

*while I am driving! Even in my own neighborhood...
.This is terrifying! Many days my head is muddled the
entire day. I get this excruciating wave of pain that
comes up from my breasts into my neck, up into my
ears and teeth! It can last all day or several hours.
My head aches, both ears ache, all my teeth ache, and
I feel drained and miserable. No words can describe
the suffering. I thought after having the implants out,
November 22, 1993, it would not happen again, but it
still does!*

*Looking back, I feel it has to be the implants that
ruined my health! In 1972, when I was implanted, I
thought I was rescuing myself. I actually sealed my
doom. How will I ever get this poison out of my body?
I can't work or retire with expenses like I have, not even
at 63 years of age!"*

*53. A Son's Story: "November, 1989: My
mom began noticing joint pain in her shoulder and hips,
her skin was extremely painful to touch on the shin and
calf, her hands had become painful and numb. She
thought she had carpal tunnel syndrome for months*

before seeing a doctor. Once she saw the doctor, he diagnosed her with Scleroderma in 1990. My mom and dad both thought this was an unusual diagnosis for a 43 year old woman with no family history of anything that even remotely resembled it. My mom had gotten silicone gel breast implants in 1979, and the physician who diagnosed the Scleroderma had given some information about the disease and some of the causes and one was a possible association with silicone breast implants. They went right back to the doctor and mentioned this correlation and the doctor and everyone else believed the silicone implants were playing a big role in her problems.

She was immediately explanted but this was only the beginning of her problems. Seven years had passed since the beginning of her illness. Her skin had become to stiff that it felt like leather, her hands so rigid that she could only close her hands to about 50% of making a fist. She had to use both of her hands to drink from a cup. Her mouth and face had become immobile. She could only open her mouth about one quarter of what she could just seven years ago. Her esophagus and stomach had virtually become useless. She was beginning to lose control of her bowels. Her lung capacity was about fifty percent, She suffered from chronic fatigue and chronic joint pain, and had numerous bouts with life threatening pneumonia.

March 1997, after many photophoresis treatments in the hospital every 28 days, my mom had a lump in her left breast. A biopsy revealed the lump was malignant. Because of the condition of her skin the biopsy was very difficult to perform, and the incision sight was healing very poorly. She was told that a mastectomy would have to be performed. She then chose to have a bilateral mastectomy.....The bilateral mastectomy would insure that the cancer would not spread to her other breast. The surgery did not go as expected. The surgeon had problems with her skin ripping after he made the initial incision because of the lack of elasticity. He was barely able to stitch the skin back together. Later on, in mid-May, she started to gain some energy, and her endurance and strength improved enough that she was able to stay up all day without having to go to bed. I was concerned about her having her first chemotherapy treatment before the incision had healed but we were assured there was no reason to worry. At this time she looked to me as though she could beat this cancer. I had to leave and go to my home in another town and the image I had of my mom waving good bye to me was the last time I saw my mother alive."

54. Testimonial, written by the loving husband, of a woman no longer with us:

"My Objectives":

A. *" To begin physical and emotional healing as soon as possible*

B. *To rid myself of silicone and begin detoxification and breast reconstruction as soon as possible.*

C. *To get the medical profession to recognize and treat silicone poisoning as a serious condition.*

D. *To receive adequate medical and emotional support throughout this ordeal.*

E. *To get the word out about the dangers of silicone to friends, loved-ones, and others so that they will not experience my hell!"*

"I have been on Social Security Disability since November, 1995, after suffering a severe nervous breakdown May, 1995; and eventually qualified for Psychiatric Treatment through Los Angeles County, where I am currently under the care of a physician.

Since this time I have been suffering from a variety of medical conditions, all of which I believe are related to the fluid silicone injections I had over 30 years ago. I came to this conclusion after realizing I had been experiencing many of the same symptoms that so many other women had. During my research, I discovered that for years my body has been fighting itself. My own body's autoimmune reaction to these injections!

Psychologically, I meet all of the DSM-IV requirements for a diagnosis of "Borderline Personality Disorder", or even "Dissociative Identity Disorder", because I was physically and sexually abused by my family as a young child. Considering that I did not begin actively pursuing suicide until sometime after I had these injections, and given what I have learned recently about the effects of silicone, and how it can even settle in the brain and create chemical imbalances, I now believe that it is highly possible that even my psychological behavior can be the direct result of an autoimmune reaction to the silicone.

November, 1997, I qualified for Medicare, as a result of my disability. In early March, 1998, I began having several canker-like lesions in my mouth, and on my tongue and gums. One even eroded the skin enough to expose my jawbone! Very soon, I began having a variety of skin lesions, or sores, which started on one leg and rapidly spread all over my body. I was immediately referred to a dermatologist who took a biopsy which came back positive for Toxic Epidermal

Necrolysis, or TENS Disease. Since I was not experiencing peeling skin, it was further concluded that I may have a mild case of Stevens-Johnson Syndrome, which was later confirmed.

A rheumatologist had put me on 180 Mgs of Prednisone per day, while he awaited the results of my Lupus tests which came back negative. At the same time I began developing bulging eyes, which an MRI showed was indicative of Grave's Disease. Since my thyroid tests came back negative, nothing has been done to treat this condition. When I developed Chronic Fatigue ,other doctors took blood and diagnosed both Entero Virus and Epstein Barr Virus, and suggested that I wait the six months necessary to confirm a diagnosis of Chronic Fatigue Syndrome, since I met all of the other criteria.

In the meantime, I have been experiencing debilitating fatigue, continuous sore throat, and unbearably painful muscle and joint pains which continue to get worse (fibromyalgia?).

In addition, I had experienced several painful breast lumps which my doctor believed should be removed. Upon consulting a surgeon, an oncologist and 2 plastic surgeons, all of whom have recommended an immediate bilateral mastectomy, my HMO (Medicare) was extremely unresponsive in providing an appropriate plastic surgeon to perform the Reconstructive plastic surgery which I believe is necessary to maintain my physical appearance and emotional health.

Since they began dragging their feet, I made three recent suicide attempts because I really couldn't deal with the situation any longer!

My husband began researching silicone breast implants by way of the Internet. Upon reviewing my medical history over the past three years we began to wonder if any or all of my diagnoses' could be related to a silicone-induced autoimmune condition? During this time I have suffered and been treated for recurrent bronchitis and pneumonia, hiatial hernia, stomach and esophageal ulcers, glossopharangeal neuralgia, and chronic wrist, arm and shoulder problems which

311

a previous doctor thought might be related to thoracic outlet syndrome.

I finally had a prosthetic radical, bilateral mastectomy nearly four months after I was first informed that I must have the surgery. They could not test me properly because of the silicone.....They dragged their feet. Why? When I wanted to get this over with? Considering I have a family history of breast cancer, and several suspicious lumps, why did the HMO cause these delays?

August, 1998, Even though I had illegal injections of silicone in 1967, after it was banned, the medical community continues to look at me and treat me as an implant complainant. Why were the injections banned? What illnesses did they cause? Where are the studies and knowledge regarding silicone injections and bio-chemistry? Why am I not being treated for complications from the illness that caused injections to be banned? Why has our government not formed a Federal Task Force to study these questions as they might apply to injectees, and rupturees? Harvard/Mayo......? How do their studies apply to me? What does my insurance carrier and the medical community intend to do to help me get well? Why won't any one respond to these questions?

February, 1999: My wife passed away in her sleep, of unknown causes! Follow-up: The Coroner has concluded that she died from idiopathic, dilated, cardiomyopathy! After a year of autoimmune symptoms, and a positive diagnosis for Entero Virus, not one of her over one dozen specialists ever suspected she had a heart problem! My immediate Internet research tells me that over 50% of cardiomyopathy is caused by an autoimmune problem, initiated by a virus!!!!......Go figure!"

55. Kelly writes about Lisa: "I don't know which company sold the implants. Lisa served in the United States Air Force, and developed breast cancer, due to her duty with Nukes!

Since she was active duty they operated, removed both breasts, and because of her young age, insisted on the implants, at the military hospital. Lisa was assured that the implants were saline filled. Some time after Lisa developed problems and sickness. After a while they tired of her complaining and medically discharged her.

Lisa went from one specialist after another, not one would remove the leaking implant, not even a V.A. doctor.

Lisa finally got desperate and removed them herself! The implants were filled with silicone which had traveled throughout her body. For more than four years Lisa suffered repeated outbreaks of sores which would be large open holes through which you could see right to the bones and tendons. At least the last four years of Lisa's life she was judged terminal! She was sent prescriptions of morphine for self injection every 4 hours. Her suffering was great and long. I personally hold the Government, the Military, Doctors, and the manufacturers guilty for her death!

In my opinion it is horrendous that our Government continues to allow our people to be used as guinea pigs....! Every one involved with the making, approving, selling, installing and taking no action at all even the President, should (in my opinion) serve life sentences. For they surely condemned Lisa to death without even a trial!"

56.   Jane writes: "My name is Jane. In view of all the questions being raised on the safety of breast implants at this time, I would like to talk to you about my daughter, Jennifer.

My daughter decided to have breast augmentation so that her clothes would fit better and to help improve her self-esteem. I asked her to please have the saline rather than the silicone just on the chance they might rupture and she agreed.

Following her consultative visit with a plastic surgeon, she discussed with me what she had been told by the surgeon. She said, "I am having silicone gel implants with a textured silicone covering because

315

the surgeon said that the chances of complications and contractures are less likely to occur with this type of implant as compared to saline implants". She, indeed, did undergo the implant surgery as planned. (These were the polyurethane/silicone FOAM implants)

Approximately 9 months following the breast augmentation surgery, my daughter began to complain of headaches. The headaches persisted so she consulted her physician after 3 weeks of suffering the headaches. She was referred to a neurologist for an evaluation. A number of tests; including a CAT scan were ordered. All these tests were negative.

The headaches persisted and visual problems also developed. She reported having blurred vision, flashing lights, seeing diagonal lines and black moving spots in her visual field. Return visits were made to physicians...Migraine headaches were diagnosed by her neurologist; this was after all diagnostic tests were performed to rule out other diseases. Medication was prescribed and changed several times in an attempt to control the headaches.

Approximately one year after the implant surgery, other symptoms were reported by me daughter. Extreme tiredness, bone and joint pain, and the headaches persisted.About fourteen months following the surgery, my daughter suffered two episodes of severe right sided pain that lasted 263 days each time! Two visits were made to the emergency room, tests were done but no conclusive diagnoses were made. She was told it might be related to ovulation pain.

At fifteen months post surgery, she began having gastrointestinal problems. She complained of having severe and persistent heartburn. Stomach x-rays were done and tested by a gastroenterologist, the results were negative for abnormal findings!

Her tiredness increased and other symptoms developed; hot flashes, breathing difficulties, chest pain, fingers, ankle and foot swelling. One of her friends also told me that she also complained of pain and tenderness in her right breast and nipple for several months.

317

She continued to work but would go to bed almost immediately upon returning home, and spent a great deal of her weekends in bed, resting.

Seventeen months after the implant surgery, my daughter arose on a Tuesday morning to go to work. As she went to the bathroom that morning, she collapsed in the floor. She had complained of a headache the previous night. By the time I got to her, she lived next door, she had slurred speech and a decreased level of consciousness. I am a registered nurse, so I immediately recognized the seriousness of this episode. An ambulance was called and she was taken to the local hospital then transferred to a larger medical facility immediately. A frontal lobe stroke was confirmed following a CAT scan of the brain.

Numerous tests were performed while she was hospitalized with the stroke. All of these tests were negative! So migraine headaches were cited as being the probable cause of the stroke.

Jennifer was able to return to work about two weeks after this happened; her deficits were minimal and her doctor told her not to allow the stroke to handicap her now! Once again, the doctor prescribed a number of medications to try and help control the headaches.

She continued to complain of being tired all of the time, but because of her daughter, she tried to maintain high spirits. Her headaches continued and she complained that some days were worse than others.

Five weeks after Jennifer had suffered the first stroke, she called me one night and said, "I have a terrible migraine, do you think I'll have another stroke when I get up in the morning? Like I did before?" That is exactly what happened!

She awoke around 7:00 a.m. and reported that she tried to sit up and was unable to do so. She said she was also weak and dizzy and could not sit up. An ambulance was called, I was already at work.

More tests were performed and a second stroke was diagnosed following an MRI. This time the stroke was in the cerebellar area of the brain. Following this stroke, she had nausea, vomiting, headaches and balance problems that persisted. Extensive testing was done by a cardiology team that was called in, in effort to determine why these strokes were happening to someone so young! In conclusion they decided that the strokes were not related to a heart condition. Other possible causes of stroke such as: vasculitis, Lupus, and Autoimmune diseases were considered but lab tests did not substantiate this.

A neurologist recommended that an angiogram be done and the next day one was. She tolerated this procedure pretty well; however, about four hours after the procedure she reported seeing diagonal lines. Her blood pressure was extremely low and remained low that evening. She remained on bed rest that evening and her neurologist was not overly concerned about the low blood pressure. His concern was controlling and preventing headaches that led to arterial spasms. I spoke with the neurologist about taking my daughter to a specialty clinic for another evaluation, he agreed that this was appropriate and helped to make the arrangements.

The next morning she called me happy that I was going to go with her and to discuss travel arrangements......That was the last conversation I had with my daughter!

After she had talked with me, her friend, who was staying with her, reported that she decided to walk to the bathroom. She was assisted and upon walking back to bed, she collapsed in the floor; suffering a third stroke! A comatose state resulted and Jennifer died two days later!

I consented to allow my daughter's organs be used for transplants...I also requested that a complete autopsy be performed.

Complicated migraine headaches were cited as being the cause of the strokes, essentially on the basis of "rule out". No other factors known to be stroke risks *could be found as reported by the pathologist. I did request that tissue be tested for silicone migration. The pathologist said he was unaware of the methods used and did not have the equipment to do so.*

The Organ Donor Association reported to me that one KIDNEY WAS UNSUITABLE FOR TRANSPLANTATION and that it was sent to a research center. I was able to locate the center and contacted them. I was told they did have a portion of the frozen kidney there. I was told it would be released to me when and how I requested. It took several weeks to contact and make arrangements with a pathologist who had a knowledgeable background in silicone tissue testing. Then he forwarded me a letter of acceptance and specific instructions for the research center regarding the best way to ship the frozen tissue. A follow-up phone call to the research center yielded that the frozen kidney tissue specimen could not be located now because "someone had probably decided to clean the freezer out and had thrown it out"! I inquired how this could happen? I had made numerous calls to verify that I wanted the tissue preserved and that it might take several weeks, or even months before I would be requesting release of the tissue to another lab. On each of my calls I was assured by a staff member there was no way anything would happen to the tissue and it would remain labeled while in storage, until I gave my permission and instructions for it to be transferred to another research laboratory.

The conclusion one draws from this tissue being discarded, is obvious! I do believe the implants were a contributing factor in the cause of her death!"

57.   Charles writes: "In the mid 1980's, my wife Joanne had silicone gel implants with the felt covering.   (Once again, polyurethane/silicone FOAM breast implants)   Three years ago she started having many symptoms. Finally she found a doctor who told her the problems were related to her implants. When she became so ill to the point that she could no longer work, she decided to have them removed.

On the day of the surgery, a mammogram revealed "no problems".   On removal, the surgeon found numerous cysts and tissue that had to be taken out. The silicone had migrated to her lymph nodes. Though the implants had not ruptured they had lost about 25 grams of material each!

The surgery was a little more than two years ago. Her condition did not improve and she passed away!

It is very important that you do what is necessary for your health. If you have implants, please have them taken out and hope that it is not too late to help! Nothing is more important than life."

Section Five - "DOW":
"Stealing Our Future", by
Charlie Cray, Greenpeace
Toxics Campaign

DOW: STEALING OUR FUTURE by Charlie Cray, Greenpeace Toxics Campaign

On May 15, 2000, the Dow Chemical Company celebrated its 100th anniversary. Dow's spin doctors came up with a new slogan to mark the event: "Proud of Our Past", "Committed to Our Future". The slogan resonates strongly with the title of a recent book on dioxin and other endocrine disrupters, "Our Stolen Future", written by Theo Colburn, a wildlife specialist who has studied the effects of dioxin in the Great Lakes, where Dow is headquartered.

How Dow could possibly be proud of its past is an issue that comes immediately to mind. Those of us who don't share the profits from $20 billion/year in revenues may be less selective in our memories than the corporate spindoctors who invented this slogan. Go to the Herbert H Dow museum in Midland and you can see an exhibit which shows how Dow grew from humble entrepreneurial beginnings in Midland, Michigan, where Herbert Dow began making bromine and chlorine from local brine deposits to today when the company operates in 157 countries around the world. *"Your products have affected everyone in the world,"* the exhibit says. Indeed! Right now there isn't a person on the planet that doesn't carry dioxin in their bodily tissues.

In any case, it would take a severe case of Vietnamnesia to be proud of a past when Dow-made Napalm was dropped on innocent villagers who burned to death in horrible agony. It is also difficult to imagine how Dow could be proud that it and other manufacturers of Agent Orange left a generation of Veterans with a litany of illnesses, or that their children and grandchildren may now be suffering from reproductive disorders, immune system deficiencies, and spina bifida. Is the company proud that it squeezed a few more years of profit out of delaying the day they had to stop making the components of Agent Orange (2,4,5-T and 2,4-D) while people were being poisoned? Do sealed court settlements make a bitter fog out of the memories utility workers have of the illnesses which they got from spraying 2,4,5-T in right-of-ways? Are Midland employees supposed to be proud of the fact *that Dow still makes 2,4-D (the other half of Agent Orange), one of the most commonly-used herbicides on the market, known to be contaminated with dioxin and to cause cancer in pets?*

Is the company proud of how Styrofoam and Saran Wrap (Dow brand products) now litter the landscape? Is the company proud that it has had a long history of litigation because of defective products such as Sarabond, a mortar additive which the Wall Street Journal reported (3/21/89) was being blamed for weakening reinforced structures and causing facades to peel away and bricks to plunge to the street below? "As plaintiffs' lawyers see it," the Journal reported, "the case is about a company unwilling to turn away from a product that it knew to be troubled but to which it had committed considerable resources. "A recurrent theme with Dow products over the past century.

Does the company feel at all embarrassed about "Informed Consent", the book which tells the tragic story of the Swansons (she a victim of Dow Corning's silicone implants and he a Dow Corning executive famous for his work on developing a company ethics program)? There are so many of these Dow stories it's no wonder Dow hired its own historian for this important anniversary. It's likely the resulting book will forget many victims, such as the scores of Costa Rican banana workers who were sterilized by working with Dow's DBCP worm killer. Dow tried to block them from suing the company in the U.S. courts at the same time that corporate lobbyists were leaving literature touting "product stewardship" (along with hefty PAC checks?) with some of the same Congressmen they would later go back to for help passing tort "reform" legislation.

It's hard to imagine that the book will reveal the cigarette science behind Dow-funded studies intended to deny the global sperm countdown referred to in "Our Stolen Future" and continuously confirmed by recent studies. How many of the people poisoned by Dursban (chlorpyrifos) and incapable of now living normal lives because of their sensitivity to most types of chemicals will be interviewed for the authorized corporate biography?

And what about the Dow legacy in the Great Lakes? Is Dow still proud that they attempted to block an EPA study from coming out in the early 1980's which revealed that the Tittabawassee River was one of the most dioxin contaminated places on earth? Does Dow forget its attempt to divert the dioxin debate away from its operations to volcanoes and forest fires (with the "Trace Chemistries Theory of Fire")? Does Dow forget that shortly after it began publicizing this thesis, scientists from Indiana University tested sediment cores in Lake Huron and Saginaw Bay and confirmed that "emission of dioxins and furans has increased greatly since 1940" when large-scale organochlorine production--and the incineration of wastes from that production-began in Midland. (Jean Czuczwa and Ronald Hites "Environmental Fate of Combustion-Generated Polychlorinated Dioxins and Furans", Environ. Sci. Technol, 1984, 18, 444-450.) Does Dow forget that it was shipping its dioxin-generating waste to a cement kiln in nearby Alpena (brown trout fishing capital of the lakes), the same year (1986) the U.S. Fish and Wildlife Service found a dead bald eagle egg in the same area with 1065 parts per trillion TCDD (dioxin) equivalents --- the highest value ever recorded in wildlife samples in U.S. Fish and Wildlife Service collections?

Instead of continuing to deny that dioxin causes cancer and other problems or that their chlorine-based operations are a major source of dioxin, the company is now trying to buy itself time with a new tactic. Dow claims it has set ambitious environmental goals for the future-including 90% dioxin reduction from its major plants in the next ten years. How it intends to do this without phasing out various chlorinated organic production lines remains unclear (unless you don't count the dioxins captured in pollution control devices and buried in landfills, salt domes and other potentially leaky reservoirs). Does Dow seriously believe anyone trusts this figure, given that it has yet to produce a baseline figure to measure its progress by? Does Dow forget that the chemical Manufacturers Association's own slogan is "Don't Trust Us, Track Us"? Will Dow apply the principles of "Responsible Care" and "product stewardship" to the dioxin that's been spread globally or that's created in accidental fires involving PVC products made from Dow-manufactured vinyl chloride?

Does Dow forget the "blob"-the huge dry-cleaning fluid (perchloroethylene) spill which spread from its Sarnia plant across the bottom of the St. Clair River in 1986? Can Dow forget that ten years later a Norwegian tanker spilled over 500 barrels of the same Dow-manufactured chemical into a commercial fishing area in the Gulf of Mexico? Or forget that Dow's Plaquemine, Louisiana plant poisoned the groundwater with massive amounts of vinyl chloride and related chemicals? Perhaps Dow has forgotten Morrissonville, the poor African-American community which settled by the Mississippi long before Dow muscled its way in and forced them to relocate because of the pollution.

Does Dow think the people in Freeland, Michigan forget the toxic train derailment in 1989 which forced them to evacuate their homes in the middle of the night?

Will the official Dow biography be a chlorinated whitewash or will it be printed on totally chlorine-free (TCF) paper, given that scientists at Radian, now a

Dow Subsidiary, once conducted a study with the EPA which suggested that TCF processes have less impact on the environment? Why doesn't Dow think of such great things when it can profit by them-Dow makes a chelating agent ----Versene----which can be used in TCF processes. Why did Dow suggest that a proposed U.S. EPA study of alternatives to chlorine (proposed after the IJC made its famous recommendation) was an "attempt to ban an element on the periodic table" when it was already beginning to invest in alternatives to chlorine-based pesticides and PVC plastics?

Why did Dow give up its aqueous cleaning business when the alternatives to "perc" and other chlorinated compounds are rapidly gaining market share because they outperform "perc" once one accounts for Superfund liabilities, occupational exposure costs and other long-term costs of doing business with Dow?

Whose future is Dow committed to? Its employees? Then why does Dow lobby for OSHA "reform" (Wash. Post 7/24/95) and disguise the cutbacks in its North American Workforce as part of a "global restructuring"

333

strategy? Multinational Monitor (10/95) asked why an agent of Dow Chemical had undertaken talks with managers of the infamous Shenyang Xinsheng Chemical Works, described as a forced labor prison camp. Is this in the interest of Dow's workforce here?

If Dow is such a big promoter of Responsible Care ("Don't Trust Us, Track Us") and other programs it suggests are intended to protect human health and the environment, then why did Dow (via the Chemical Manufacturers Association) sue the U.S. EPA to prevent it from adding chemicals to the Toxics Release Inventory-The principle tool that the public and NGOs use in the U.S. to track the company's progress on waste reduction. If Dow wants to operate in an open and responsible manner then why was Dow and its affiliates (e.g. DowElanco) listed as supporting more corporate front groups than any other single company in Essential Information's report, "Masks of Deception"?

As early as 1972, Carl A Gerstacker, then the Chairman of Dow Chemical Company, confided to the White House Conference on the Industrial World Ahead that he dreamed of buying "an island owned by no nation" and on "such truly neutral ground" he would locate the world headquarters of Dow so that "we could then really operate on the U.S. as U.S. citizens, in Japan as Japanese citizens, and in Brazil as Brazilians rather than being governed in prime by the laws of the United States". Isn't it obvious that "Citizen Dow" wants to enjoy the rights that the doctrine of corporate personhood grants the company, without the responsibilities that the rest of us have to pick up the tab for? Dow may continue to deliver hefty profits to the company's shareholders, who for that reason may be proud of Dow's past and committed to its future. The rest of us are left with the challenge of figuring out how we can rightfully take back our own stolen future. In light of this document written and researched by Mr. Cray; how can we as citizens "Trust" anything the manufacturers might tell us?

Section Six - "The Burson Marsteller Plan" - The Largest Public Relations Firm in the World......Hired by Dow Corning and Dow Corning Wright

THE "BURSON MARSTELLER PLAN

(The largest public relations firm in the world, hired by Dow Corning and Dow Corning Wright)

1991

"Marie, Jeff and I did the Heartguide program which involved somewhat similar "behind the scenes" work on behalf of a client. The difference here is that Burson will stay behind the scenes too, and the American Society of Plastic and Reconstructive Surgeons (ASPRS) doctors and their patients will be the visible participants."

"ASPRS is not our client, Dow Corning and Dow Corning Wright, its' subsidiary that makes breast implants, are." Morris, Jeff and I have been working with them for several months. They will support ASPRS in the efforts we'll be discussing tomorrow. However, that knowledge, the meeting, and our working with ASPRS, and particularly the knowledge

we have of Weiss's pressure on Kessler, need to be
kept confidential."

"If you remember, I was not going to put this in
writing, but wanted you both to be up to speed-and
there's too much information for you to have to listen
to it all verbally. With the FDA's new penchant for
walking into ad agencies and demanding to look at
documents, I hope you'll give this a toss once you've
read it."

What follows is more than you ever wanted to
know about breast implants-and the issues DC/DCW
face. Please give me a call if you'd like to discuss this
once you've had time to read it. I leave for the airport
about 4:15, Eastern time. If we miss each other, I'll be
at the Park Hyatt tonight.

"SITUATION: Breast Implants and other medical
devices have long been grandfathered in by the FDA and
have not gone through the usual FDA approval process.
In late November,1990, implant manufacturers (in an

expected move) were told to submit research on breast implants."

On December 10, 1990, the Connie Chung Show aired with horror stories about women who had become ill because of their breast implants. The most common illnesses indicated were connective tissue diseases/ illnesses of the immune system such as scleroderma, lupus, arthritis, joint pain and fatigue, among others. There were also rumors of implants causing cancer. The horror stories were compelling and other media jumped on the bandwagon. Since that time there have been almost 2,000 stories, 74% of them negative."

"Research (USC study of 3000 women over 11 years) indicates that there is no greater incidence of breast cancer in women with implants than in those who do not have them. Connective tissue diseases are not so easy to quantify. There are no clear records of the incidence of connective tissue disease. However, the incidence in women with implants is no greater than the accepted rate to the general population."

"No one really knows why the women who have problems have them. It may be just two major events in a woman's life, implants and disease, with no connection, as is true with many things. It may be that hearing the horror stories, and being egged on by people like Sid Wolfe, the plaintiff's bar (two major players on this issue are Dan Bolton and Denise Dunleavy), and others, some women are blaming unrelated problems on implants."

"It may be that there are women with an allergic reaction to the silicone gel that in minute particles leaks out of the implants. This is unlikely because silicone in other forms is so pervasive in our lives. It's in Digel, on the tips of IV needles, in the coating of capsules and in beer as an antifoaming agent. It's also used to make a number of artificial joints and tubes for implantation."

DC's main product is silicone, hence the need to protect it.....(I remember when DC & DCW said that the silicone industry was only 1% of their business?)....They could walk away from manufacturing implants tomorrow and save money because of the dollars spent on research and lawsuits. They're good people, sincerely concerned about women with problems, and concerned too about their company's reputation."

"On July 9, along with other breast implant manufacturers DC/DCW submitted its PMA (pre-market approval) as required to the FDA. At that time DC also made public thirty years of proprietary research." ....(This so-called research was skewed)

"August 22---FDA sent DC/DCW a form letter, sent also to the other manufacturers who were not turned down, indicating fileability of their submission. Fileability letter from FDA stated that further information would be required and that by September 13, FDA would indicate to manufacturers what the information would be.

*   "Advisory panel hearing will be in November-further information from manufacturers due by then."

*   "January 8, 1992, --FDA final decision"

"ISSUE: We now believe that Kessler plans to take implants off the market entirely. The one exception may be for use in reconstruction after breast cancer, (Evidently FDA had planned to disallow all PMA's thereby effectively taking implants off the market in August. However, doing it in that way would take longer than going through the current process). We believe the pressure is coming from Congressman Ted Weiss, who along with Sid Wolfe, have stated openly their desire to have implants banned."

"It is believed that we have the window between now and an unknown date in November, when the advisory panel hearings will be held "to influence this decision". While we have programs in place "to help change 'misperceptions' caused by current negative media" coverage, they are longer term. This new information "requires immediate activity to 'inform' Kessler of the opposition to his proposed move" and to 'influence' him to leave implants on the market"."

"If our information is faulty, the need still exists "to create as soon as possible an atmosphere that makes

it more comfortable for the FDA to approve implants and less comfortable for them not to approve"."

WHAT DOW CORNING/DOW CORNING WRIGHT/BRISTOL MYERS HAVE DONE:

* made safety and efficacy data public through public release of 30 years of proprietary research

* established Implant Information Center #800. (These two steps resulted in the only positive media coverage to date). * launched two major studies

--NYU-to study any causal relationship between breast cancer/implants

--University of Michigan-to study any causal relationship between connective tissue disease such as scleroderma and implants

* private meetings with influential plastic surgeons to discuss the issue and what they might do.

344

"The Burson Marsteller Plan" - The Largest Public Relations Firm in the World......Hired by Dow Corning and Dow Corning Wright

* *Dan Hayes, CEO, Dow Corning Wright, spoke at 8/31 meeting of 350 breast implant surgeons in Santa Fe informing them of FDA stance and the need for action. Handouts on "what to do" were given out.*

CURRENT DOW CORNING/DOW CORNING WRIGHT/BRISTOL MYERS PROGRAMS:

* *patient grassroots program*

--beginning stages of qualifying spokeswomen

--spokeswomen to write letters to FDA/Congress, letters to editor op-ed pieces, speak to local groups-will probably not be up and running in time to have enough influence for November deadline

--Dow Corning Wright patient relations person in place-Joy Murray

* *Surgeon grassroots program*

--36 surgeons to be trained as spokespersons September 21, at ASPRS annual meeting in Seattle

--Dr. Norman Cole to give "Call to Action" speech at business meeting. We will provide handouts. Handouts to include addresses of key legislators, regulators, active reporters, women's groups and bullet points for speaking/letters

--handouts to include response mechanism to Dave Fellers, Executive Director, ASPRS, so follow up letters can be sent to nudge those not participating and to track what's being done

--handouts to be mailed out immediately to those not present under Dr. Cole's cover letter

--later handouts to include videotape and speech for presentations

--DCW professional relations person in place-Gene Jakubczak

--*Dr. Cole also to speak at Seattle meeting of plastic surgery nurses*

--*Dr. Brody to speak at plastic surgery office administrators meeting.*

--*ASPRS leadership attempting to set up meeting with Kessler*

The strategy that we would like your help in carrying out is how to influence Kessler and Weiss through other Congressmen.

*   *We are suggesting that doctors with their patients visit their own congressmen and Senators along with those on the appropriate committees with oversight as well as Jamie Whitten's Appropriations Committee.*

*   *The thrust of this effort will be getting women angry about having the right to make their own decision about implants taken away from them. One approach is "How dare two men who are only tangentially* *involved, try to make this decision on behalf of the millions of women involved""*

* We also want to place regional, and if possible, national media stories on the need for keeping this option open to women. (Focus groups and congressional testimony indicate that for many women with breast cancer who have had mastectomies, breast implants let them look in the mirror without being reminded of their cancer every day.) While these are only 15-25% of implant patients-the rest are augmentation-they engender more sympathy.

Over two million women have had breast implants since they were developed thirty years ago, less than a hundred have had problems. However, those are the vocal ones. Even most of those, most notably Sybil Goldrich and Kathleen Annekens who have formed a group called Command Trust Network, don't say that implants should be banned. Just that doctors should give more information to their patients and that women should make a careful decision based on all the information available.

That until now has been the FDA position too. DC/DCW are in complete agreement. Women who call their implant information center can get the package insert among other items. It gives every possible and potential complication. One of the problems is that the physicians, as is their won't do, haven't wanted to bother the pretty little heads of their patients with all this information. The manufacturers, at least DC/DCW, have provided it to the docs and they haven't always passed it on. No point in irritating Norm or Gary with this. They know some of their own have dropped the ball in this regard. They are sincere and eager to move forward, evidenced by their changing surgery schedules for tomorrow's meeting.

This is a lot of information---thanks for taking the time to go over it. Look forward to seeing you tomorrow." END BM 005146

This "piece" that follows was written around 1992.........

"CONFIDENCE GAME: Burson-Marsteller's Public Relations Plan for Silicone Breast Implants"by: John C. Stuber and Sheldon Rampton

"Once reviled as corporate villains, the manufacturers of silicone breast implants have made a stunning comeback recently in the court of public opinion. A series of scientific studies and news stories have emerged, arguing that breast implants are in fact harmless, and that companies such as Dow Corning and Bristol-Myers are hapless victims of misguided women, greedy attorneys and manipulated juries.

This turnaround is no accident. PR Watch has obtained internal documents from Burson-Marsteller, the PR firm which engineered Dow Corning's PR strategy in the early 1990's. These documents provide an intriguing peek into a massive, expensive, and carefully orchestrated campaign that integrates state-of-the-art grassroots PR with subtle manipulations of science and the legal process.

The PR story begins in 1985, when Burson-Marsteller warned Dow Corning of 'the potential for a corporate media crisis' after a federal jury in San Francisco ordered the company it pay $1.7 million to Maria Stern in Carson City, Nevada, for what the court judged were 'defectively designed and manufactured' breast implants. The jury judged Dow Corning guilty of fraud, based on internal corporate memos and studies showing that the company had failed to inform the public of health risks related to implants.

Although the Stern case received slight media coverage, Burson-Marsteller wrote an analysis titled 'Silicone Medical Implants as a Public Issue', in which the PR firm predicted that 'the combination of human suffering, large financial awards, big business and big medicine....represent a potentially volatile media situation for the company'."

"FROM COVER-UP to BLOW-UP"

"After unsuccessful attempts to overturn the Stern verdict, Dow's lawyers negotiated a settlement *in which the company agreed to pay the judgment in exchange for a 'protective order' blocking public access to embarrassing internal documents and testimony which had emerged during the trial. In a series of subsequent cases filed by other plaintiffs, Dow settled out of court, again obtaining secrecy orders to keep damaging information from reaching the public.*

In the late 1980's; however, Dr. Sidney Wolfe, the head of Ralph Nader's Public Citizen Health Research Group, became an outspoken critic of implants. Women's groups also began pressuring the FDA to ban silicone implants.

December, 1990, the story hit big on Connie Chung's Face to Face, on CBS-TV, which featured interviews with a series of seriously ill women who blamed implants for their conditions. The show touched off a frenzy among women with implants, and the FDA came under additional public pressure. March, 1991, a New York City court awarded $4.5 million to a woman who claimed that implants had caused her cancer.

Juries judged Dow Corning guilty of fraud, based on internal corporate memos, documents showing that the company failed to inform the public of health risks related to implants.

As the crisis grew, so did the company's PR campaign. In 1990, Burson-Marsteller billed a paltry $6,000.00 in PR fees to Dow Corning, but 'From May 1991, through February, 1992, our billings have been $3,776,000 with gross income of $1,384,000', stated Burson-Marsteller Senior Vice President Johnna Matthews, in a March 10, 1992, letter marked 'confidential' to Larry Snodden, President of Burson-Marsteller/ Europe.

According to Matthews, Dow's PR crisis exploded when yet another implant recipient, Marianne Hopkins, sued the company and the 'jury reached a verdict in December, 1991. They found Dow Corning guilty of fraud, oppression and malice with damages of $7.4 million. Damning memos on issues of quality control and safety, which had been under protective orders, reached the public and we've been playing catch-up *ever since.....Our job has become damage control of language that compares breast implants to the 'Pinto gas tank' and a multitude of other comments' in memos which are 'almost impossible to defend in court and certainly in the 'court of public opinion'."*

By 1992, the FDA had imposed a ban on further breast implants, and implant manufacturers faced lawsuits worth billions of dollars. Dow began to fear for its very survival, as breast implants threatened to become a wedge opening the company to even wider scrutiny. 'There are other issues on the horizon for them', Matthews wrote. 'All silicones may be attacked, their other medical devices like joints are under attack and they have some environmental issues too.'

In a separate strategy document, Burson-Marsteller advised, 'We must aggressively fight a world in which 'silicone-free' becomes a labeling boast'.'

"MOBILIZING THE MASSES"

As the FDA moved toward hearings on the implant controversy, Dow and the plastic surgeons launched a fierce PR counterattack. Burson-Marsteller and its subsidiary, Gold & Liebengood, led the charge for Dow, while the plastic surgeons retained the firms of Kent & O'Connor, along with Black, Manafort, Stone & Kelly, another Burson-Marsteller subsidiary.

One of Dow's internal memos from that period has been cited by critics of the company as evidence that the company was engaged in deliberate deception. Plaintiffs and their attorneys have emphasized a sentence from the memo in which Dow CEO Dan Hayes states, 'The issue of cover-up is going well from a long-term perspective'.

Less attention; however, has been given to the remainder of the Hayes memo, in which he describes clearly the company's PR strategy. 'The number one issue in my mind is the establishment of networks,' Hayes states. 'This is the largest single issue on our *platter because it affects not only the next 2-3 years of profitability....but also ultimately has a big impact on the long term ethics and believability issues....I have started to initiate surgeon contact.....to organize the plastic surgery community....The place we have the biggest hole still missing......is in this whole arena of getting the patient grassroots movement going.'*

'These women (including celebrities) will be trained and testimony will be written for them to deliver before Congressional committees.' (internal Burson-Marsteller PR document)

'Grassroots' has become a corporate buzzword for a PR strategy which uses corporate wealth to subsidize orchestrated mass campaigns that put seemingly independent citizens on the front lines as activists for corporate causes. Phillip Morris, for example, has paid Burson-Marsteller tens of millions of dollars to organize smokers into the National Smokers' Alliance, which effectively lobbies for the company in the name of 'smokers rights'.

*"The Burson Marsteller Plan" - The Largest Public Relations Firm
in the World......Hired by Dow Corning and Dow Corning Wright*

Johnna Matthews described Burson-Marsteller's grassroots strategy for Dow in a confidential letter on September 9, 1991, addressed to Burson-Marsteller subsidiary Gold & Liebengood. 'I was not going to put this into writing, but wanted you both to be up to speed---and there is too much information for you to have to listen to it al verbally', Matthews wrote. 'With the FDA's new penchant for walking into ad agencies and demanding to look at documents, I hope you'll give this a toss once you've read it.'

According to Matthews, 'No one really knows why the women who have problems have them......It may be that there are women with an allergic reaction to the silicone gel,' although she termed this 'unlikely'.

Worried that the FDA was considering a ban on silicone breast implants, Matthews outlined a strategy for 'getting women angry about having the right to make their own decision about implants taken away from them......We also want to place regional, and if possible, national media stories on the need for keeping this option open to women.'

357

"STAR SEARCH"

Another internal document describes Burson-Marsteller's grassroots organizing tactics in more detail: 'Utilize a well-known celebrity who has breast implants for reconstructive purposes to speak out on the benefits of them. Utilize spokespeople drawn from women's cancer support groups in major markets to defend implants by writing letters to the editor, participating in media interviews, and communicating positive messages to women's groups in their regions.'

Burson-Marsteller turned to the American Society of Plastic and Reconstructive Surgeons for help in identifying patients who could be recruited as spokespeople. After regional spokespersons had been enrolled around the country, 'we can announce the celebrity chairperson as head of the national women's cancer support organization (name to be determined)...(Dow Corning) makes corporate grant to this organization....Agency to provide day-to-day media support for this group....These women (including

celebrities) will be trained and testimony will be written
for them to deliver before Congressional committees.'

In a preliminary budget, Burson-Marsteller
suggested that Dow should be prepared to pay
$891,000 to get the grassroots program up and
running, including a $300,000 'participation fee' to its
celebrity spokesperson.

In practice, it appears that Dow was never able
to find an adequate celebrity willing to fill the desired
role. Only two celebrities have gone public talking
about their experiences with implants----talk show host
Jennie Jones and 'Waltons' actress Mary McDonough,
both of whom have spoken out against health problems
which they believe were caused by their implants. (To
date, there are several celebrities who are outspoken
about the toxicity of silicone and saline breast implants.
circa, 2000)

"SEEKING SYMPATHY"

Burson-Marsteller's focus groups showed that it could get the most favorable press coverage by highlighting cases of women with breast cancer who have had mastectomies and used implants for the purpose of breast reconstruction. 'While these are only 15-25% of implant patients---the rest are augmentation---they engender more sympathy', Matthews wrote.

For similar reasons, Burson-Marsteller advised that cancer specialists should be recruited as 'spokesdoctors' to defend the company in the top 15 media markets in the United States, because 'an oncologist obviously has more credibility than a plastic surgeon'.

As Dow Corning geared up for the hearings on implant safety scheduled for November 14, 1991, Burson-Marsteller worked to organize a massive 'Washington fly-in'. Burson-Marsteller staffer Cindee Castronovo was in charge of bringing up to 1,000 women to Washington to rally in favor of implants, with Dow Corning footing the bills for their travel and lodging plus several days of rehearsals and training prior to actual testimony.

Participants in the fly-in included a writer named Karen Berger and breast cancer support groups Y-ME, the Susan B. Komen Foundation, and the National Alliance of Breast Cancer Organizations (NABC). Y-ME was given the assignment to generate 175,000 letters to Congress. (Are you starting to see how this all worked now?)

Berger, a former schoolteacher, was neither a cancer survivor nor an implant recipient. Her authority as an expert on implants was based on her authorship of 'A Woman's Decision: Breast Care, Treatment and Reconstruction'. Co-authored with plastic surgeon John Bostwick, III, the book encourages women to seek reconstructive surgery following mastectomies. Burson-Marsteller pitched her to the press as the author of 'survey work' which 'shows that the majority of breast cancer patients who have been reconstructed find implants very valuable'.

361

Berger's name appears repeatedly on internal Burson-Marsteller documents, which describe her as a 'primary recruiter' for the Washington fly-in. In a profile; however, Berger is described as an 'independent medical publisher' who 'says she has no connection with any organization'.

'The suggestion that women should martyr themselves...by remaining breastless is a throwback to the Middle Ages,' Berger argued in one news release. She even went so far as to claim that banning implants would lead to an increase in cancer deaths among women. Without the implant option, she argued, women would avoid seeking diagnosis and treatment of their cancers.

"ONE-HAND WASHES ANOTHER"

Burson-Marsteller documents suggest that financial incentives helped Dow great the skids with cancer support groups such as Y-ME and the Susan B. Komen Foundation. The Komen Foundation, for example, sponsors running marathons in several cities to fundraise and promote awareness of the need for breast cancer checkups. In an October, 1991, strategy note, Burson-Marsteller noted that the foundation 'wants Dow Corning to sponsor upcoming race in Atlanta'.

Burson-Marsteller also offered its assistance on what is called an 'I scratch your back' basis to the breast cancer coalition 'to pump dollars for [breast cancer] research'.

Some breast cancer survivors, such as Darcy Sixt, publicly acknowledged that they had become paid spokespersons for Dow Corning. Others either worked for free or made no mention of who paid them.

Although the hundreds of women who rallied during the Washington fly-in had their expenses paid, Burson-Marsteller planned to avoid payments to people who would be testifying before the FDA. It made a special exception to this rule in one case---Timmie Jean

Lindsey, who in 1962, became the first woman to receive a set of breast implants.

'We will be paying for Timmie Jean Lindsey to testify---based on the fact that she could not take on the financial responsibility', states a Burson-Marsteller document.

In fact, Lindsey's full story could strengthen the argument of women who say implants cause connective-tissue disorders. In the 1970's, she suffered joint pain, rashes, dry mouth, dry eyes, and a chronic fatigue. More recently, she underwent surgery to replace a knee joint, a problem she attributes to age but which might be interpreted as a symptom of silicone-induced arthritis. Her daughter and a sister-in-law, both of whom she encouraged to receive implants, have joined the class action lawsuit that plaintiffs have filed against implant manufacturers, with her daughter alleging that the implants gave her lupus.

The plastic surgeons' efforts to recruit spokespersons backfired completely in the case of

Terry Davis of Palm Beach Gardens, Florida. 'My doctor told me to lobby the FDA to keep implants', she told the FDA panel. Instead, she attended so she could describe the complications she had suffered with her implants following a double mastectomy four years previously.

"BOWING OUT"

In the March 1992, letter from Burson-Marsteller's Johnna Matthews to co-worker Larry Snodden, she credited Burson-Marsteller's grassroots strategy with 'turning around the media coverage on the issue from strongly negative. It culminated briefly in November's FDA Advisory Panel Hearings where by bringing in a tremendous number of women to testify, we also helped turn those hearings around. The result was that the panel recommended to FDA Commissioner David Kessler that the implants remain on the market- -a major victory.'

Victory notwithstanding, Dow Corning was almost outlining plans to withdraw from the breast implant market, which had become both controversial and unprofitable. In a strategy document dated December 19, 1991, Burson-Marsteller warned that 'the company's motives are going to be questioned'. You can't say in November, 'We are very concerned about the patients, and will do anything the FDA requires for us to keep the product widely available,' and then say in January, 'We are withdrawing from the marketplace.' "

From a Public Relations perspective, Burson-Marsteller advised Dow that it could 'minimize negative comments' by timing its withdrawal to coincide with an 'adverse FDA decision' that could serve as 'a highly defensible public reason for withdrawing from the business'.

The anticipated 'adverse FDA decision' came with two rulings in early 1992. Although Kessler made an exemption so that breast cancer patients could continue to receive silicone implants despite the ban, Dow's grassroots network continues to accuse the FDA of limiting options for breast reconstruction.

As recently as August, 1995, Y-ME Executive Director Sharon Green testified before Congress that 'The implant debate is out of control---and, as a result, we all lose'. Another Y-ME activist, Rosemary Locke, described silicone implants as 'a benefit to women not only in the breast cancer community, but to some degree to all women'.

"COSMETIC CONSTRUCTION"

In order to rehabilitate its battered image, Dow Corning reshuffled management in 1992, bringing in Keith McKennon as its new chairman. McKennon's background included crisis management for Dow Chemical during the parent company's own prior scandals. The Washington Post noted that McKennon had handled 'public relations fights over dioxin and Agent Orange.....This background is very pertinent to a meaningful resolution of the mammary issue.'

Dow also hired Griffin Bell, former U.S. Attorney General under President Carter, to perform an 'independent review' of the company. Since leaving *public office, Bell has performed similar high-profile services for clients including Exxon in the wake of the Valdez oil spill, General Motors after the discovery that pickup trucks were exploding in auto collisions; Virginia Military Institute in its effort to bar women students; and A. H. Robbins during its Dalkon Shield controversy.*

'What does the company need from Griffin Bell?' asked one Burson-Marsteller document. 'Not a 'clean bill of health'----which would be a disaster.' Burson-Marsteller even suggested toughening the Bell review by adding a 'representative of a responsible public interest group' or a 'major medical association'. If the findings are a bit rougher than they might otherwise have been, from a PR perspective, that's not a problem. It gives the company a chance to show credibility, responsiveness, willingness to change.'

Bell prepared a report based on his investigation, along with a three-page letter of recommendations for changes in company policy. Dow released the letter with an accompanying statement of the company's

intent to comply with these 'reforms'. The statement
claimed that Bell's team had exhaustively reviewed
300,000 pages of corporate information. Citing attorney-
client privilege; however, Dow refused to release the
documents for public review, or even to release Bell's
full report.

As you can see.....the compelling evidence of
manipulation and distortion of facts was in place
from the very beginning. The so called "grass roots"
efforts consisted of arranging and paying for groups
of women to speak out in behalf of the breast implant
manufacturers while playing on the "choices" women are
given for breast reconstruction after radical mastectomy
and for augmentation purposes. There is no regard
for what adverse effects these toxic "medical devices"
might have on the human body, and absolutely nothing
regarding the effects of putting these 38 toxic chemicals
into a body that has already been compromised by
cancer!!!!!!!!

Section Seven - Transcript of the "Connie Chung Interview" - Aired on CBS - TV, December 10, 1990

This next section is the ORIGINAL Connie Chung Interview of December 10, 1990.

It has been taken from evidentiary disks/BMS 28413 Misspelled names are as they appeared in the transcript.

TRANSCRIPT OF CONNIE CHUNG INTERVIEW

December 10, 1990

9:00-10:00 PM (CT)

CBS-TV

Connie Chung

Connie Chung, host:

"Most of us know little about breast implants. We have seen the adds; we have heard the rumors about which celebrities have them and which don't. But we don't know anything about the dangers. Since the

early 1960's, some two million women have had breast implants. It is a simple device; the most common ones look like this: it has an outer shell made of silicone, with silicone gel on he inside. The operation takes a few hours, and if all goes well, the implants should last a lifetime, at least that is what most women believe, but not the women we interviewed. In fact, it couldn't be further from the truth.

Dr. Douglas Shanklin (Pathologist, University of Tennessee at Memphis): "Nobody came out and said, "We have an announcement to make. We are about to experiment on two million American women. But from a certain view, that is what has happened. We have done a large-scale clinical experiment on an unproven, probably unsafe medical device which is placed inside the body where the body can react." "

Chung: "For almost thirty years, American women have been getting breast implants. An astonishing average of three hundred and fifty implant operations a day. But what is shocking is that these devices have never been approved by the federal government. Only now is the government looking at the dangers. For some women, it may be too late."

Judy Taylor (Breast Implant Recipient): "I knew many women that have had implants, many women. And, you know, I have asked, How did it go? You know, Were there any problems, you know, How does it feel? Do they hurt? And it was fine. I just didn't talk to the right women, the women that were sick."

Chung: "Six years ago Judy Taylor received silicone implants after a double mastectomy. You thought everything was going to be just fine."

Taylor: "And it was."

Chung: "For how long?"

Taylor: "Approximately one year, and then I started getting sick."

Chung: "What were your symptoms?"

Taylor: "It was flu-like symptoms: swollen glands, fevers, chills, sweats, sore throats, and many, many trips to the doctor. And I got more tired, and more tired, and joint pain. And it was very difficult to go up and down a stair."

Chung: "How long did this go on?"

Taylor: "This went on for almost five years."

Chung: "Five years!"

Taylor: "Yes."

Chung: "Doctors insisted she had a virus, until finally one physician told Judy her system was being poisoned."

"When the doctor told you what her thought was wrong with you, how did he explain it?"

Taylor: "He told me that I had silicone-associated disease, or human adjuvant (sic) disease."

Chung: "What did that mean to you?"

Taylor: "Absolutely nothing." 'You know, and &'

Chung: "It meant her implants would have to be removed, and when they were, what the doctor found surprised him. The implants were intact, but as this photo shows, silicone had leaked into the surrounding scar tissue of her breasts, and traveled to her lymph glands."

Shanklin: "Silicone gets right into the heart of the immune response system, and is processed in a way that causes the formation of abnormal antibodies."

Chung: "And these antibodies," says Dr. Shanklin, "not only attack the silicone, but can turn on the human system as well, causing the body to go haywire." Shanklin is a pathologist at the University of Tennessee in Memphis, where he has spent six years studying tissue from women with implants. He has found evidence of silicone in almost every part of the body."

Shanklin: "I found it in the thyroid gland here in the neck. I found it in the spleen, which in most people is in the abdomen on the upper left side. I have seen it in the liver. I have seen it in the other lymph nodes in the body. I have not found it so far, in one case, where I looked at the ovaries."

Janice Buck (Breast Implant Recipient): "They do say, "Mom, I'll take care of you" "Don't worry about anything", you know."

Chung: "Janice Buck is convinced that silicone is also at the root of her health problems. Eleven years ago, tumors in her breasts forced her to have mastectomies, breast implants. Today, she can barely walk. She is plagued with illnesses."

Buck: "I suffer constant pain constant pain and constant fatigue. I take a total of between four and dive hundred dollars of medication a month to try to keep me going."

Chung: "When the doctor told you that maybe it might be the breast implants, and that you ought to have them removed, what did you think?"

Buck: "I would have done anything if I thought it would help me get better, but it was probably the hardest thing I ever had to do, because it was so hard losing my breasts once, let alone having to lose them twice."

Chung: "Sybil Golridge gave up on implants after five operations left her breasts mangled and infected. She allowed us to use this photo as a graphic example of her ordeal. Today she is demanding that doctors warn women of all the dangers they may face."

Golridge: "If every doctor would simply read the package insert to the patient, the woman would then have enough information to make her decision. Simply read the list of complications to the patient, and let her

decide whether she wants to risk these complications.
The complications they list are known. Just tell her
what is there. She is not getting that information.
Nobody is getting that information."

Chung: "This is a typical insert that
manufacturers include with their implants. It says that
is the surgeon's responsibility to tell the patient about
any possible risks of complications. They include
implant rupture, or tearing from excessive stress such
as massage or vigorous exercise, silicone bleeding
or leaking, and a warning that implants may cause
severe joint pain, swollen glands, and hair loss."

"None of the women is this story had access to
this information. That is because manufacturers didn't
start disclosing it until five years ago. We spoke with
more than forty doctors around the country, and were
surprised to learn that less than a third mentioned
these complications to their patients."

Karen Valleya (Breast Implant Recipient): "Had
I known that these things could rupture, I would never

have had this done, because I would have been afraid of leaking silicone."

Chung: "Initially, where you had the implants, how long did you think they were going to last?'

Valleya: "A lifetime."

Chung: "Karen Valleya is a nurse and mother of two. Before deciding on implants for cosmetic reasons, she had asked about the dangers. She thought she knew everything that could possibly go wrong."

Valleya: "I was quite happy with the way I looked. I was really pleased with the surgery. I think I even wrote the surgeon a letter telling him this, you know, how much that it did for my self-esteem."

Chung: "When did you start noticing some problems?"

Valleya: "Six months after breast augments I started to experience extreme fatigue, fatigue to the point where I couldn't care for my children, mouth ulcers, just eroded my mouth completely, fevers, pneumonia, chest pain, hair loss, bizarre skin rashes, and all of those things. And I just knew something was wrong."

Chung: "Karen would later be diagnosed with a disease of the immune system called lupus, but there were other symptoms that no one could explain."

Valleya: "I had leakage of a clear fluid from my right breast, and a lump there &"

Chung: "Leakage?"

Valleya: "Leakage from a nipple. I was absolutely shocked to find out that it was silicone that had been leaking out of me for two-and-a-half years."

Chung: "And surgery confirmed what she had feared: the right implant had ruptured. Karen had them both removed."

"Karen, what are you left with now?"

Valleya: "I'm left with, you know, just about no breast tissue. I wear, I wear a prosthesis, just like someone with a mastectomy."

Chung: "But silicone isn't the only danger women face. Since the early 1980's more and more women have been turning to this: It is called Meme™. It is a silicone implant covered with soft polyurethane foam. Although doctors had their concerns about this foam decades earlier, in recent years the makers of the Meme™ have called it the new answer to keeping the breast tissue from turning hard."

"The Meme™ was the implant of choice for Janice Cruz. She couldn't imagine what her doctor would find when he removed them seven years later."

Janice Cruz (Breast Implant Recipient): "The polyurethane cover was completely dissolved. What was supposed to be a two-and-a-half hour surgery to remove implants turned into seven hours of dipping, what he referred to as a green, slimy-looking gelatin from my chest wall and everywhere he could reach."

Chung: "In his laboratory in Canada, Dr. Pierre Blais has spent ten years researching what happens to polyurethane once it is in a woman's breast."

Dr. Pierre Blais (Researcher): "After about a month, it looks like this, the foam has gone in part, and it is beginning to peel away from the surface. After about six months to a year, half of the foam has gone away, dissolved. They produce debris, which is potentially toxic."

Chung: "The foam is made here at a factory outside of Philadelphia. It is an industrial polyurethane like that found in air conditioning and carburetor filters. When it breaks down, it can produce a chemical. Tolulene-diamine, or TDA. A known animal carcinogen already banned in hair dyes. But the makers of the Meme™, Surgitek, insist their studies show the foam is safe."

383

"We asked Surgitek to talk to us about the Meme ™, the foam, and its dangers. But officials not only refused to go on camera, they asked us to leave their property."

Golridge: "Nobody has done the kind of studies that are required for this kind of product. Just as I say that it is my belief that the implants are harmful, the drug companies and the manufacturers don't have any proof that it is not. Why should we be in the catch-22 situation thirty years after the fact. There's got to be something wrong there."

Chung: "The FDA will not grant us an interview on Meme™ or any other implant. But in a statement the FDA did say it is in the process of collecting date from the manufacturers, and that it may take years before any decisions are made about their safety."

"In the meantime, more than a hundred thousand women each year are still receiving implants."

Valleys: "It is very difficult to tell people about what has happened to me, because I find it is somewhat embarrassing. Not that I did anything wrong, but just personal. But I feel that if someone doesn't speak out, and talk about this....I believe that there are probably many women like me, but how many want to tell the world this, you know. It is hard to do."

Chung: "There are no statistics on how many women have become ill because of their implants. No agency, no study has kept track of them. While questions continue to be raised about the safety of breast implants, only the state of Maryland requires doctors to inform their patients of all the known risks and complications. It took five years to get that law passed."

To date, mid-March, 2004.....Breast implants are still not approved for safety by the FDA, or the federal government.

The manufacturers now, seem to be targeting the very young teenagers for breast augmentation.

385

Parents are agreeing to this and paying for the surgeries as graduation gifts.........Something tells me that the manufacturers, doctors and government agencies who are supposed to be overseeing this are not......Are all of the risks being given to these teens and their parents so they can make an informed decision? I think not!

I am involved with thousands of women in silicone related support groups all over the United States and Iceland, Britain, Australia, Switzerland, South America and other countries, to my knowledge not a single woman, who received implants for either augmentation or for Reconstructive surgery after mastectomy, was told of the hazards associated with silicone breast implants.

Section Eight - Letter Written by Dr. Norman D. Anderson of the Johns Hopkins Hospital to Dr. David Kessler of the F D A

From Dr. Norman D. Anderson, Associate Professor, Medicine and Surgery, The Johns Hopkins Hospital....December 12, 1991.

THE JOHNS HOPKINS HOSPITAL
600 North Wolfe Street
Baltimore, Maryland 21205
December 12, 1991
Dr. David Kessler
Commissioner, Food and Drug Administration
5700 Fishers Lane
Rockville, Maryland 20857

Dear Dr. Kessler:

"I am writing as a member of the present General and Plastic Surgery Advisory Committee, and past chairman of that same panel during FDA reviews of breast implant usage in 1983 and 1988, to urge that all gel-filled silicone breast implants be promptly removed from the public marketplace and made available for continued use only under controls provided by investigational device exemption until further research

provides reasonable assurances of their long term safety and efficiency."

"This appeal is not made lightly. In past years, I have witnessed attempts by some breast implant proponents to suborn governmental regulation by: editing their research data, selectively reporting device-related complaints, discrediting their scientific critics, demeaning patients with adverse outcomes, and substituting political influence for their own faulty science. Many such activities were equally evident preceding and during the November panel meeting. Yet, at the time of closing it seemed entirely plausible that the responsible marketing practices promised by the manufacturers under the glare of public scrutiny might suffice to protect consumer interests until all scientific uncertainties over the gel-filled implants were resolved under time tables to be established by the FDA."

"Regrettably, those hopes for ending public ignorance on the long term sequelae of breast implants have been extinguished by corporate maneuvering. Although Dow Corning Wright has openly stated that

it fully disclosed all relevant information to support the PMA (pre market approval) applications reviewed by the advisory panel in November, I am now in possession of unprotected court documents which indicate this was not done. That overt breach of the public trust is exemplified by remembering that in the panel meeting I repeatedly asked Dr. LaVier for data on the incidence of implant rupture, any evidence for biodegradation of retrieved implants and explanations for Dow Corning Wright's "limited warranties". His response was to state that such information did not exist and that he was insulted by my questions."

"Attachments to this letter from the case of Cardinal v. Dow Corning in the Michigan Court of Appeals # 138959, establish that, in tact, Dow Corning Wright possessed such information and has used it to direct business practices since 1970. The following listing of office memos from the business records of Dow Corning Wright leaves little doubt of their misrepresentation of the facts:"

*Letter Written by Dr. Norman D. Anderson of the Johns Hopkins
Hospital to Dr. David Kessler of the F D A*

1.   *Memo from Koning to Mantle: "Increasing
incidence of Ruptures"; June 1970*

2.   *Memo from Caterer to Woodward: "Dr.
Bader - Rupture"; January, 1971*

3.   *Memo by Koning: "Envelope Degradation";
January, 1971*

4.   *Memo by Koning: "Envelope degradation";
February, 1971*

5.   *Memo from Morgan to Koning: "Envelope
Degradation"; March, 1971*

6.   *Memo by Koning: "Mammary Return";
March, 1971*

7.   *Memo by Koning: "Extravasation"; April,
1971*

8.   *Memo by Koning: "Rupture"; May, 1972*

9. *Memo by Rathjen to Baecker: "Request for Information on Breakage Rate of Silastic Round Prostheses"; April, 1973*

10. *Memo from Lewis to Hinsch: "Mammary Prostheses Ruptures"; December, 1977*

11. *Memo from Lewis to Hinsch: "Report of Excessive Ruptures and Loss of Business"; March, 1978*

12. *Memo by Peters to Hinsch: "Physical Properties Versus Time for Silastic II and Standard Prostheses"; November, 1981*

13. *Handwritten analysis/Report by Peters: "Returned Mammaries Made in 1976"; May, 1982*

14. *Memo from Jakubczek to Matherly: "Silastic II Mammaries-Loose Gel HH023099 (Drums, 1,2)": April, 1983*

15. Memo by Frisch to Dumas: "Returned Breast Implants"; February, 1984

16. Paper by Grow, et al: "The Biodegradability of Organo-Silicone: Clinical Management Implications"

17. Letter from Dr. Motley to Hayes: "Termination of Relationship with Dow Corning due to Ruptures"; October, 1985

In light of these disclosures, I must urge that FDA initiate a full investigation and immediate review of all Dow Corning Wright business and records alluded to in the above court proceedings. At the very least, this compilation of citations suggests that a series of implants marketed between the mid-1970's through the mid-1980's pose potential hazards to their wearers that have never been conveyed to patients or physicians.

It is equally obvious that good faith actions by the FDA cannot be substituted for good science when vested interests run counter to the public need for resolving 30 years of controversy. I believe the FDA must now act firmly to restore scientific credibility to regulatory processes that are in danger of being molded by PAC's and political influence peddling. Justification for these concerns are illustrated in additional attachments accompanying this letter. However, they can be summarized here by noting that following the November panel meeting, the manufacturers and proponents of breast implants have reverted to skillfully devised programs of "spin management" which frequently equate with misleading pronouncements and unsubstantiated claims of device safety. Those practices may be routine business fare for influencing public opinion and mobilizing congressional support, but they should never prevail in matters of consumer health.

More flagrant are actions billed as good public relations efforts which utilize media advertising to direct the health concerns of individual consumers into corporate telephone centers where neither the content nor the accuracy of the advice rendered by "trained staff" is scrutinized by the FDA. I have telephoned these centers seeking advice as a distraught husband whose wife is uncertain about breast reconstruction and received counsel given warmly but replete with glaring inaccuracy's that clearly represent a corporate version of insidious deceit which can only be recognized by those who are quite knowledgeable about the implant controversy.

Dr. Kessler, I invite you and your staff to make similar assessments through your own telephone conversations with these "information centers". If you conclude, as I have, that they are designed to protect the product and not the consumer, then the time has come to place all silicone gel-filled implants in a mandatory IDE status. Any compromises short of that regulatory status will surely be countered by the "spin makers" who have voided every good faith previously extended by the FDA. I will also point out that such policies would be entirely consistent with your past demands for fair labeling practices in the food industry and with the actions you have taken against the "Misty Gold" breast prosthesis because of unsubstantiated claims without your having to make any determinations on implant safety from the paucity of meaningful available data.

I must also express grave concerns that the process pursued by the FDA in the recent panel meeting inadvertently contributed to the misinformation that is now being used by 'spin makers' to mold public opinion on breast implants. By designating an advisory panel of 11 voting members where only 4 had any semblance of familiarity with breast implants, the FDA created a body of novices susceptible to the one-sided testimony of experts selected by the manufacturers and the stature of professional societies advocating continued marketing of these devices. This strategy did work well in the panel's review of PMA data submitted by the four manufacturers because the corporate stances were effectively offset by excellent scientific appraisals from the FDA staff members who are to be commended for their fine work. But in the equally important task of defining a public health need for continued availability of these devices. The outcome was in shambles because there was scant balancing testimony from scientists who have studied the putative medical problems attributed to silicone implants and statements from Dr. Steven Wiener and Dr. Frank Vasey were not included in the proceedings. In such a titled playing field, the opinions of psychologists and psychiatrists who have studied only the happier outcomes of breast implant usage easily carried the day for the manufacturers, while the testimony from 10 women clearly injured by failed implant surgery was dismissed as anecdotal irrelevance. Such edited deliberations by a body of experts who reviewed data restricted to the best devices currently available could only lead to flawed implications because they made no considerations for the possible hazards posed today for more than one million women who are wearing vintage implants of antiquated shell designs, variable gel consistencies and uncertain gel formulations. To leave such questions unresolved would be an unpardonable omission by the FDA. Yet, these potential health risks were ignored unwittingly by the panel, the media and official FDA pronouncements which immediately began categorizing all such devices under the generic label of silicone breast implants.

Perhaps an even greater error came after the panel meeting in the FDA's Talk Paper issued on November 15. That publication states: "The panel chairperson, Dr. Elizabeth Connell of Emory University School of Medicine, emphasized that the group did not find evidence that implants are unsafe, but rather that there was not enough information about the risks and benefits of their use." While Dr. Connell may be quoted correctly here, I do not recall that I ever voted to express that precise opinion. In any event, the use of a double negative in the first phrase of that sentence has proven unfortunate for it is now being widely quoted out of context as official FDA endorsement of breast implant safety. For example, in my recent telephone call to the Dow Corning Information Center, the counselor advised me that the "FDA found no evidence that breast implants aren't safe, and somehow neglected to mention the qualifiers included in the second half of the sentence cited above. From that conversation, I can only conclude that the Talk Paper provided just the right grist for the needs of the "spin makers".

You should also know that in this conversation, the same Dow Corning counselor stated that continued marketing approval was assured in your pending January, 1992, decision. However, she did suggest that a "minor condition" would be attached "to ensure informed consent using a patient information pamphlet similar to that required by the law in Maryland". I sincerely hope this is simply another corporate misstatement, since I helped write the Maryland pamphlet and its use has done nothing to dispel my worries about the long term safety of many, if not all, silicone gel-filled implants.

During the dozen years I have worked with the FDA, I have conversed with hundreds of women wearing breast implants. While hardly scientific simple cataloguing of their statements reveals that approximately 96% of those experiencing implant rupture developed local, chest wall, upper arm and/ or vague systemic symptoms that are reminiscent of the sequelae described after liquid silicone injections into the breast. Because the majority of these women received implants for reconstruction following simple or modified radical mastectomies, such outcomes may relate to the scant protection provided for the implants by the remaining local tissues-but with times to implant rupture typically ranging from 7 to 9 years. I fear that in vivo degradation of implant shell could be a contributing factor that would be relevant to all women wearing implants. To help resolve these issues, I am requesting your permission to work with the FDA scientific staff without compensation in reviewing case materials from the 400 women who have reported device rupture to your agency over the past 2 years. Since the manufacturers have publicly stated that they do not test explanted devices, I again urge that you establish such a test facility and an appropriate registry for explanted breast prostheses within the FDA or by contract with reputable biomaterials testing firms. Nothing short of these actions can determine the health risks faced by women wearing implants of older design that were previously produced by existing manufacturers or companies that have gone out of business.

*In closing I must apologize for burdening you
with such a lengthy letter filled with requests. I do
recognize the heavy burdens of responsibility you
face in determining the future course of breast implant
regulation in this country and trust that your decisions
will be well reasoned and correct. Please recognize that
I am at your service and would be privileged to meet
with you to discuss any issues raised by this letter, if
you so desire.*

Sincerely yours,

Norman D. Anderson, M.D.
Associate Professor, Medicine & Surgery

Enclosures
cc: Carol Scheman
Ruth Markatz

NDA/ mja

*Dr. Norman Anderson was not unlike many
physicians who dared to question the ethics of the FDA,*

the manufacturers, and the public relations firms hired by the manufacturers to "spin out" the truths into a more palatable awareness of silicone breast implants. Remember that to date.....these devices have NEVER been approved for safety by the FDA.

Dr. Diana Zukerman, a proponent of victims of silicone breast implant recipients, was a Professional Staff Member of the House of Representatives, Human Resources and Intergovernmental Relations Subcommittee of the Committee on Government Operations in 1991, wrote a letter to Ted Weiss, deceased now but also a proponent of silicone breast implant victims. The letter is difficult to read but I will quote a majority of the letter here as follows:

September 12, 1991

"The statisticians that reviewed the clinical studies by McGhan, Mentor, and Bioplasty explicitly recommended that the PMA's for each of these companies not be filed because of major flaws in those

studies. And yet, all of the PMA's were accepted by filing by FDA.

Despite the subcommittee request for all documents regarding the PMA's, we have not received any written justification that explain why the scientists' recommendations were overruled. In fact, there is no written justification of any kind regarding why the seven PMA's were filed by the FDA. This is unusual, within every agency of the HHS there is usually a written justification for any decision of this importance. Since we have been assured by the FDA that the subcommittee has received all documents on this matter, we have to assume that there are no FDA documents supporting the filing of any PMA's for breast implants."

"DOW CORNING. In an August 12 memo to the file, the Task Leader of the FDA Breast Prosthesis PMA Task Force wrote that the Dow Corning clinical studies are 'so weak that they cannot provide reasonable assurance of the safety and effectiveness of these devices' because they provide 'no assurance that the full range of complications are included, no dependable

measure of the incidences of complications, no reliable measure of the revision rate and no quantitative measure of patient benefit'. In his detailed criticism, he specified that the physicians who conducted the research were instructed 'to report only complications associated with the implant. As a result, the only complications reported are those at the implant site. This prevents those investigating from detecting systemic adverse effects or complications resulting from implantation of the devices'. He also stated this 'causes an underestimate of both types and incidence of complications'. Furthermore, each patient was examined only once after surgery and the number of patients examined at each time point is very small' making it difficult to determine the rate of complications at any point in time."

"MCGHAN. The statistician who reviewed the McGhan PMA pointed out many major problems in their studies of women. For example, in the McGhan prospective clinical study, 10% of the 118 patients were not evaluated at the time they were discharged, and only one-third of the implants were assessed at the second required visit (3-6 months). The statistician

pointed out that the lack of follow-up makes it impossible
to draw any conclusions about long-term safety or
effectiveness. In addition, only three reconstruction
patients were in the study, making it impossible to
draw any conclusions about their experiences. The
statistician reported that the company's 'historical
cohort study' suffered from 'strong potential for bias'
and was; therefore, of no use in providing support for
safety and effectiveness. An FDA biologist pointed out
that the company studied only two of the four models
listed on the PMA. This obviously makes it impossible
to determine safety or effectiveness for the two 'multi-
lumen' models (made from saline and silicone) that
were to be studied. Moreover, only 39 reconstruction
patients and 101 augmentation patients were studied,
which isn't enough to determine problems (even fatal
ones) that affect a small percentage of patients. In
addition, many potential medical problems, such as
breast disease or carcinoma, were not evaluated for
all patients. My review of that PMA indicates that
two-thirds of the women included in that study had
prostheses implanted in 1989 or 1990; therefore, the

study could not under any circumstances assess long-term risk."

"BIOPLASTY. Similarly, a statistician reported that in the study of 260 patients with Bioplasty's MISTI single or Double lumen implants, only 6% of the patients were assessed at the 2 year follow-up, and yet the company calculated their claims of safety and effectiveness as if they had followed large numbers of patients for 2 years. There were only 21 reconstruction patients, which importantly, the company stated that the physicians conducting the study refused to all the company to contact the patients to ask about autoimmune disorders or cancer, 'fearing that it may cause undue concern or violate patient confidentiality'. The company blamed the media, saying 'it created an environment in which gathering that information was, at best difficult'."

'MENTOR. There were three PMA's submitted by Mentor, for three different types of implants. This in itself is interesting, since most companies submitted one PMA for several types of implants. The studies

for the three types of implants were identical, and the statistician criticized the applications for failing to include important information, such as when patients were assessed subsequent to surgery, or whether appropriate steps were taken to avoid bias in the study. My review of the application reveals that the (number is illegible) patients in one study were apparently evaluated on the basis of the medical records, which did not necessarily provide any long-term information. For a second study, 128 women of those (number is illegible) patients were interviewed on the telephone to evaluate their satisfaction with the implants. The 128 women represent 37% of the patients who were selected for the interview: it is; therefore, impossible to draw any conclusions about patient satisfaction based on that sample. In a third study by Mentor, 273 augmentation patients were included in a retrospective study of complications, but the information available was for an unspecified time and based on available medical records of the plastic surgeon. Since such records would not be expected to include information on autoimmune disease or cancer, this study is inadequate in the safety information it provides."

"CONCLUSIONS. When new drugs or devices are introduced onto the market, the number of patients evaluated is necessarily small. However, in the case of breast implants, there is a 30 year history involving more than 2 million American women. It is hard to understand why the companies, which have known since at least 1982, that they would probably be required to provide safety data, and which were warned more than three years ago that data would definitely be required, waited so long before they started conducting major studies. In fact, many of the studies were started in 1990 or 1991. Although prospective studies that followed women for many years would have been considered ideal, a reasonable alternative would be to start a study in 1990 that asked patients from the 1970's or 1980's about any medical problems they have had since their implant surgery. That kind of thorough retrospective study was not conducted by any of the manufacturers."

"In summary, there are several major problems with most of the studies.

1. *Most do not study women for more than two years at the most; this is not sufficient to evaluate the safety of a medical device that is meant to be permanent, especially when allegations have been made that they are likely to rupture after several years.*

2. *In many cases, the majority of women are lost to the study after a few months; it is therefore impossible to say whether an implant is safe if there is no information at all on most of the women who had the surgery.*

3. *In several studies, there are no relevant questions regarding autoimmune disorders, cancer, or other possible risks that have been associated with implants. It is not enough to look at medical records kept by plastic surgeons, since women will only return to their plastic surgeon for complications that they recognize to be associated with the surgery.*

4. *The number of reconstruction patients in most of the studies is so small, that they could*

not provide persuasive evidence of safety. Robert Sheridan informed me that for the purposes of filing, FDA assumed that the experiences of augmentation patients would be the same as those for reconstruction patients. That assumption is impossible to defend, since there is no data to back it up.

5. Several manufacturers have no studies of women with certain models of implants that they sell, or they have studied fewer than 10 women with particular types of implants. Again, Robert Sheridan told me that for the purposes of filing, the assumption was made that the safety of one model was the same as for other models. Again, that assumption is impossible to defend, since there is no data to back it up."

"It will take years to provide meaningful long-term safety and to determine the average lifetime of breast prostheses that have been implanted in women. In some cases, well designed studies are planned but have not yet been started."

In reading the above one certainly might understand the complexity of this ongoing issue. We as the victims of this whole mess continue to be "corralled" or herded into "generalities" by the manufacturers, the media, and by some of our attorneys. Many studies on our behalf have been completed but for reasons unknown are not contained in the prestigious journals or if they are published, disappear very quickly along with the scientist writing it suffering discredit to his work. The term "junk science" was given to any researcher who discovered any material that might be detrimental to the manufacturers products.

Some of the abstracts of studies researching the affects of silicone gel breast implants included here are:

Cook PD, Osborne BM, Connor RL, Strauss JF American Journal of Surgical Pathology 1995, June 19: 6 712-7

Follicular lymphoma adjacent to foreign body granulomatous inflammation and fibrosis surrounding silicone breast prosthesis.

Silicone lymphadenopathy associated with fracture and/or erosive breakdown of silastic implants in joint replacements and is also known to occur with cosmetic and reconstructive breast implant surgery. Rare malignant lymphomas have been reported in association with silicone granulomas in lymph nodes; whether silicone is a causative agent remains controversial.

Painful capsular contractures and palpable 2-cm nodule medial to silicone mammary implant. The mass comprised an extra nodal follicular mixed lymphoma with surrounding granulomatous response to polarizable foreign body material.

Frey C, Naritoku W, Kerr R, Halikus N Foot Ankle 1993 September 14: 7 407-10

Tarsal tunnel syndrome secondary to cosmetic silicone implants

Silicone has been implicated as a cause of inflammatory disorders in the body including synovitis and lymphangitis. Silicone particulate matter has been shown to cause a fairly severe chronic foreign body reaction with the use of silicone prosthesis. There are 2 reports of malignant lymphoma found with silicate lymphadenopathy.

Roux H, Imbert I, Roudier J, Quinsat D, Catane'o-Fontaine J Rev Med Interne 1987 November-December 8: 5 475-80

Seven years after bilateral implantation of silicone breast prostheses' a woman presented with a seropositive rheumatoid arthritis involving the shoulders, wrists, metacarpophalangeal and interphalangeal joints of both hands, as well as the knees and ankles. Six months after the onset of the arthritis, she developed a Raynaud's syndrome and a lachrymal and salivary dry syndrome with unilateral axillary lymphadenopathy.

Tang L, Eaton JW American Clinical Pathology 1995 April 103: 4 466-71

Host proteins that spontaneously associate with implant surfaces are important determinants of the acute inflammatory response. In this regard, absorbed fibrinogen appears particularly pro-inflammatory. Chronic inflammatory processes, in many cases in response to fragments of implanted biomaterials, may cause implant failure. In the case of silicone-filled mammary prostheses, the extravasation of silicone gel has been held responsible for a number of complications, including silicone granuloma, synovitis, connective-tissue disease, and lymphadenopathy. In some instances, material-mediated inflammatory responses may even cause degradation of the material itself (via oxidative products released by implant-associated inflammatory cells).

Tabatowski K, Elson CE, Johnston WW Acta Cytol 1990 January-February 34: 1 10-4

Fine needle aspiration biopsy of an enlarged axillary lymph node in a patient with an intact mammary prosthesis yielded a cellular sample in which there were numerous macrophages containing large cytoplasmic vacuoles, a picture suggestive of granulomatous inflammation of the foreign-body type. Subsequent excision of the lymph node confirmed the diagnosis. Analytical electron microscopy identified the foreign material as silicone.

Truong LD, Cartwright J Jr., Goodman MD. Woznicki D American Journal of Surgical Pathology 1988 June 12: 6 484-91

Silicone Lymphadenopathy (SL)-defined as the presence of silicone in a lymph node-is a rare side effect of mammary augmentation either by injection of liquid silicone or by placement of a bag-gel prosthesis. Nine new cases in eight patients are herein reported and compared with six previously documented cases. The available data showed that SL was frequently detected as an incidental finding of no clinical significance during mastectomy and nodal dissection for associated breast carcinoma (nine cases), but may present as a painful or nontender enlarged lymph node (six cases). The latter presentation was almost always associated with a history of injection of liquid silicone or rupture of the prosthesis. All or some of the following findings were present in an affected lymph node: coarse vacuoles, fine vacuoles, and multinucleated giant cells. All lymph nodes contained a variable amount of an unstained, nonbirefringent, refractile material that, in seven of our cases, was shown to contain elemental silicon by energy-dispersive x-ray elemental analysis.....

Falk S, Neudert H, Radeljic A Geburtshilfe Frauenheilkd 1996 January 56: 1 55-7

Reported on a case of axillary lymphadenopathy in a woman secondary to a bilateral silicone augmentation mammoplasty which occurred 10 years after surgery. Microscopic silicone leakage ("bleeding") from an intact prosthesis lead to sizable lymph node enlargement.

Sever CE, Leith CP, Appenzeller J, Foucar K Arch Pathol Lab Med 1996 April 120: 4 380-5

The simultaneous occurrence of KD and silicone lymphadenopathy in an axillary lymph node of a patient with a leaking silicone breast implant is reported. Since both KD and silicone implants have been implicated in autoimmune diseases, including systemic lupus erythematosus, serologic tests for antinuclear antibodies and rheumatoid factor were performed. RESULTS: Axillary lymph nodes showed both silicone lymphadenopathy, as well as classic morphologic and immunophenotypic features of KD.

CONCLUSIONS: Silicone compounds may be associated with transient abnormal immune reactions and lend further support to the hypothesis that KD represents an exuberant T-cell-mediated immune response to a variety of nonspecific stimuli.

Vasey FB, Havice DL, Bocanegra TS, Seleznick MJ, Bridgeford PH, Martinez-Osuna P, Espinoza LR Semin Arthritis Rheum 1994 August 24: 1 Suppl 1 22-8

Clinical findings reported in a series of women with silicone breast implants (SBI) and rheumatic disease.

These findings represent the first 50 patients seen at the University of South Florida Medical Clinic between March, 1977, and January, 1991. The average age was 44 years with a range of 30 to 66 years. The most common clinical findings included chronic fatigue, muscle pain, joint pain, joint swelling, and lymphadenopathy. Seventeen women with an average Steinbrocker functional class of 1.8 decided not to remove the implants. An average of 14 months later, follow-up showed no change in their condition. Thirty-three women, with an average functional class of 2.5 underwent implant removal. Twelve of the 33 had documented implant rupture. During an average follow-up of 22 months after implant removal, 24 women improved clinically, 8 did not change, and 1 worsened. We believe this series supports a relationship between silicone breast implants and rheumatic disease signs and symptoms.

Travis WD, Balogh K, Abraham JL Human Pathology 1985 January 16:1 19-27

Since silicone is rapidly becoming one of the most commonly used biomaterials in modern medicine, pathologists will be observing increasing numbers of cases of silicone-related disease. Although numerous case reports have established that silicone elicits a characteristic response in tissues, the varying tissue reactions to silicone gels, liquids, and elastomers (rubber) have not been emphasized. Three cases are reported, and the literature is reviewed to illustrate the varying features of tissue reaction to silicone in its different forms. The first case is an example of silicon lymphadenopathy in an inguinal lymph node. This case demonstrated exuberant foreign body granuloma formation in response to particles of silicone elastomer. The second case involves a patient who had facial subcutaneous liquid silicone injections, and the third case is that of a woman in whom breast carcinoma developed 13 years after mammary augmentation with liquid silicone injections. These two cases illustrate the characteristic reaction to silicone liquid, with numerous cystic spaces and vacuoles in the soft tissues but minimal or no foreign body giant cell reaction. Scanning electron microscopy and energy dispersive x-ray analysis were performed in the first two cases, confirming the presence of silicon. Silicone migration and the clinical significance of various silicone-induced lesions are discussed.

Rogers LA, Longtine JA, Garnick MB, Pinkus GS
Human Pathology 1988 October 19: 10 1237-9

A 33-year old male runner, who had undergone a Swanson silastic prosthetic implant for degenerative joint disease of the first metatarsal head and proximal phalanx of the right great toe, presented with unilateral inguinal lymphadenopathy. Biopsy revealed confluent, non-caseating granulomas containing silastic material. Silicone lymphadenopathy is unusual and most frequently presents as axillary adenopathy in patients with rheumatoid arthritis as a sequelae of prosthetic surgery. This case is clinically distinctive for its site of presentation in a healthy athlete and is histologically remarkable for the marked granulomatous response to the silastic elastomers.

Murakata LA, Rangwala AF Journal of Rheumatology 1989 November 16: 11 1480-3

Six cases of axillary lymphadenopathy induced by silicone elastomer following silastic finger joint arthroplasty have been reported; 2 cases had associated malignant lymphoma. This is the 3rd reported case of malignant lymphoma with concomitant silicone lymphadenopathy discovered 8 years after insertion of silastic finger joint arthroplasty for long-standing rheumatoid arthritis. Histology revealed a partially replaced reactive lymph node with immunoblastic lymphoma. Both sides contained single and clusters of multinucleated giant cells with silastic particles, as well as formed asteroid bodies.

Malignant lymphoma is associated with rheumatoid disease, but to date, silicone particles have not been linked to malignant lymphoma.

Benjamin E, Ahmed A, Rashid AT, Wright DH Diagnostic Histopathology 1982 April-June 5: 2 133-41

Two cases of axillary lymphadenopathy induced by foreign body reaction to silicone particles are presented. Both were patients with long-standing arthritis who had silastic metacarpophalangeal joint implants; one patient also had concomitant lymphoma. The material was conclusively identified as silicone by electron microprobe analysis.

(These abstracts go on and on.......There are so many studies which do, in fact, relate silicone to disease and complications in the human body. The risks allude not only to the obvious failure of the prosthesis but also of migration of the particulate debris resulting from "bleeding" of the silicone elastomers. These particles are

carried by the bloodstream to ALL organs, tissues.......

EVERYWHERE IN THE BODY!)

FACTS: As of March, 2000

Report of Problems with Silicone Gel
Implants via MEDWATCH
127,770
109 Deaths

Report of problems with Saline Implants
65,720
14 Deaths

This is nearly 200,000 ADVERSE REPORTS......

..THIS IS JUST A FRACTION OF THE TRUE numbers!

Section Nine - Symptoms Frequently Associated with Silicone Gel Filled Breast Implants

Symptoms Frequently Associated with Silicone Implants

As Defined by: Andrew Campbell, M.D., who has seen over 5,600 patients with silicone prosthetic devices which he has examined since the mid - 1980's

Breast pain and tenderness

Burning pain in the breasts, chest, arms or axilla (under the arms)

Swallowing problems (dysphasia)

Mouth ulcers

Paraesthesia (change in feeling; neurological)

Loss of sensation to pinprick, vibration, touch or position Tingling, Paraesthesia (change in sensation) or burning pain in the extremities.

Elevation of one or more Immunoglobulins (IgG, IgA, IgM)

Fatigue which gradually worsens, often made worse by exercise

Cognitive function problems such as attention deficit disorder, calculation difficulties, memory disturbance, spatial disorientation, frequently saying the wrong word

Short-term memory loss

Psychological problems; depression, anxiety, personality changes, mood swings, Sleep disturbance and non-restorative sleep

Headaches of greater intensity than before implantation

High Cholesterol, i.e., over 250 even with a low fat diet

Positive ANA; 1:40 titer+ (approximately 35% of those who are symptomatic have a positive ANA); often a precursor to autoimmune disorders or a signal that one already exists

Elevated Sed Rate (20+): sign of inflammation in the body positive Anti-thyroid, Anti-adrenal and/or Anti-parietal (95% with fatigue and a silicone implant have at least one of these three positive!)

Changes in vision

Seizures

Numbness and tingling

Loss of balance; falling for no reason

Lightheadedness

Ringing in the ears

Paralysis

Severe muscular weakness

Intolerance of bright lights or sunshine

Intolerance of alcohol

Decreased libido

Joint pains

Diffuse muscle aching/ hurting

Muscle tremors

Recurrent flu-like illness

Severe allergies or worsen after implantation

Asthma; acquired after implantation or worse afterwards

Weight Gain

Irritable bowel syndrome

Low grade fevers

Night sweats

Abnormal heart rhythm

Uncomfortable urination

Hair loss

Chest pain

Dry eyes and mouth

Cough

Canker sores in the mouth

Raynaud's phenomenon (example: cold fingertips)

Low back pain

Enlarged thyroid

Shortness of breath and breathing problems

Skin changes and/or rashes

Photosensitive dermatitis; the skin is affected by exposure to the sun

Diffuse petechiae on torso: small red spots on the chest and abdomen

Livido reticularis: Purple, lace-like pattern on the arms or legs caused by abnormalities of blood vessels

Malar or discoed rash: a rash over the cheeks, often looks like a butterfly, or face and upper back and chest,

Optic neuritis

Lymphadenopathy: enlarged lymph glands in the neck, under the arms (axilla) and groin

Asymmetrical breast from unilateral of bilateral breast rupture, migration of implant

Capsule formation (hardening), unilateral or bilateral Migration of the implant, usually laterally and superior lieu, unilateral or bilateral

Abdominal pain on palpation

Upper back pain

Abnormal neurological exam with increased or decreased deep tendon reflexes

Muscle pain and tenderness of numerous of eighteen tender points on palpitation

Diffuse muscle pain/aching/hurting (not in joints; muscles)

Pathology (normally at explant): granulomas or siliconomas or chronic inflammatory response

Burning/ acid pain---particularly in breast(s)

Section Ten - MY THOUGHTS AND A SURVEY

I feel that Silicone Breast Implants CAN Produce Autoimmune Illnesses. "Since their introduction in 1962, silicone breast implants have been surgically emplaced in over 2 million American women. Some women get them as part of breast reconstruction therapy following mastectomy for breast cancer, but the majority of women get them because they want larger breasts.

Now, 38 years later, it is alarmingly apparent that bigger, siliconized breasts can be hazardous to your health. We are just now beginning to understand that the real cost of cosmetic breast enhancement may not be the $ 6,000.00 in surgical fees to implant them, but a host of autoimmune disorders and symptoms and strange illnesses that can crop up, typically within about seven years of implantation. "450,000 Siliconized Women Sue"

Not everyone sees it this way of course. The subject of silicone breast implants is clouded and controversial, marked by denials, cover-ups, stonewalling, suppressed research, bankruptcy, and class action lawsuits. There is also much suffering involved. Thousands of women who have had their implants for one or two decades now are seeking medical help for mysterious symptoms which resemble arthritis, fibromyalgia, scleroderma, connective tissue disorders, Multiple Sclerosis, Lupus, and/or immune dysfunction. As medical authorities and scientific experts continually downplay the risks of implants and assert that no association between breast implants and symptoms has been proven, the case for silicone implant toxicity is growing, fueled in large measure by the facts. Research now is showing the negative effects of silicone and saline breast implants. For many years, Dow Corning conducted experiments on silicone breast implants. Dow found that the implants leak and rupture, spreading silicone throughout the entire body.(1)

They learned that the silicone in the implants kills roaches (2), is not biologically inert (3), and stimulates a human immune response (4). Tragically. "DOW KEPT THIS SCIENCE HIDDEN".

437

In recent years; however, a host of articles have been published in scientific journals pointing to the negative health effects of silicone breast implants. A Canadian study found that 40% of implants leak or rupture after six years. And 95% leak or rupture after 12 years (5). Other studies are finding a rupture rate after 10 years of 70%(6). A Mayo Clinic study found that 25% of women require surgery within five years after implantation (7). A report in the Archives of Dermatology shows the unmistakable link between local pain, numbness and deformity and deposits of silicone that had migrated from a ruptured implant (8). It has also been documented that silicone leaks from women's nipples (9). A 1996 Harvard study found a 24% increase in connective tissue disease, both classical and atypical, for women with breast implants (10). A 1997 report in The Lancet found an abnormal immune response in women with silicone implants (11). A University of Michigan study found women with implants had three times the risk of developing an unusual connective tissue disease (12). Other studies have documented that silicone provokes an immune reaction in humans and in animals (13).

The manufacturers' public relations machine has led many people (in fact most people) to believe that implants have been proven safe! Nothing could be further from the TRUTH! There is abundant scientific evidence confirming that thousands of women are suffering the effects of faulty, broken, dangerous silicone and saline breast implants.

a. *"These medical devices have never been approved by the F D A (An F D A Panel Advisory Hearing held in October, 2003, decided against allowing silicone breast implants back on the market until 10 more years of research is completed)*

b. *There are numerous reports of silicone shells filled with medical grade, isotonic saline causing autoimmune and other diseases*

c. *All breast implants leak because the silicone shells are porous---an undebatable fact*

d. The silicone shell will "slough off" silicone particles, which in turn will migrate throughout the body, and lodge in major organs

e. The implant manufacturers, who previously advertised implants would last a lifetime, had actual knowledge that implants could fall apart after just 5 years or less!

f. The manufacturers of saline-filled breast implants still have never tested their products to determine if there would be long-term health risks, prior to putting their "new improved" implants on the market.

g. Sadly, no one tells a patient, that the children she might bear after implants are in her body, could be adversely affected all of their lives.

A SURVEY OFFERED TO THE I.O.M (Institute of Medicine) July, 1998

These figures were obtained from a survey done on the Internet, 1996-1997. There were 72 respondents. The most classic symptoms women with silicone related diseases were posted and it didn't seem to make any difference whether the implants were for reconstruction or augmentation. Here are the responses:

Breast Reconstruction for Radical Mastectomy 35

Simple Mastectomy   7

Modified Mastectomy   13

There were 8 Lumpectomies

There was 1 Latissimus Dorsi Flap

7 Abdominal Flap

5 Free Flap

2 Skin Graft

6 Nipple Graft

26 Had two or more augmentations

Type of Implants for women in percentages:

90.2% were Silicone

19.4% were Saline

4% were Foam

5.5% were a combination

The number of ruptures was 64%, More than four to one.(All of the Heyer Schulte implants were ruptured)

Other questions included: Have you had breast implants removed? Responses: 81.9% YES

If implants were removed were capsules also removed? 62.5% Responses: YES

If capsules were tested after removal, what were the results?

Responses: Almost 50% reported infections consisting of Staph- 45.5%, Strep -34.1%, 22.7% - E-coli

Conclusions: The average respondent to the survey was married, between the age of 35 and 45 at the time of implantation, and had their implants over a period of ten years.

At the time the surveys were completed, 35% of the respondents were on disability. That percentage has increased since then. Some of these women began drawing disability before the age of 50.

Thirty five percent of the women have no insurance to cover the cost of an explantation Thirty three percent of the women have problems dressing while over 50% have difficulty with sexual intimacy, walking, and housework such as vacuuming.

Using the MDL (Multi District Litigation) figure of 440,000 thousand participants and the responses in percentage from the survey, one could expect:

154,000 Women on Disability

421,000 Experiencing Chronic Fatigue Syndrome

Using again, the MDL figure:

145,200 Women cannot even comb their hair without difficulty

246,000 cannot perform household tasks, i.e. Vacuuming

242,000 cannot enjoy walking

220,000 cannot enjoy sexual intimacy

Remembering "Life before breast implants" these same women felt their health rated an average of 9.52% on a scale of 1 - 10.....In comparison, after breast implantation, to a 3.04%. That is more than 50% LOSS of QUALITY OF LIFE!

Sixty Eight Percent of the women did not use the same plastic surgeon for explantation as well as implantation! Sixty Percent would NOT recommend their plastic surgeon. Once again, COPIES OF THIS SURVEY WERE PRESENTED TO THE INSTITUTE OF MEDICINE, July, 1998, AND ALSO TO THE JUDICIARY COMMITTEES OF THE HOUSE OF REPRESENTATIVES AND TO THE SENATE....July, 1998!!!!!!!

Section Eleven - "Silicone"

* SILICONE IS A BIOLOGICALLY ACTIVE AND "TOXIC" SUBSTANCE

The original statement by Dow Chemical Company in the 1940's, repeated hundreds of times since, that SILICONE is biologically inert and nontoxic, was based on a single "one-week study" of rats and guinea pigs. (In 1943, Dow Chemical Company and Corning Glassworks formed Dow Corning Corporation to market SILICONE and SILICONE breast implants.)

The basic gel implant filler- DC 360 SILICONE fluid was once considered worth following up for development by Dow Corning scientists as a potent "insecticide", one of the few known substances capable of killing cockroaches.

Dow Chemical researchers also studied SILICONE as a possible better "CHEMICAL WARFARE" and riot control agent, according to a 1969 internal memorandum obtained by the PSC.

The silicone gel is not a single substance but a fluid comprised of numerous different versions of silicone, such that it is better termed a "chemical soup".

Research collected by the PSC shows that silicone has marked effects on the adrenal glands and liver, induces chronic inflammation, and degrades into smaller molecules, including silica.

Silicone fed to rabbits produced widespread toxic effects including kidney and spleen damage within four months! (Stanford Medical Bulletin, 10:1 [1952], 23-26.)

* That silicone is toxic in both animals and man is well proven, stated John S. Sergent, MD, and colleagues in Textbook of Rheumatology (W. B. Saunders Company, 1993). Silicone degrades into silica, usually at the surface of the gel implant, then fragments and subdivides into millions of microdroplets capable of migrating throughout the body (PSC Records No. 1352, 7010: These are documents produced by

Dow Corning in national litigation). Silica in the body is a toxic, carcinogenic substance, damaging the immune system, killing cells, and producing silicosis.

Silicone and its contaminants which bleed through its surrounding implant envelope into neighboring tissue have the potential for significant toxicity in the implant recipient. (Seminars in Arthritis and Rheumatology 24:1 Suppl 1 [August 1994], 11-17.) Dow Chemical and Dow Corning have been aware of the toxic effects of silicone and silica since the 1950's, based on their own studies, but never published the data. They knew these substances were bioreactive, immunogenic, toxic, and inflammatory, when introduced into the human body. (Update on breast implants, January 1998, website http://consumerlawpage.com)

As early as 1956, Dow Chemical researchers knew that liquid silicone, when injected into the body, migrates to all the major organs, including the spleen, heart, lungs, and brain. (PSC Record No. 0006.)

Studies by both Dow Corning and Dow Chemical in 1970 confirmed that silicone, after injection, migrates to the bone marrow of animals and changes the brain weight. They also showed that silicone particles migrate from a human finger joint into the lymph nodes.

(PSC Record No. 0018, 7038.)

Researchers at Baylor College of Medicine in Texas found that silicone is widely distributed throughout the body of mice after a SINGLE injection, MIGRATING to TEN different organs from the brain to the uterus and persisting in these organs over time. (American Journal of Pathology 152:3 [March 1998], 645-649.)

Researchers at the Medical College of Wisconsin in Milwaukee found that following silicone implant rupture, silicone gel migrated into the arm of a woman, where it produced nerve pain, dysfunction, and fibrosis. (Plastic Reconstructive Surgery 89:5 [May 1992], 949-952.)

Physicians at Massachusetts General Hospital in Charlestown, using magnetic resonance imaging, found that a significant amount of free silicone had migrated from an implant (not noticeably ruptured) into the liver and spleen of a woman (Magnetic Resonance Medicine 36:3 [September 1996], 498-501. Researchers also found that silicone in the liver could be detected in the first three to four years after a woman received her implant. (Magnetic Resonance Medicine 33:1 [January 1995], 8-17.)

Of 39 women with silicone implants, 27 (69%) showed signs of silicone in their livers, and of the 20 whose implant had ruptured, silicone was detected in the livers of 17 (85%). In other words, whether the implants rupture or not, SILICONE LEAKS AND MIGRATES TO THE LIVER. (Radiology 201 [1996], 777-783; PSC Record No. 0050.)

In 1989, studies by Dow Corning showed that silicone, given orally to rats, increased liver size and weight by up to 45% and suggested the enlargement might be interpreted as a CARCINOGENIC response. (PSC Record No. 0482.)

Based in large part upon animal experimentation conducted by a scientist, Steve Carson (1), who was later convicted of fraud on the FDA (2), and upon admittedly misrepresented evaluations by Dow Corning's own Silas Braley (3), silicone gel became a popular substitute for breast tissue in the 1970's. Enclosed in a balloon constructed of amorphous silica and PDMS (polydimethalsiloxane), silicone gel breast implants were marketed and sold as SAFE, LIFETIME DEVISES.

Lawyers for implant manufacturers assert that silicone was tested and evaluated more thoroughly than any other product. The FACTS are; however, that NO CLINICAL TRIALS were conducted prior to marketing, and only ONE such TRIAL was in progress as late as 1983. That trial, the Gregory Study, had no controls and it's only reported finding, which was NEVER MADE PUBLIC, was a 40% reoperation rate (4). After discovering the friability of the product, manufacturers *began communicating this defect to operating surgeons in vaguely worded cautions contained in package inserts. Most of the surgeons probably never even knew the product contained a package insert! Indeed, former Professor Hans Norberg, M.D., so testified (5).*

(1) Steve Carson worked at FDRL (Food and Drug Research Laboratory). He reported observations in at least 14 studies on silicone, including Rees and Ashley's early work. As early as 1968, his work was described as "not providing complete confidence", KMM 128723-24. Industrial BioTech (I. B. T.) was the other major research facility. Its work was generally suspect in the industry and thought unreliable (M-170037) (Note all document references are to the MDL Bates stamp number.)

(2) On December 14, 1979, Carson was convicted of conspiracy to make false statements to the FDA. USA v. Carson, U. S. D. C., District of New Jersey, Cr. 79-00202 (04).

(3) "Medtox": DCCX-MM298322.

454

(4) See MEM000033210. This remarkable document, known as the Betty Locke memo of February 2, 1983, MEM000033208-13, contains a wealth of information. For example, a lawyer from 3M told Ms. Locke that his company would get out of the business if Silicone Breast Implants (SBI's) were made Class III devices. This memo; however, has never been adequately covered in any Locke deposition.

(5) Dr. Hans Norberg practices plastic surgery in Tulsa. He formerly was a Professor of Medicine at the Oklahoma Medical School from 1979 - 1985. Norberg deposition, pp. 107-109, Byron v. Dow Corning, et al. #945-6071, 44th Judicial District, Dallas County, Texas.

Attorney, Sanders (6) for Bristol Myers Squibb and Hayes (7) for Dow concluded there was not "a chance in hell" that a surgeon would read a package insert before surgery! This mode of communication to the doctors (via package insert) has been labeled even by the manufacturers as inadequate and ineffective.

Did manufacturers represent that silicone gel breast implants would last a lifetime? Here are the facts:

1. Dow Corning: In 1976 Dow Corning provided doctors a printed handout for patients which says that the product is expected to last a lifetime. (8)

2. BMS (Bristol Myers Squibb: As late as 1991, BMS was asserting publicly that its implants lasted a lifetime. (9)

3. Heyer-Schulte: In 1973, Heyer-Schulte stated that only its elastomer's outside surface ever came in contact with body tissue. (10)

4. 3M: In its training manual 3M taught its salesmen that: Implants lasted a lifetime. (11)

5. Natural Y: Claimed in 1982 that its implants did not rupture or even bleed. (12) BMS reiterated this claim for this poly product after the 1987 acquisition from Cooper. (13) Jan Varner, formerly at Dow, Heyer-Schulte, McGhan, 3M and INAMED testified that until the mid eighties silicone implants were marketed and sold as lifetime devices. Coyne,currently the MAN at 3M, in an early deposition said the same thing. (14)

(6) Sanders MDL Depo. Pp. 205-210, Vol. 8, May 26, 1994.

(7) Hayes Harris County Depo. Pp. 123-125, Vol. I. Sept. 27, 1994.

(8) M-650014

(9) & (10) MED 000029432

(11) McG 7243

(12) TCC000040882

(13) MED 000024622-27, 29431

(14) Varner Harris County Depo. Pp. 208-212, Vol. II, December 12, 1992. Coyne MDL Depo. Pp. 0124 Vol. I (120993).

The FACTS are: Implants WEAR OUT over time. Average life expectancy for an implant is probably between 2 and 10 years. (15)

There seems little question; therefore, that EVERY MANUFACTURER engaged in FRAUDULENT practices. As Judge Fawsett found in a trial against BMS and MEC (Medical Engineering Company) in Florida: "MEC misrepresented its product through advertising and marketing"****. Barrow v. BMS, et al, 1998 WL 812318, 812345 (U.S.D.C.M.D. Fla, 1998). "Defendant intended to induce reliance upon such misrepresentation" Id at 812345.

"As a consequence of justifiable reliance on the misrepresentations and omissions of Defendant, Plaintiff suffered damages. Relying upon the misinformation given to her by her doctor, Plaintiff chose to be implanted with MEC's silicone gel breast implants. As a consequence, Plaintiff suffered a chronic foreign body reaction to the leaking silicone gel. She had inflammation of tissue in her breast area.

After implantation Plaintiff suffered severe capsular contracture, on numerous occasions she had to undergo closed capsulotomies, and one of the Plaintiff's implants became deformed and produced the appearance of a bulge on her breast. She also suffered continuous foreign body reaction and chronic inflammation. She had an explant operation performed. Silicone gel remained in her breast tissue area and in her lymph nodes even after explantation. A significant amount of tissue was removed from Plaintiff upon explantation, and she has permanent scars on her breasts from removal of the implants, capsular contracture, and adjacent breast tissue. She also suffers numbness in her breasts after explantation. Accordingly, Plaintiff is owed monetary damages to compensate for such injuries." Ibid.

Barrow was affirmed by the Eleventh Circuit, without opinion. BMS v. Barrow, 190 F, 3d 541 (11ᵗʰ Cir. 1999) (15) The first study reporting in vivo deterioration of implants was by Van Rappard,

Annals of Plas. Surg. 21: 566 (1988). His findings were confirmed in a virtually unimpeachable study by Phillips - Plast. And Reconst. Surg. 97, #6, pp. 1215-1225 (1996). In vivo durability was also examined by Robinson, Annals of Plast. Surg., Vol. 34, #1, pp. 1-7 (1995), among others.

Section Twelve - Medical Engineering and Surgitek Prosthetic Systems Corporate History, According to Dr. Pierre Blais

MEDICAL ENGINEERING AND SURGITEK PROSTHETIC SYSTEMS

Corporate History: According to Dr. Pierre Blais

Surgitek is a trade name associated with the Medical Engineering Corporation (MEC) of Racine, Wisconsin. MEC was founded circa 1968. Originally known as Surgitool, it was initially connected to Travenol Laboratories Artificial Organ Division. Travenol is a precursor to Baxter Travenol. This organization had been involved in the manufacturing of implants in the early-seventies through Surgitool. This firm produced the Beall-Surgitool and the Cromie-McGovern cardiac valve prosthesis.

These valves had been developed at Baylor-Methodist Hospital of Houston at about the same time as the "Cronin Breast Prosthesis". The valves created a major health care crisis circa 1969 when they were found to DISINTEGRATE and EMBOLIZE (or move) after a few years of use. The associated morbidity and mortality continued throughout most of the seventies

462

and ultimately, surviving salvageable patients who constituted a significant part of the original ten thousand valve users had to undergo replacement of their faulty cardiac valves. Surprisingly, the same valves reappeared in NEW FORMS as part of the Surgitek product line of MEC in the seventies.

MEC reincorporated under several names and evidently conducted pre-commercial development of medical devices under the name of "Lakeside Engineering" in the late sixties and early seventies. In 1972, the firm formally entered the rapidly developing cosmetic surgery market. Some of its first products included mammary prostheses developed in Canada. Its first products in this area included largely analogs of devices made by other U.S. manufacturers of medical implants. It released primitive silicone gel-filled mammary implants such as the Papillon-Perras silicone-polycarbonate "bag" implants and the Snyder contoured implants. The line was later broadened to include variations of devices which completed their product line and made it very similar to those 169 sold

463

by Dow Corning, McGhan Medical and Heyer Schulte Corporation.

Late in 1982, MEC was sold and became a wholly-owned subsidiary of Bristol-Myers, a pharmaceutical products corporation. MEC was one of several acquisitions by Bristol- Myers in the medical devices area. In 1988, Bristol-Myers authorized the MEC Corporation to purchase "Cooper Surgical Specialties", a division of CooperVision International. The acquired assets included the Cooper Aesthetech manufacturing facility in Paso Robles, California.

Cooper-Aesthetech was engaged in the production of plastic surgery items which duplicated to some extent MEC's lines. This acquisition markedly reduced the competition in the sector and concentrated a significant fraction of the international cosmetic surgery implant business in a single enterprise. The product line included the then controversial "POLYURETHANE FOAM-COVERED IMPLANTS". The transaction was consummated for approximately $20 million dollars.

The original Cooper-Aesthetech plant of Paso Robles was beset with many administrative, personnel and technical problems. It had FAILED FDA inspections in 1987 and 1988. Information on regulatory entanglements with California regulatory agencies, the FDA and similar organizations in Canada and abroad became public shortly after the acquisition.

Many devices sold to foreign markets incorporated major fabrication defects. Some were investigational items, others were production rejects. MEC documents confirm the existence of policies which habitually directed products with deviant attributes or defects to foreign markets. Liquidation of marginal products was also undertaken.

MEC subsequently transferred parts of the Paso Robles implant manufacturing operations to Racine, Wisconsin in 1990. Regulatory problems continued. The FDA later demanded pre-market documentation for breast implants. Documentation provided by MEC in response failed to acquire approval. A moratorium on further use of all silicone gel-filled implants was *later enacted by the FDA. Production at the Racine facility was terminated in September, 1991, and the assets were sold. SIMILAR PRODUCTS ARE NOW MADE ABROAD AND SEVERAL FORMER EMPLOYEES OF SURGITEK/MEC ARE INVOLVED IN THE NEW PRODUCTION LOCATIONS.......These things are still being manufactured and sold!*

Bristol Myers merged with Squibb Pharmaceuticals to become Bristol Myers Squibb in 1991. Difficulties from continuing litigation have surrounded the activities of the firm. Increasing numbers of claims of adverse reactions by users of the products are currently under investigation; numerous cases are currently filed with federal and state courts. It is generally understood that Bristol Myers Squibb is responsible for post-market follow-up of Surgitek products. The exact relationship between Surgitool, Surgitek, Travenol, Baxter Travenol, Baxter Healthcare and MEC is UNKNOWN!......

Surgitek breast implants were made by the Medical Engineering Corporation (MEC) of Racine,

Wisconsin. These items appeared in 1970-73 and most early items embodied the same technology as the contemporary competing products. Many of the items were generic equivalents of existing popular designs. GENERAL ELECTRIC silicone-based materials as well as other materials intended for GENERAL INDUSTRIAL USE were incorporated into the products until about 1976-77. Dow Corning elastomers and gel are found in later issues. Production was generally CRUDE and the finished items often exhibited MAJOR DEFECTS. Some products had MAJOR SAFETY, EFFICACY and DURABILITY PROBLEMS and were withdrawn early. Some Surgitek products were initially named after prominent consulting surgeons for promotional purposes. Later nomenclature deleted such references.

MEC was primarily a cosmetic surgery products manufacturer, prior to discontinuation of all of its product lines. Some examples of secondary products manufactured by MEC as well as the mammary implants were: urology implants and genito-urinary devices for surgery; included are: penile implants, vaginal stints, catheters and products generally intended for reconstructive purposes. Other typical examples include chin, malar, orbital floor, ear cartilage, nasal inserts for rhinoplasty and lines of custom-made implants mostly for cranio-facial and chest reconstruction. A significant number of these products are based on "gel-in-shell" technologies. In effect, much of the Corporation's activity related to such implants amongst which are breast and chest defect devices, in addition to small facial implants assembled from shells that are later filled with soft silicone gels. Many of those devices remain on the market through secondary distributors. THERE IS CONTINUING MANUFACTURING ACTIVITY OF THESE PRODUCTS OUTSIDE OF NORTH AMERICA FROM SUCCESSOR CORPORATIONS WHO ACQUIRED ASSETS DISPOSED OF BY THE MEC OPERATIONS.

(There is a reason I am writing so much about these particular implants...I had implants made by this manufacturer for only two years. I was implanted in September, 1990, and explanted completely July, 1992....I say completely because after having them only about 5 weeks, the right one became terribly infected and the surgeon told me I must have it removed or I

would DIE in 48 hours! I had it removed and replaced 3 months later with the same type...... MEME ™ was the name of the type of implants I received.)

Surgitek mammary implants were made by the Medical Engineering Corporation (MEC) of Racine, Wisconsin. These items appeared in 1970-73, and most early items embodied the same technology as the contemporary competing products. Many of the items were generic equivalents of existing popular designs. General Electric silicone-based materials as well as other" materials intended for general industrial use" were incorporated into the products until about 1976-77. Dow Corning elastomers and gel are found in later issues. Production was generally "crude" and the finished items often exhibited "major defects". Some products had major "safety, efficacy and durability problems" and were withdrawn early. Some Surgitek products were initially named after prominent consulting surgeons for promotional purposes. Later nomenclature deleted such references.

Some examples of secondary products MEC manufactures are: urology implants and genito-urinary devices for surgery including penile implants, vaginal stints, catheters and products generally intended for reconstructive purposes. Other classes of manufactured items comprise cardiovascular implants and items for cardiothoracic life support. A much larger group of small volume devices are also comprised as part of the cosmetic surgery lines.

Typical examples include chin, malar, orbital floor, ear cartilage, nasal inserts for rhinoplasty and lines of custom-made implants mostly for cranial-facial and chest reconstruction. A significant number of these products are based on "gel in shell' technologies. In effect, much of the Corporation's activity related to such implants.

EARLY PRODUCTS; The Perras-Papillon Gel Filled Mammary Implants:

The Perras-Papillon designs are among the earliest Surgitek plastic surgery items. They are *described in a patent credited to the two plastic surgeons from Montreal, Canada. The devices are mechanically similar to existing products but the assembly methods and the shells material differ. They are a fixation type design and incorporate fixation fabric on the posterior side.*

Commercial versions had shells made from polycarbonate-silicone copolymers. A complex array of fabric and adhesive were used to seal the shells at the mold extraction opening. The gel was "unstable" and "reverted to REACTIVE oil", the shell walls were thin and the polycarbonate-based polymer "degraded rapidly and embrittled" leading to "drastic changes" in properties.

Several modifications were issued and were sold until the early-eighties. Evidently, they were not widely used. Most ruptured early and were removed for medical reasons. The "inflammatory reaction" that followed shell perforation led to "grossly contaminated breasts", "oily granulomata" and "calcification of tissues" with "pathological conditions" similar to what is found in patients who received silicone oil injections. Such patients are occasionally encountered among long term users who present with "advanced stages of breast diseases and undergo extensive breast resection" because of large "atypical tumors", "advanced stages of oil dissemination" or other "late complications" and "adverse reactions" of prostheses sold in the sixties and seventies.

Dahl Gel-Filled "Inflatable" Implants:

These were made in small numbers by MEC from about 1972. They were spherical prostheses supplied as empty shells and provided with a separate container of gel precursor fluid. They copied some concepts used in an earlier Japanese product credited to Akiyama. They had valve shells similar to the contemporary saline's and the "kit" included a container of conventional pre-catalyzed liquid gel precursors. The filled prostheses then required exposure to sterilizer temperatures in order to "vulcanize" the fluid and form the felled substance deemed suitable for the claimed purpose. The product evidently did not sell well and was withdrawn DISCREETLY circa 1974-76; RECALLS WERE NEVER CONDUCTED!!!!!

"Adverse reactions and cosmetic failures's surrounded the product. It appears that the instructions for use were "faulty" and were "misinterpreted" by surgeons. Instead of filling the shell and vulcanizing it before implantation, "most users placed the shell in the surgical pocket and then filled it with the supplied material". Heat treatments were INFREQUENTLY CONDUCTED!

This resulted in" thin, oily and mobile filling substances with residual reactivity and intensely inflammatory properties". The mixture altered the shell elastomer and early "ruptures were commonplace". Most Dahl "30000" Series prostheses were explanted early. Many users required "extensive resection of granulomatous tissue" that formed around the ruptured devices.

473

Other Early Surgitek Gel-Filled Prostheses:

Other contemporary gel-filled round and oval/ contour Surgitek products were conventional technology products similar to the competitors. Some were sold under surgeons' names and took a significant market share. They later evolved into the main Surgitek product lines and sales continued until the early nineties.

The "10000" Series were oval antecedents to the popular round and "anatomic" gel prostheses. Several designs were released; some were listed under different product numbers in successive catalogs depending on year of production. On occasions, the same devices appeared in different sizes with CONFUSING catalog numbers suggesting different Series. Most were thin wall, gel-filled prostheses similar to other common products already in the marketplace. The items were manufactured at the Racine, Wisconsin plant of the MEC. The devices were also called "Snyders", "Snyder designs", or "Snyder Technique" depending of the year of release. The "Georgiade Design" was another variant. It had an approximately equivalent shape with subtle shell differences and was marketed concurrently.

Unlike the round versions, the Snyders and oval devices had small orientation loops bonded to the bottom edge of the patch. This orientation loop "leaked profusely" and was a "common site of failure" for the devices. It "eroded through the shell after a few years" and a "progressive tear advanced towards the middle from that point". The oval variants were made in smaller numbers than the round ones. Most early products also used General Electric silicone materials. The technology of fabrication differed slightly from the later issues bearing similar names. The "quality of workmanship was EXTREMELY POOR". "Some items had scissor cut or torn components and permanently molded fingerprints were often noted on the adhesive zones". The gel fill hole seal, a small dot of adhesive used to close the shell after filling with the gel precursor, as well as the orientation tab bonding area, were "notoriously irregular" and "leaked for most items". The performance of the early variants was NO BETTER THAN THE LATER ISSUES which used more precisely made components BUT THINNER SHELLS AND Dow Corning MATERIALS. Very few of these items have ever been recovered in the UNPERFORATED STATE. THE LIFE EXPECTANCY BEFORE PERFORATION WAS OF THE ORDER OF 4 to 6 years AND THE AGGRESSIVE GEL WAS "NOTORIOUS FOR SYSTEMIC ADVERSE REACTIONS"!

Now we come to the MEME ME: (The ones I was implanted with)

The Meme implants were made in multiple forms. Early versions were THIN WALL products. The Meme designs appear to have been motivated primarily by COST CONTAINMENT consideration and a wish to develop the cosmetic augmentation market. Very early models of this implant are rare and are believed to have been made according to processes similar to those used by the breast implant industry in general. Typically, a separate shell would be formed on a mandril or form, removed, patched and filled with gel precursors. This superficially conventional prosthesis would then be coated with POLYURETHANE FOAM using RTV-

based adhesives according to the earlier process. It shared the same PROBLEMS OF ALL OTHER FOAM IMPLANTS, including ELEVATED RISK of SURVIVING MICRO-ORGANISMS "DEEPLY EMBEDDED WITHIN THE SURFACE STRUCTURE AND ADHESIVE LAYERS.

However, in the late-seventies, a patent aiming to produce implants without shells for the purpose of creating a "contracture resistant" prosthesis appeared; It was credited to J. Cavon, a Newport Beach, California surgeon. This was not new! The concept had already been used on some variations. In this case; however, a new element was introduced. Accordingly, a device was to be made with a TEMPORARY, RESORBABLE OR FRANGIBLE SHELL DESIGNED "TO BREAK OR DISAPPEAR "sometime after surgical implantation. Thus, the shell would somehow DISINTEGRATE to RELEASE THE SEMI-LIQUID SILICONE GEL CORE FILLING WITHIN A TISSUE CAPSULE which was EXPECTED to form around the temporary shell!!!!! This process was tantamount to silicone oil-gel injections which were popular in the late-forties, fifties and sixties. Its primary appeal was that the procedure would be performed in a single surgical session. It was claimed to confer a lasting "CONTRACTURE-RESISTANT" cosmetic result to the subject. It appears that this device credited to Dr. Joseph Cavon, was initially manufactured under a contract by the Cox Uphoff Corporation. Later, staff from Cox Uphoff formed a competing corporation, the Aesthetech Surgical Specialties Corporation of Paso Robles, California. They produced such devices and later introduced subtle variations known formally as the MEME ME ™. These products although not formerly made of resorbable shell materials, still fulfilled the Cavon requirements and had the ability to RUPTURE, DISINTEGRATE or "DISAPPEAR" shortly after implantation.

Thus, the process used by Aesthetech which consisted of coating a pre-vulcanized or "cured" "uncontained" gel core with SOLVENT-DILUTED RTV yielded "EASILY BROKEN AND FRANGIBLE SHELLS"! Such implants have been HABITUALLY recovered with FRANK RUPTURES, PARTIAL DISAPPEARANCE OF THE SHELL and GROSS INFILTRATION OF THE GEL INTO THE SURROUNDING TISSUE!

The shell making and foam coating processes were essentially analogous to that used in early Natural-Y devices produced by predecessor manufacturing plants. It amounted to casting a similar semi-solid shape of gel and subsequently coating this gel "lump" with a much thinner layer of RTV. In effect, it was more like a "paint layer". Because of the presence of SOLVENT in this "RTV paint", the produced "shell" had a very large amount of diluent and for practical purposes, was POROUS in addition to BEING EXTREMELY WEAK. Furthermore, the solvent in the paint consisting generally of TOLUENE (known carcinogen) or CHLOROETHANES, RAPIDLY ABSORBED INTO THE GEL CORE AND MUCH OF IT REMAINED TENACIOUSLY BOUND DESPITE STRONG HEATING!!!! THE PROCESS REQUIRED REPEATED HANDLING AND FURTHER ENHANCED THE BIOBURDEN OF THE DEVICES. THE OILY AND TACKY SURFACE AFFORDED FURTHER PROTECTION FOR HARDY MICRO-ORGANISMS ENCOUNTERED IN THE "UNCONTROLLED PRODUCTION ENVIRONMENT". STERILIZATION DEEMED TO HAVE SUFFICIENT LETHALITY TO ENSURE MEDICAL SUITABILITY WAS

SO AGGRESSIVE THAT IN EFFECT, IT DESTROYED THE PRODUCT! THEREFORE, VIRTUALLY ALL SUCH PRODUCTS WHICH SURVIVED THE STERILIZATION PROCESS MECHANICALLY WOULD HAVE HAD A "HIGH PROBABILITY OF NON-STERILITY"!!!!!

The addition of a POLYURETHANE FOAM coating and its adhesive initially contributed to reinforcing this weak structure so that it withstood the rigors of packaging and surgical handling. Upon implantation, the POLYURETHANE FOAM WOULD DISINTEGRATE WITHIN THE TISSUE BY DESIGN AND THE LARGE MASS OF SOLVENT AND SOLVENT IMPURITIES CONTAINING SILICONE GEL WAS THEN RELEASED INTO THE CAPSULE POCKET! This effect was evidently sought by the promoter! In retrospect, it appears that this "rupture process", followed by DISINTEGRATION and PARTIAL ABSORPTION of the silicone gel mass by the surrounding tissue, IS WHAT ACCOUNTED FOR THE APPARENTLY" REDUCED" INCIDENCE OF CONTRACTURE.

Outwardly these devices looked like gel-in-shell prostheses except there was no shell patch and the tactile characteristics of the bare shells were widely different from the expected properties for these ELASTOMERS. Their life cycle in vivo (in the body) was extremely brief with frequent intrasurgical ruptures and inevitable multi-site rupture-dissolution and disintegration taking place within the order to 2-3 years at best!!!!! In many cases, disintegration took place even earlier and left little more than fragments of shell to be recovered intermingled with tissue and a mass of partly liquefied gel!!!!!

This process was abandoned during the early-eighties because of litigation between the inventor of the process and the promoters...and the MEME ME ™ was discontinued amidst reports of adverse reactions, shell failures and problems with lasting health consequences.

PROBLEMS WITH ASSEMBLED FOAM-COATED IMPLANTABLE PRODUCTS

Injury Mechanisms for Foam-Coated Implants: Foam implants were widely used in the 1980-91 period; they became a significant part of the volume of commerce in breast augmentation products and drastically affected the sales of contemporary conventional products. However, the devices were not of consistent composition and quality. Several suppliers and numerous processes were used to manufacture the various prostheses which were sold during that period. In the latter years of production, the manufacturing site was also changed several times.

THE MANUFACTURER WAS REPRIMANDED BY THE FOOD AND DRUG ADMINISTRATION IN 1988-89, FOR "DEVIANT" MANUFACTURING PRACTICES INCLUDING MAJOR SHORTCOMINGS IN THE "HYGIENE" OF THE PRODUCT LINE. IN ONE INSTANCE, AN FDA INSPECTOR NOTED PRODUCTION STAFF "BLOWING INTO SHELLS" TO VERIFY THE ABSENCE OF PERFORATIONS!!! Items manufactured after 1989 were significantly different in design and production methodology from earlier versions. Production records in the 1980-91 period are FREQUENTLY SPARSE AND CREDIBILITY GAPS ARE EVIDENT! THERE ARE; THEREFORE, LINGERING UNCERTAINTIES IN COMPOSITION, PREDICTABILITY AND SAFETY OF PRODUCTS ISSUING FROM THESE PRODUCTION FACILITIES.

Technical, ethical and clinical problems surround these implants and their marketing. The most OBVIOUS IS THAT THE FOAM COATING ITSELF WAS "INCOMPATIBLE WITH LONG TERM MEDICAL IMPLANTATION AND WAS "NEVER INTENDED FOR THAT PURPOSE BY ITS MANUFACTURERS""!!!!! Its chemical constitution made it a likely candidate for the production of TOXIC SUBSTANCES and the manufacturing process failed to control the level of IMPURITY of this material at time of release!!! Furthermore, the material "DETERIORATED ON THE SHELF" because of large amounts of REACTIVE BY-PRODUCTS. This led to a gradually increasing level of CONTAMINATION with time, thus making the performance and characteristics of the product dependent on the delay between manufacturing and clinical use!

THE MOST OBVIOUS FEATURE OF THE PRODUCT UNDER CLINICAL USE WAS THE RAPID LOSS OF ADHESION AND DETACHMENT OF THE FOAM FROM THE ADHESIVE COATED CORE IN-VIVO. ONCE DETACHED, THE MATERIAL "BROKE UP" LEAVING "MICROSCOPIC DEBRIS" WHICH "REMAINED IN PATIENTS' TISSUES FOR A VARIABLE PERIOD OF TIME DURING WHICH "CYTOTOXIC METABOLITES" APPEARED IN "BREAST MILK", "BLOOD" AND "URINE". Fragments of adhesive remained as initiating centers for "FOREIGN BODY REACTIONS AND INFLAMMATORY ACTIVITY which further complicated the prosthetic environment!!!!

Interaction Of FOAM and TISSUE:

The fate of the VERY FINE FOAM "FRAGMENTS" over the long term is still the object of kinetic studies. What is known is that the very fine DEBRIS is LONG

LASTING. Depending on the in-dwelling time of the prostheses', residual FOAM and material can vary from a fractional percent to as much as 80% percent of the original mass of FOAM into PROXIMAL TISSUE!

The FRAGMENTATION and DISPERSAL of the silicone-based adhesive is a SLOWER process but INCREASES gradually with in-dwelling time. The POLYURETHANE RESORPTION RATE is STRONGLY AFFECTED by the simultaneous presence of silicone oils and gel which act as protective coatings that delay exposure of the foam and retard degradation of the foam. The adhesive layer used to bond the foam to the shell is also vulnerable to biodegradation but by a different process. Its terminal condition consists of very FINE FIBROSIS-INDUCING FRAGMENTS which are readily carried away from the implant site and which ELICIT MACROPHAGE ACTIVITY (T-cells which fight infection). In summary, the surgical retrieval of spallated (migrated) debris from coatings of this kind is a long and uncertain task with attendant risks which increase, in particular with the use of Bovie and thermal cautery.

Electrosurgery Surrounding FOAM PROSTHESES:

The use of electrosurgical procedures such as electro-dissection and electrocautery, two procedures believed essential for the safe removal of breast prostheses with mature capsules, led to the formation of significant amounts of INJURIOUS SUBSTANCES. The pyrolysis (decomposition) of POLYURETHANE DEBRIS and silicone-based material results in TOXIC, MUTAGENIC and IMMUNOLOGENIC SUBSTANCES such as AMINEOXIDES, AMINES, CARBAMATES, SILICA, as well as other COMBUSTION products suspected of adverse BIOACTIVE EFFECTS.

FOAM RESIDUALS:

Foam DEBRIS cannot be removed exhaustively without elaborate extracapsular capsulectomy procedures. Predictably, loss of tissue and CONTAMINATION of the surgical site is more severe for these patients and adds to the risks of these implants.

These factors contribute to the creation of an environment which is propitious for aberrant biochemical and biophysical processes. It also makes the site well suited for TENACIOUS INFECTIONS. In combination with shell rupture and gel leakage and/or extravasation, these phenomena also pose major radiological interpretation difficulties. Patients with a history of infection are potentially even more complex. The ability of the prosthetic sites to HARBOR and PROTECT COLONIES of ATYPICAL MICRO-ORGANISMS is another dimension in the complex impact of these devices. An environment supportive of ENCAPSULATED INFECTION, is well suited for secondary phenomena. Studies on prevalence of T cell lymphoma and immunological aberrations suggest LONG TERM IMPACT of protected infections, in particular with common infections such as staphylococci.

Prolonged use of these leaky devices increases the risk of SYSTEMIC DISEASES in proportion to the time that the devices are worn and the rate of ingress of foreign material into tissue. The presence of foam debris and adhesive fragments exacerbate these effects. They stimulate phagocytotic (cells ingesting microorganisms or other cells or and/or foreign particles) activity in the area. All of these factors appear to be at their optimum for ADVERSE REACTIONS from foam prostheses. This may explain the rapid deterioration of some patients who have a history of multiple implants and where the last implant is a foam device.

Foam develops LARGE QUANTITIES OF DEGRADED RESIDUALS upon "standing", in other words these devices have a "shelf life". This adds to substances already present as a result of the manufacturing process. Acids from the foam adhesive attacks the foam and creates water-soluble derivatives. Foam is thermally and photochemically REACTIVE; this creates other FAMILIES of CONTAMINATES with concentrations that rise with handling and storage!!

Foam implants EFFUSE OIL from the gel core during the storage period. The foam progressively absorbs oil, reaching levels sometimes in excess of 30% percent of the foam's dry weight. During the post-implantation period the foam DISSOLVES

QUICKLY leaving behind an INFLAMMATORY, FINELY DISPERSED ADULTERATED silicone oil in the immature capsule. The use of a foam implant about 3 years or less after its release or manufacture date amounts to INJECTING a BOLUS of IMPURE SILICONE OIL of ABOUT 2 - 3 GRAMS.

Contamination of the space between the capsules and the implants by viable MICRO-ORGANISMS compounds the problems of implant compatibility. For foam implants with deep microscopic channels with ongoing resorption of polyurethane spicules, the process is even more HAZARDOUS and virtually IMPOSSIBLE TO CONTROL with antibiotics. Most of these types of infections may be credited mostly to common micro-organisms from the skin which frequently enter and populate the intracapsular space.

More serious situations develop when the colonization is from more aggressive nosocomial entities such as staphylococcus aureus. If the population of micro-organisms is large enough, significant amounts of TOXINS may be produced from the natural metabolism of the organisms. Capsule formation protects these organisms from natural body defenses and post-surgical antibiotics. This leads to progressive fibrosis over a BRIEF PERIOD of time. The micro-organisms receive additional nutrients from leakage of blood and plasma into the intracapsular space. Closed compression capsulotomies, or frequently prescribed "implant movement exercises" or massage, often lead to rupture of small blood vessels and intracapsular bleeding. This may occur early, in particular if the patient complies with recommendations from plastic surgeons for preventing "contracture".

*Additional complications result from major blood infiltration leading to outwardly visible or palpable hematomas and seromas close, around or under the prosthetic space. Such events are COMMON. In severe cases, they can be LIFE THREATENING; it may become necessary to have the devices removed, the area debrided, disinfected and the hematomas evacuated. **(This is what happened to me!)** Infected hematomas/seromas are often discovered by surgeons who describe "malodorous and serosanguinous* exudates" (bad odor and containing serum and blood) surrounding GROSSLY INFECTED prostheses.

Such phenomena should be cause for concern. Mixtures of this kind have potential to create entities that function as "super antigens", in particular with prosthetic oils. These mixtures are EXPECTED to stimulate formation of antibodies directed against the micelles (living matter) consisting of fragments of altered autogenous tissue. The key role of microbiological debris in such mixtures was recognized by early workers in immunochemistry and there is current evidence validating the early data in the context of chronically infected, silicone-oil contaminated prosthetic sites. It probably explains the prevalence of ATYPICAL AUTOIMMUNE DISEASES in patients bearing prostheses with large amounts of oily or particulate debris. Phenomena of this kind also provide possible explanations for the occurrence of T cell LYMPHOMAS in patients. (Cancers)

My thoughts: "No matter what the century, no matter what the time or place, any one who KNOWS *something is harmful to others and continues doing it, selling it, implanting it, and/or states there is NO DOCUMENTED PROOF that it is DANGEROUS; However, KNOWS IT IS, is committing a heinous crime! These devices should never ever have been allowed on the market for implantation!"*

Section Thirteen - "One Woman's Theory About 'Silicone Disease'"

One Woman's Theory About Silicone Disease - This woman is a member of one of the many support groups around the world!

"We do not need to prove the statement., "Breast Implants Cause Systemic Disease"." "We do not need to make the statement, "We Need to Wait Until There is Sufficient Funding to do the Research". "Nor do we need to be disappointed the Judge-Appointed Panel- of "Experts" Could Not Conclude There is Enough Evidence to Prove Breast Implants Cause Systemic Illness". "All that is needed to show injury, and most importantly, to inform women of possible risks, is to change our perspective. This altered perspective is not new. It is basic fundamental science, easy to observe, easy to demonstrate and already proven! This theory ends the drama as it answers the questions; "Why do some women get sick from their breast implants and others do not?" and "Why do some women have similar symptoms who do not have breast implants?"

"This perspective is: Until the moment of death, the human body attempts to heal body tissues and

balance the complex chemistry of the body. Each person's immune or auto-immune response to an invasion or trauma is unique and highly individual. Countless environmental and genetic factors contribute to the uniqueness of each individuals' response to disease. No disease is in and of itself. All diseases are the effect of the body's response to an event. This theory deals with the subject of breast implants in relationship to the basic, fundamental, scientific principles."

"For example; a decayed tooth root that is not extracted will be reabsorbed by the action of the immune system. The reabsorption process (the body's attempt to remove decayed, dead tissue, or to remove a foreign substance) is a common observation in dental science. Obviously, a surgical steel pin, rod, or plate cannot be broken down as readily as a decayed tooth root. Hard, medical grade silicone is also resistant to body enzymes. However, the soft silicone envelope of a breast implant is readily broken down for absorption.

Whereas absorbing a decayed tooth will not stress the vital organs, all the body's organs are overburdened and stressed when it attempts to breakdown, absorb and excrete silicone."

The body attempts to encapsulate silicone with a collagen capsule to keep silicone away from direct exposure to body enzymes and immune properties of the blood. In the case of free-floating silicone in the body, the body attempts to encapsulate the silicone particles throughout the body. These appear as granulomas. In the case of unresolved infections, encapsulation walls-off infection by forming a cyst-like bag (capsule). Each silicone granuloma found during surgical exploration is an example of the absorption process." "We must cease trying to prove that silicone causes "CLASSIC SYSTEMIC DISEASE". "Symptoms women with breast implants have are the effects of their individual and varied responses to silicone coming in contact with the immune properties of the blood.

Some women with breast implants do not have symptoms of organ stress, experience rejection or absorption into their bodies. However, many women with breast implants experience organ stress *symptoms such as non-viral hepatitis, nephritis, colitis and otherwise unexplained skin eruptions, muscle pain, joint pain, night sweats, fatigue, and headaches. These women are experiencing the effects of their body's effort to absorb and excrete the silicone. Some women's organs will be stressed to the point of failure. This is an individual response. The risks can be calculated only if an endless number of factors are taken into consideration regarding the woman's lifestyle, environment, general health, and genetic make up. Science cannot conclusively predict the eventual outcome of an individual's attempt to heal a wound, destroy a viral or bacterial invasion, remove decayed or necrosed tissue, excrete poison or a foreign substance because of these factors. However, science does stipulate that the person with healthy organ function has a better prognosis for healing."*

"Keeping this scientific principle in consideration, it is doubtful anyone can prove that breast implants cause systemic disease. Continuing the attempt to prove causation of systemic illness by reviewing statistics gathered from subjective questions, or performing

laboratory tests will not work! We fail to prove breast implants cause disease because each person's body responds uniquely to the event that manifests disease symptoms in the body."

"This is true of all so-called diseases whether it is cancer, polio, arthritis, arteriosclerosis, head cold, and so on. Science cannot prove why some people have multiple sclerosis, nor can they prove why others' don't. In the case of cystic fibrosis, science cannot predict conclusively if a child will have CF even if both parents carry the genetic factor. Scientists can only gather statistics and inform parents of the percent of risk for their children." "Take the case of tobacco. It is obvious every smoker does not develop lung cancer. And it is equally obvious that some people who have never smoked, or breathed second hand smoke, will develop lung cancer. How does tobacco cause disease? Can it be proven?"

This theory suggests that a person's immune and autoimmune response to the inhaled tobacco smoke may cause organ stress and failure. Or, failure may occur from the mutation of developing cells because of repeated, direct exposure to foreign material. This is demonstrated when the body ceases to replicate functional cells. This example does not suggest that silicone is carcinogenic (I believe it is!). However, tobacco related illnesses are an example demonstrating that "hard" science is not conclusive."

"Further demonstrating the uniqueness of each individual's responses, consider the common cold. Science does not conclusively know why only one of three exposed persons will catch a cold. In fact, research to cure the common cold has revealed that the rhinovirus itself does not cause the cold symptoms-they are caused by the body's response to the rhinovirus-the body's attempt to eliminate the virus." It is interesting that new cancer treatment research is proving the efficacy of vaccine to stimulate the immune systems of cancer patients to dissolve (or absorb) malignant tumors."

"If one remains skeptical that the immune system attempts to breakdown the silicone and remove it from *the body, consider the organ transplant patient. Ask them about the immune-suppression drugs they take for the rest of their lives. Or ask the family dentist what happens to a decayed tooth root that is not extracted."*

"Consider the microscopic lab reports of body tissue surgically removed with a ruptured implant. There are hypertrophied cells, thick collagen tissue with a blood supply. In some women there are frank tumors in the axillary area (arm pit), near the clavicle bone, and throughout the fatty tissue surrounding the breast glands. These symptoms of body stress are not localized to the breast area. There is a systemic effort by the body to remove the foreign silicone. The immune system is complex and the effects on an individual's body will vary. This fundamental scientific observation is undeniable."

"The immune/autoimmune response is a total body response, not a local response. It may appear that a festering wooden splinter in the hand is localized, but that is not true-all immune responses come from a complex, chemical systemic feedback system. This fundamental scientific fact explains why some women

do not become ill when the silicone comes into contact with blood or the lymph system and others do. Just as some persons have no complications from a splinter while another does." "NO totally inert material has been developed for the breast implant envelope. The silicone shell of a saline implant comes in direct contact with the blood and lymph system. It is unlikely that the protective collagen capsule will remain flexible, pliable and never tear. "Assuming" the saline solution is uncontaminated, the saline will probably not cause an immune response. However, if the liquid is contaminated with mold, fungus, or bacteria, the body will mount its defenses. At this point the roll of the dice begins. Will her body absorb the implant and its contents and possibly stress vital organs?"

"In the 1970's the manufacturers received letters from numerous surgeons regarding the degraded appearance of breast implants after explantation. Nevertheless, the implants continued to be manufactured and sold, disregarding the responsibility to advise surgeons of risks or to continue research."

We can factually state that women's systemic injuries are the results of a repeated, failed immune response to prevent silicone from coming into direct contact with body enzymes. Scientists know that each person's immune system varies in its ability to defend against invasion of a foreign substance and ability to protect cellular integrity when foreign substances are introduced. Repeated attempts to absorb or remove a foreign substance may cause excretory organs such as the lungs, liver, kidneys, skin, and colon to become stressed. When excretory organs are stressed, debilitating systemic symptoms are experienced."

(My thoughts on this: "Most of the substances contained in the manufacturing process of these implants whether silicone, silicone/polyurethane, or silicone/saline are highly toxic." "I can see no reason for the manufacture, marketing, sales, or promotion of a toxic substance.....purporting to be a "medical device" to be used for human implantation, cosmetically or for reconstruction." which is TOXIC and potentially hazardous or even fatal!!!)

What the Implant Manufacturers WON'T tell potential users:

They have paid millions of dollars to cover-up the hazards of silicone

They knew from the early 1950's silicone is dangerous

They knew silicone gel attracted and killed cockroaches

They knew silicone crossed the placenta in pregnancy and caused hormonal changes

They knew silicone shrank the testicles of mice

They knew silicone was biologically ACTIVE in the human body and NOT INERT

They BOUGHT science by paying for RIGGED "made up" studies

503

They PAID for the MAYO and HARVARD studies

They contributed $ 7 million dollars to the hospital where the studies were done

They controlled science by BUYING EDITORS of medical journals

Peter Schur, Editor of Arthritis and Rheumatism, made $300.00 per hour on their payroll

They conspired with plastic surgeons to COVER-UP the risks

Plastic surgeons and the manufacturers inflated the number of women with implants to 2 million

Implants contain SILICA, BENZENE, FORMALDEHYDE, VINYL CHLORIDE, ALUMINUM and Non-Organic PLATINUM

Silicone MIGRATES to ALL organs of the body and to the BRAIN

Silicone BREAKS DOWN into CRYSTALLINE SILICA in the body

The mixture of CHEMICALS in implants are TOXIC and even create a CHEMOTHERAPY drug in the implants

Implants become CONTAMINATED with body fluids

Some implants contain FUNGUS not normally seen in humans (some resemble mushrooms)

The manufacturers FALSIFIED documents

These are TRUTHS that we as women affected by these devices have uncovered through research of thousands of pages of documents which were "sealed" in courts by the manufacturers and judges in some of the original litigation undertaken against them. It

505

is; therefore, understandable, at least to me, that the women are justified completely in their attempts to recover monetary remuneration for their illnesses, loss of careers, lifestyles, families, in essence their lives before "implants"!   WOMEN NEVER WERE GIVEN SUFFICIENT INFORMATION ABOUT THESE DEVICES TO MAKE ANY KIND OF RESPONSIBLE "INFORMED" DECISION WITH REGARDS TO HAVING THEM SURGICALLY IMPLANTED IN THEIR BODIES!

The FDA allowed them on the market under a "grandfather clause" and never knew anything about their being implanted inside of the human body they never questioned as to their safety until 1991!   We all accepted the "facts" we were told: "They will last a lifetime":   "They are perfectly safe with NO risks to health": On and on.

Section Fourteen - March 2000, F D A Hearings on Saline Breast Implants

During March, 2000, the FDA held meetings to review information about saline implants manufactured by several companies. Among these were Inamed and Mentor. The decision was made to approve these two companies for manufacture of saline implants. This decision, according to Dr. Diana Zukerman, Ph.D. Executive Director of the National Center for Policy Research for Women and Families, "brings FDA's standard of safety to a new low." "The FDA's decision is baffling on many levels. On the scientific level, it is baffling because the manufacturers' own studies, analyzed by FDA scientists, showed that between 73% - 82% percent of the breast cancer patients who tried saline implants had COMPLICATIONS within three or four years of surgery." Those complications included additional surgery, implant deflation, excruciating pain, and serious infections - not the kinds of outcome a reasonable person would call "safe"." Says Dr. Zukerman.

"On the medical level, it is baffling because breast implants are known to interfere with mammograms, sometimes obscuring cancer in its early stages. Of the *two million women who already have implants, 20,000 - 40,000 will be diagnosed with cancer at a later stage as a result."*

She states, "On the political level, the decision was baffling because the FDA seems to have turned a deaf ear to the Clinton Administration's efforts to improve health care in America. Improving access to care has been a major focus of this Administration, but not providing a strong watchdog when medical products are reviewed is also and essential component of health care. The approval of saline implants is just the latest FDA "mis-step", which has included the approval of numerous medical products that were recently removed from the market after KILLING and SERIOUSLY INJURING patients."

She further states, "Women are smart enough to make their own choices, but they need accurate information to do so. Why would any woman put a questionable product in her body, knowing that IT WILL BREAK after a few years, knowing that it can GROW BACTERIA or FUNGUS inside, knowing that her breast may get HARD and PAINFUL, and knowing that each additional surgery will result in the removal of her healthy breast tissue and new scars where the implants are inserted and removed? Unfortunately, the answer seems to be that women DON'T KNOW THE FACTS. The FDA hopes to improve that situation by providing an informative brochure to warn women about the RISKS. They will try to require that plastic surgeons distribute this brochure, but the FDA is UNLIKELY to ENFORCE THAT."

Lastly she states, "Since virtually everyone - at the FDA and elsewhere - agrees that better, longer-term research is NEEDED, it would have made sense to require additional research before approving these products. Consumers HAVE NOT BEEN PROTECTED by the FDA's decision: LET THE BUYER BEWARE."

Section Fifteen - Associated Press Article regarding: "Classification of 'silica' as A Hazardous Material"

PUBLISHED: TUESDAY, APRIL 18, 2000

"Department of Natural Resources may classify silica as hazardous material"

ASSOCIATED PRESS MILWAUKEE

"Businesses that deal with a powdery form of one of Earth's most common minerals object to new state rules that would classify it as hazardous to public health."

"The Wisconsin Department of Natural Resources (DNR) plans to expand its 1988 list of toxic airborne substances and wants to include crystalline silica."

"Silica is found throughout the world. It is the basic ingredient of quartz, which commonly occurs as beach sand, is used as glass and can often be found in granite."

"The 'DNR' proposal would regulate airborne or breathable silica, referring to tiny particles that get loose when rock is crushed or a grinder is applied to a silica product in a foundry."

"Inhaled silica is suspected of causing a disease known as silicosis that can lead to cancer."

"Gregory Wagner of the National Institute of Occupational Safety and Health in Morgantown, West Virginia, says nearly 2,800 people died of silicosis between 1987 and 1996."

"They included 109 in Wisconsin, giving the state the eighth-highest death rate in that period, Wagner said."

"The DNR regulation would not apply to the workplace. However, the U.S. Occupational Safety and Health Administration is considering strengthening its silica regulations, OSHA Milwaukee director George Yoksas said."

"Crystalline silica is among about 200 substances the DNR proposes adding to the 450 currently identified in its toxic air regulations, DNR toxicologist Jeff Myers said." 196

"The rules are known as' NR445' and have not been brought up to date since 1988, hesaid." *"An advisory group representing health, environmental, labor, industry and other organizations has formed to discuss the changes."*

"Public hearings could be held next spring. The department could announce a decision by autumn 2001, Myers said."

"In January, some employees and retired foundry workers sued Badger Mining Corporation of Berlin, Wisconsin's largest producer of silica sand."

"They argue they suffered lung diseases because they were exposed to silica dust."

"The International Agency for Research on Cancer and the National Toxicology Program calls it a CARCINOGEN, leading the DNR to propose adding it to the list, Myers said."

"Opponents say there is no evidence that silica is hazardous to the general population." (Does this sound familiar??)

"Requiring industry to cut down on silica emissions will have no appreciable effect on the silica in the air, said Joe Shapiro, a vice president of Unimen Corporation, a New Canaan, Connecticut, industrial mining company."

"'That's the problem', said Linda Sturnot, vice president of the Mining Impact Coalition of Wisconsin. 'I don't think quarry operators and owners understand the seriousness of silicosis'."

"The DNR has not announced what an acceptable exposure limit might be. Businesses fear the department will select a guideline that would make compliance impossible, said Gary Mosher, vice president of environmental health for the American Foundry Society."

"'The technology doesn't exist to comply with these levels,' Mosher said of those that some states have."

"'They don't do a risk assessment.'. 'They don't do a hazard analysis.' 'It's an accounting exercise, not a health effects risk exercise,' Mosher said."

"'None of these regulatory agencies (has) done any studies to determine if silica is a danger to those who live around these quarries,' Sturnot said." "And until they prove it's not a hazard to the general public, we're taking the position that it is.'"

("Some of my hopes for this book are that it will promote a better sense of responsibility by large corporations, the United States Government, and the policy makers, as well as the general public to be more concerned about the laws that are passed which affect us all.

We are a "global" community now. The Internet, television, fax machines, and immediate recognition through email has brought us all much closer together. We have a responsibility to ourselves and to the planet upon which we live to be custodians and care takers of our resources so that there will be a place for others' to live with the bounties that we enjoy long after we are gone.)

There are so many of us women who have died as a direct result of silicone poisoning!

You never read about them in the Media.....So many who have ended their lives by suicide because they cannot handle the pain any longer. The medical society, in general, chooses to ignore our symptoms and illnesses saying, "It's all in your head!"

"You need psychiatric help!" Ha! Alas, we do need help! Yes, we do....We need to tell our stories, we need the general public to understand what has happened to us and what continues to happen to us each day. We are suffering, it seems no one cares!

I hope this book, which contains the TRUTH, will be accepted and we will obtain the health care we so desperately need, we will be then able to go on with whatever lifestyle we can manage to the best of our ability, and will be free to help others' who are just beginning to become ill from the TOXINS in these so-called "Medical Devices"!

We never know who will be the next victim of silicone! The manufacturers have "played" this "game" very well. The cover-up has been effective!

We are not being "tracked" by anyone. Not the FDA, not the government, no agency is keeping *records on us....What has happened to each and every woman....No one is counting the deaths!*

These huge corporations will continue to pollute the air, our water, our bodies, and our food supplies! They take chemicals which have been banned here in the U.S. to third world countries and use them there; it all returns right back here! The poor individuals in these other countries are being toxically poisoned daily, we sit here watching and this is a sickening tragedy. What can we do?

These manufacturers have been cutting deals for years! They most assuredly knew what they were doing! So does our own government! We know, all of us, who produced these chemicals for war, they had them produced to destroy others! We have toxically poisoned our own military for years and yet the government continues to deny that as well. How about "Agent Orange", how about "Seron Gas", how about "Desert Storm"? Hopefully together we can unite to STOP those who continue to use these TOXIC poisons and make this a safer world to live in."

Section Sixteen - Excerpts from Dr. Frank B. Vasey's Book entitled: "The Silicone Breast Implant CONTROVERSY," "What Women Need to Know"

By Frank B. Vasey, M.D. and Josh Feldstein. Dr. Vasey's Book: "The Silicone Breast Implant Controversy", "What Women Need To Know"

Dr. Frank B. Vasey is Professor of Medicine, Department of Internal Medicine, and Chief, Division of Rheumatology, at the University of South Florida College of Medicine, Tampa. Dr. Vasey has served as an advisor to the F D A and provided testimony before the Human Resources and Intergovernmental Relations Subcommittee of the Committee on Government Operations. He has published numerous scientific articles in the field of Rheumatology. He has also provided testimony as an expert witness in silicone implant cases.

Josh Feldstein, is a medical writer, editor, and marketing specialist, is President of Marcom Group International, Inc., a health care public relations/ marketing communications agency with offices in New York City and Montgomery County, Maryland.

THE DIFFICULTIES IN DIAGNOSING SILICONE-INDUCED DISEASE

"Not every woman who gets implants becomes sick-many are lucky and never do-but those who do, go from doctor to doctor and from test to test and get nowhere because there are so few doctors who understand silicone disease." "Countless patients confirm this experience." "Many have wiped out their savings in the process due to a lack of insurance coverage, or due to their existing insurance excluding them." Some women have even been told by their doctor(s) that they simply do not want to see them again! (Insurance companies are now declining to insure "people" if they have a silicone implant of any kind.)

"Silicone disease, due to its varied nature, is an illness that requires a fitting together of a constellation of signs and symptoms. Unfortunately, a single lab test to confirm silicone disease such as the one used to confirm Strep throat, does not yet exist. Hence few physicians have been able to identify the disease in

521

their patients, and therefore have instituted a long chain of blind testing and trial medications."

"To make diagnostic matters even more complex, great skill is required to conduct a pathological evaluation with a standard laboratory microscope in order to catch silicone particles in tissue. Far more sophisticated and expensive technologies, such as high-powered electron microscopy/X-ray dispersive analysis, can be used to identify silicone in the body, but this is far beyond what is generally available in most doctors' offices."

"Additionally, the early signs of silicone disease are often nonspecific, the types of symptoms that can occur in anyone. Later, as the illness proceeds, its symptoms often evolve into conditions that appear similar to nonsilicone-induced rheumatic diseases, such as rheumatoid arthritis, lupus, and scleroderma. This combination of nonspecific and rheumatic symptoms, all of which appear to be similar to other illnesses, makes mis-diagnosis easy. What's more, a physician who sees only an occasional silicone disease patient

may easily misdiagnose her symptoms as a rheumatic ailment not linked to her implants. But should the physician develop an interest in silicone disease and see hundreds of patients with the same patterns, the constellation of silicone-induced signs and symptoms soon becomes clear."

"Simply put, surgeons tend to focus on a single problem or area of the body. They will take a generally healthy patient, address a specific surgical problem-an infected gallbladder, for example-remove it, and be finished. Medical problems that might occur following surgery would normally be referred to an internist, family practitioner, or other medical specialist, because that's not what the surgeon handles. Internal medicine, on the other hand-and rheumatology is a subspecialty of internal medicine-is oriented toward the assessment of all the body systems and how these systems integrate."

THE UNFOLDING OF A DISEASE

"The first women believed to have their breasts enlarged with silicone were Japanese, possibly in the mid-to-late 1940's. In these cases, liquid silicone gel, as well as paraffin and other substances, were injected by syringe directly into the breasts. Many of these women were prostitutes who had discovered that American servicemen preferred women with larger busts than were common in Japanese women. Concern about their health was apparently a very low priority."

Beginning in the 1950's, physicians in the United States began using injections of liquid silicone as well, in addition to implanting sponges directly into women's breasts. The practice was continued for years. According to a report in the American Journal of Nursing, it was finally banned by the F D A due to a wide range of "disastrous" complications, including infections from improperly sterilized silicone materials and patient injuries and deaths."

Excerpts from Dr. Frank B. Vasey's Book entitled: "The Silicone Breast Implant CONTROVERSY," "What Women Need to Know"

"The search for a healthier and safer way to introduce silicone into the female breast for the purpose of physical enhancement led to a major advance in 1961. That year, Drs. Thomas Cronin and Frank Gerow, who later joined implant manufacturer Dow Corning, first combined rubbery and liquid silicone to create a soft but firm gel. They enclosed the gel in a silicone-rubber envelope. The implant was surgically placed in a Houston woman in 1962, and the era of surgical breast enhancement began."

"Silicone-gel implants have been widely used since 1976. Saline-filled silicone envelope devices have also been implanted, (at the writing of his book in 1993) but less frequently; they have the same silicone shell as gel implants but are filled with a sterile saltwater solution." ("Since the F D A 's moratorium on gel-filled implants in 1992, these have been the only legal implant prostheses unless a woman is enrolled in a clinical trial. However, saline implants are now also under F D A investigation.") (Of course now, we know that the saline breast implants acquire bacteria, fungus and mold and can cause illnesses in women also.)

525

"Plastic surgeons and others may argue that the date implicating silicone implants definitively in the cause of serious illness is not as yet strong enough. But based on the suffering of patients, as well as the 'burden of proving safety', according to the F D A (which sadly, was articulated 20 years too late), it is our opinion that silicone implants are dangerous and unproven. In fact, according to a Medical Devices Bulletin issued by the F D A, following testimony provided by a panel of medical experts in late 1991 prior to Dr. David Kessler's decision 'to remove silicone breast implants from the market', the F D A noted that date from 'all four' manufacturers "did not provide reasonable assurance of safety" in the areas of:

"Implant Rupture"

"Gel bleed and the potential of silicone migration (throughout the body)"

"Chemical information on silicone and silicone gel"

"Toxicity regarding the immune system, cancer, and birth defects"

"Tumor detection"

"Psychological issues."

"To make matters worse, implant manufacturers had known since 1979-when the medical device law statute was passed, "grandfathering" medical devices (including implants) already on the market (that is, excluding them from providing additional safety data)---that they would one day be called upon to provide the F D A with additional scientific evidence of safety. Well, more than 15 years later, as demonstrated by the F D A panel's findings, the manufacturers still had not done their safety data homework. The obvious question is, did they know something they wanted to keep secret?"

WAS EVIDENCE ABOUT SILICONE DANGERS AVAILABLE TO DOCTORS?

"Silicone had been successfully used for many years in a host of medical devices, with virtually no bad publicity regarding biological or autoimmune incompatibility. So the medical establishment embraced the practice of placing foreign silicone objects into women's bodies "before" those objects were rigorously tested for safety." "In addition to erroneous assumptions about safety, six other factors have delayed the medical community's full knowledge of silicone's potentially dangerous nature."

1. *"Lack of access to foreign studies."*

2. *"Implants were not evaluated for safety by the F D A"*

3. *"Company communications lacking"*

4. *"Follow-up studies by plastic surgeons on patients receiving silicone implants ended too soon"*

5. *"Autoimmune disorders are often outside the expertise and general interest of plastic surgeons"*

6. *"Doctors may not realize that their patients have implants"*

(All of these seem to be legitimate reasons; however, it might also have been a convenient means by which the plastic surgeons could avoid taking a closer look into the extremely lucrative business of surgically placing implants in a human body!)

SILICONE MIGRATION A LEAKAGE: THE STARTING POINT FOR DISEASE

"Implant manufacturers have maintained for many years that silicone implants are safe and inert. Yet simply placing an implant of a paper napkin will produce an observable absorption of gel on the paper within hours. While this "bleeding" effect does not, in itself, prove toxicity, it certainly raises reasonable doubts about silicone safely remaining within the

implant. This "bleeding", moreover, occurs in all implant recipients, and is the first- and fastest-means by which the body can be exposed to silicone." "Wherever the silicone goes, scarring, swelling, and inflammation may occur." (How about rupture?)

RHEUMATIC REACTIONS TO SILICONE: A NEW DISEASE?

"Rheumatic conditions affect the body's joints, muscles, and connective tissue (which hold together the structure of the body), including tendons and cartilage. Silicone exposure can affect the entire musculoskeletal system in numerous and serious ways."

"Under normal circumstances, inflammation is an important component of the healing process: it creates an environment conducive to tissue repair and to the elimination of bacterial invaders. In the case of rheumatic ailments, this same healing process turns injurious, adversely affecting healthy joints, muscles, and connective tissues adjacent to the areas of inflammation. Should these inflammatory conditions

last for a prolonged period of time, the localized rheumatic effects may become systemic, appearing in all parts of the body. And since exposure to silicone in women with implants is most often measured in years, such long-term exposure can induce chronic inflammation." "Some women with implants show atypical combinations of clinical findings. When the manifestations of silicone-associated connective tissue disease are severe and widespread, it comprises a syndrome not typically encountered by physicians: severe chronic fatigue causing a patient to sleep as much as 10 hours but awakening exhausted; fibromyalgia pain (musculoskeletal pain and stiffness) with diffusely tender muscular trigger zones; joint pain, generally without swelling, but occasionally with mild swelling of wrists and ankles; swollen lymph nodes (lymphadenopathy) in the underarm and neck that wax and wane; and mysterious burning/crawling sensations indicative of peripheral nerve malfunction. In a woman with silicone disease, all this in the absence of a "butterfly" facial rash on the cheeks or kidney disease (which would suggest instead that the patient has systemic lupus erythematosus)."

"The presence of antinuclear antibodies in a woman's blood, while typical of systemic lupus erythematosus, is not unique to that disorder. In fact, most women with a positive ANA do not have lupus. The test really serves as an indication of immune stimulation occurring in a variety of clinical situations ranging from chronic infectious hepatitis to cancer, to multiple chronic inflammatory rheumatic diseases. Research in this area continues with several new publications. Richard Silver, M.D., a rheumatologist from Charleston, found elemental silicone in the skin, joint lining, and lung tissue of three women with breast implants using X-ray dispersive analysis and electron microscopy.

Henry Claman, M.D., an immunologist from Denver, reported the prevalence of antinuclear antibodies in groups of women with and without breast implants. While normal women without implants had a 5 percent prevalence of a positive ANA, asymptomatic women with implants had a 30 percent prevalence of positive ANA. What's more, symptomatic women with implants but without defined connective tissue disease had a 50 percent prevalence. Finally, women with implants and defined connective tissue disease showed a 90 percent prevalence."

"Additionally, Eric Gershwin, M.D., and co-workers in rheumatology from the University of California at Davis, have recently described anti-collagen antibodies in women with breast implants."

"While none of these observations are definitive, the all support the concept that silicone may diffuse widely throughout the body and is a stimulant to the immune system." Next, Fibromyalgia. "Fibromyalgia, when rheumatologists use this term, they mean tender knots of muscle (trigger zones) caused by a combination of injury, strain, and overuse, as well as a light, nonrestorative sleep pattern in a tense, anxious/compulsive individual resulting in chronic pain. Immune malfunction is not thought by most rheumatologists to play a central role. In fibromyalgia patients, there is pain and tenderness in muscles and around joints, but

not typically 'in" joints-a clinical manifestation seen far more often 'only' in silicone patients."

"Additional evidence supporting the association of silicone and connective tissue disease comes from observations of women with traumatic breast implant rupture. Our research in a small group of women who were in good health while the implants were in place has shown that shortly following implant rupture, these women developed the typical muscle pain, joint pain, and swelling of rheumatic disease, which improved or stabilized once the rupture was recognized and the implants removed. In addition, women known to have experienced a silicone-gel breast implant rupture at a certain time (following a specific traumatic event, for example) have developed chronic fatigue, and muscle and joint pain, shortly thereafter."

"While there is no way to be certain that silicone other than coincidental factors is causing an immune response and clinical illness, the University of South Florida rheumatologists have observed that a 'common constellation of symptoms shows up in a

high percentage of women with implants who develop problems'. As mentioned earlier, these symptoms appear on average a little more than four years after implantation, but the range extends from 'immediately' after surgery to 22 years later. Here are the most common symptoms of silicone disease documented thus far, in order of frequency:"

"Chronic Fatigue"

"Inflammation and muscle pain (myalgia), initially in the anterior chest, back, and neck (pain may radiate beyond these areas)"

"Joint pain and swelling"

"Swollen lymph nodes (from pea-sized to lima bean-sized lumps) in the chest, neck, underarms, and groin (junction of legs and abdomen)."

"Low-grade fever (100 to 101 degrees)"

"Gastrointestinal symptoms, including cramping and abdominal pain"

"Other symptoms include:"

"Night sweats"

"Memory loss"

"Dry eyes and mouth"

"Headache"

"Rashes"

"Difficulty swallowing"

"Bladder problems, including interstitial cystitis (chronic inflammation of the bladder) and frequent urination in the absence of infection"

"Sinus irritation"

"Numbness and altered sensation in the body"

"Skin tightening, either locally or bodywide"

"Lung problems such as chronic cough, shortness of breath, pulmonary fibrosis (scarring and thickening of lung tissue), pleural effusion (accumulation of fluid between the membrane lining of the lung and chest cavity), and recurrent pneumonia"

"Decreased sex drive"

"Depression and thoughts of giving up or suicide"

"Not all women susceptible to silicone-associated disease will experience all of these symptoms, and the severity varies widely according to each individual's duration and extent of exposure, as well as genetic make-up and immune system."

"As mentioned earlier, unfortunately there's no one blood test or other technique that can confirm

the presence of silicone-induced autoimmune disease. Batteries of test results have varied widely from woman to woman. For example there have been reports of patients with silicone-related symptoms who have cholesterol levels of over 480 (under 200 is ideal) and white blood cell counts of 33,000 per cubic millimeter of blood (normal range is 4,500 to 11,000), while others with the same symptoms have had normal test results. In fact, with the exception of uric acid crystals (gout) or bacteria growing in joint fluid, testing for rheumatic conditions rarely confirms a diagnosis; nor do test results determine treatment."

"Although still inconclusive, the following results have been found to correlate with the disease in some implant recipients:"

"Elevated sedimentation rate, a non-specific measure of inflammation in the body, based on the presence of certain proteins in the blood, has shown up in about 24 percent of patients"

"Elevated levels of antinuclear antibodies (ANA), which are antibodies that tend to react with components of cell nuclei." ("ANA tests are positive in 30 percent of patients with silicone implants, but in only 1 percent to 2 percent of the general population.")

"Positive test for toxic porphyria, a disorder caused by overaccumulation in the body of coproporphyrin. 'Porphyrins' are chemicals that play a key role in the manufacture of hemoglobin and other important body substances. Symptoms of porphyria may include extreme sensitivity to light, a rash, skin blistering, abdominal pain, and nervous system disturbances. ("At the University of South Florida, a small number of women treated with implant-related problems have tested positive for this condition and their tests returned to normal after implant removal.")

THE EVIDENCE SUPPORTING A RELATIONSHIP BETWEEN SILICONE AND RHEUMATIC SYMPTOMS

"The following points represent some of the most compelling evidence to date suggesting these materials as a perpetrator of autoimmune disorders."

"Silica exposure is hazardous" - "Silica has a well-documented record of damage to humans exposed to it on an ongoing basis. People in occupations such as sandblasting who inhale many silica particles may develop silicosis, a form of pulmonary fibrosis. This scarring and thickening of lung tissue usually results from inflammation and typically causes shortness of breath. In many cases, the condition is irreversible. When especially severe, it can lead to heart failure. Pulmonary fibrosis has been diagnosed in some U S F breast implant patients."

"Silica is an immunogen" - "Silica ("which is a sandlike material") is a proven immunogen, that is, a substance that stimulates the body's immune system to attack normal body tissue. The shell for both gel-and

saline-filled implants is made of a polymer with a 30 percent silicone dioxide filler. The silica helps solidify the envelope, or implant jacket."

"Since congregations of macrophages have been found on the surface of silicone implant jackets, it appears that these immune-system cells attack the jacket itself-whether silicone is leaking from it. In support of the shell-destruction/erosion hypothesis, Nir Kossovsky, a pathologist at University of / California, Los Angeles (UCLA), has obtained compelling evidence using an electron microscopic X-ray technique on implants removed from patients. Dr. Kossovsky, who presented his scientific findings to a congressional subcommittee, demonstrated how the body's macrophages attack the silicone shell of the breast implant. This process can be likened to 'gophers chewing' into and through the implant's wall, chiseling off microscopic pieces of silicone, which then lodge in neighboring body tissue. Eventually, this cellular assault weakens the outer envelope to the point where it may rupture."

"Silicone has been found in tissues peripheral to the breast even in the absence of implant rupture, which further implies that attacking macrophages can cause bits of the silicone envelope to break off. The immune process itself may also activate normal cells in the area. More research is required to determine the specifics of this process."

ANIMAL AND HUMAN STUDIES SHOW IMMUNE RESPONSE

"Silicone oils were recognized as potential adjuvants in the 1960's by researchers. Adjuvants are substances that alter natural, 'friendly' cells into activated cells capable of attacking the body."

"Macrophages containing silicone particles have been found in test animals' adrenal glands, lymph nodes, liver, kidney, (brain, lungs), spleen, pancreas, and ovaries. Results from Dow Corning's biosafety animal study reports have included findings of liver toxicity, stillbirths, fetal abnormalities, respiratory diseases, lesions, cancer, hemorrhages, and death. In

mid-1982, for example, Dow initiated a project with an internal mammary gel formulation labeled "Q7-2159A" to address the issues of gel cohesivity and bleed, the results of which 'showed the extreme sensitivity of the formulated gel to penetration and bleed'. Further studies with this particular formulation, variously conducted over a decade, revealed "metastatic sarcomas", "enlarged lymph nodes", "pituitary adenomas", and "hair loss (that) may be associated with thyroid disorders". A subchronic toxicity study with formulation D5, contracted to the University of Mississippi Medical Center in 1989, found the gel to "induce (liver enlargement), with recovery after cessation of dosing", and it "resembled phenobarbital" in its ability to induce certain enzymatic activity"."

"The potential of free silicone migration was also raised to company officials in at least one report submitted in 1976, by an outside testing laboratory. Injecting a series of gel formulations labeled "TX1228", "TX1229", and TX1234", the researchers noted a "possibility that the test material may have migrated away from the implant sites"."

"When viewed under a microscope, tissue next to silicone implants has, in some women, show an exceptionally high accumulation of scavenger cell-devouring macrophages. Unlike the finite healing of a particular wound, the assault of macrophages around the silicone implant does not stop, because the body continues to respond to the tiny, but potentially widespread, silicone particles."

"In many women who receive silicone breast implants, the macrophages keep accumulating month after month, year after year. As more cells arrive, the scar tissue becomes increasingly thicker-often creating a series of hard, painful lumps or overall hardening of the breast, in addition to the likelihood of changes in the physical contour of the breast itself."

SILICONE *"BLEEDS"* THROUGH, AND SHEDS FROM, THE ENVELOPE

"Numerous reports in the medical literature, as well as findings by manufacturers, have shown that a

certain amount of silicone leaks, or "bleeds", through the outer casing of the implant jacket in every case, even when there is no rupture. This means that all women with silicone implants will experience some exposure to the gel."

"Silicone particles may come off the outside of the envelope, perhaps creating potential hazards for women with saline-filled silicone envelop implants as well."

SILICONE FOUND IN FIBROUS TISSUE AROUND THE IMPLANT

"Unpublished correlations between the amount of silicone in capsular tissue that surrounds an implant and the total amount of this tissue have been made by some researchers, but these findings have not yet been substantiated. The theory;, however, is that silicone/silica appears directly related to the development of fibrosis, the overgrowth of scar or connective tissue around the prosthesis itself." (keep in mind Dr. Vasey wrote this book in 1993)

THE BODY MAKES ANTIBODIES AGAINST SILICONE

"Studies conducted in the 1970's by John Paul Heggers of the University of Texas Medical Center at Galveston showed that the human immune system reacts to silicone in breast implants by making antibodies against it, according to a January 18, 1992, news report in 'The New York Times'. He found that these antibodies (which help macrophages and other immune-system components to destroy harmful invaders) attacked the silicone "as well as the body's own tissues" associated with it-a classic symptom of an autoimmune disorder. More such studies need to be conducted to confirm and isolate specific antibodies created by the body against silicone."

EPIDEMIOLOGIC STUDIES SHOW SYMPTOMS AMONG BREAST IMPLANT RECIPIENTS

"Michael Weisman, a rheumatologist at the University of California, San Diego, published a survey in a 1988 issue of the "Journal of Plastic and

Reconstructive Surgery" of women who underwent silicone implant surgery for cosmetic purposes during a 12-year period. Of 125 women, 30 percent reported rheumatic complaints. None of the patients had rheumatoid arthritis or scleroderma, causing Weisman to believe it was a negative study. About 30 percent of the responding women (average age: 48) had musculoskeletal complaints. There was no control group for comparison."

"University of South Florida's Divisions of Plastic Surgery, Dermatology, and Rheumatology pursued the silicone-rheumatic disease connection further in 1988 with a survey of 370 women who had received silicone-gel breast implants and a control group who had undergone nonsilicone plastic surgery procedures. The women in the silicone group had their implants for an average of five years, and their average age was 37. The average age of the control group was 46."

"Even though the women in the silicone group averaged six years younger than the control group, they were discovered to be eight times more likely to suffer *from tender lymph nodes under the are (8 percent) than the control group (1 percent), as well as four times more likely to develop swollen lymph nodes under the arm (12 percent vs. 3 percent respectively). Muscle pain, joint pain, joint swelling, and chronic fatigue were more common in the silicone patients, but these symptoms did not reach the 95 percent certainty level."*

MORE SYMPTOMS OCCUR NEAR IMPLANT LOCATION

"In some women who have only one silicone implant due to unilateral mastectomy or breast asymmetry, symptoms of pain and inflammation tend to be more pronounced on the side of the body where the implant is located. Some of these women, as well as women known to have experienced a rupture in only one breast have developed muscle pain and swelling in the arm on the affected side only. This asymmetrical reaction implies that a localized stimulation of the immune system occurs in the affected area."

CONNECTIVE TISSUE DISEASE IN WOMEN WITH BREAST IMPLANTS MAY DIFFER FROM THE NATURALLY OCCURRING DISEASE

"Lupus": "One of the first cases of silicone-associated connective tissue disease seen at USF was a woman treated for a condition similar to systemic lupus erythematosus (SLE) in 1987. This case was distinguished by a milky fluid with a high fat content in the membrane that lines the lungs and chest cavity, a condition known as chylous pleural effusion. We could find no similar reports of this specific problem occurring previously in natural SLE. Apparently, the woman's thoracic duct (a large duct of the lymphatic system located between the neck and the abdomen) had been inflamed and blocked by silicone granules and/or activated immune cells."

"After she had her implants removed and was treated with cortisone, her symptoms resolved within six months. When the cortisone was stopped, her symptoms did not recur. Similar complete remissions

have occurred in the natural disease, but are unusual. She continues to do well five years later." (at the time of printing of his book -1993-)

SCLERODERMA

"While this serious condition is extremely rare in the general population-approximately 50 cases per million people-a sclerodermalike illness has been documented in numerous women with silicone implants."

"Steve Weiner, a Los Angeles-based rheumatologist, sent out a questionnaire to the Scleroderma Foundation and found 50 such women in the Los Angeles area alone."

"Harry Spiera, a rheumatologist based in New York City, has reported that 4.4 percent of his scleroderma patients have implants-as opposed to only 0.3 percent of his rheumatoid arthritis patients. Although the percentages are low in both of these group[s, what is significant is that he found over 14

times as many of his implant patients suffering from scleroderma as nonimplant patients."

"In the medical literature, about half of the women with scleroderma have improved after implant removal, whereas remission of natural scleroderma without treatment occurs uncommonly."

LUNG DISEASES

"Studies of patients at USF show that some of those who have connective tissue disease also have lung disease. This suggests that silicone and possibly silica can make their way past regional lymph nodes into the right side of the heart and out to the lungs. This could result in lung inflammation and/or fibrosis."

"Lucy Love and Fred Miller, at the F D A, reported an interesting clinical difference between naturally occurring dermatomyositis/polymyositis and the same disease in women with breast implants. The implant patients were found to have a higher prevalence of pulmonary fibrosis than nonimplant patients

551

(about 50 percent versus 20 percent). Although this observation is preliminary since it is based on fewer than 20 women with implants who have the disease, it nontheless suggests that implants are playing a role in this illness."

SJOGREN'S SYNDROME:

"Bruce Freundlich, a rheumatologist from the University of Pennsylvania, reported at the American College of Rheumatology meeting in October 1992, that women with breast implants exhibited the immune-mediated symptoms of dry eyes and dry mouth."

CHRONIC FATIGUE AND SWOLLEN LYMPH NODES HAVE BEEN OBSERVED

"Many women with silicone disease suffer from chronic fatigue. Based on the USF 1988 questionnaire, 15 percent of the silicone group reported having chronic fatigue compared with only 11 percent in the control group without implants. Statistically, this is suggestive

(more likely than not) but not definitive (that is, below 95 percent certain)."

(Dr. Vasey continues to make reference in his book to this "1988 questionnaire". For the record, at this time I knew of NO problems with breast implants-there was NO media coverage, nothing from The Department of Health, that I knew of, Nothing controversial about breast implants-Only statements that the implants would "last a lifetime". Also, Dr. Vasey's reference to swollen and painful lymph nodes is extraordinary at the time he wrote this. He was the only physician to mention this at this early time of the breast implant issues.)

"Clinical observation of lymph node swelling is more dramatic in silicone-related lupus and other connective tissue diseases than in nonsilicone versions of these diseases. Through a method not yet understood, silicone particles can enter the lymphatic system (a network of glands and fluid-carrying ducts) and become lodged in lymph nodes under the arm, in the neck, and in the groin. The silicone, combined with *various immune-system cells, can then travel via the lymphatic system to stimulate a dangerous cycle of immune and lymphatic system 'excitation', one that builds and builds. Should this occur, some women experience swollen and painful lymph nodes in their breasts, necks, underarms, and groin. This diverse swelling indicates that the immune system has been stimulated throughout the body, not just at the site of the implant."*

"As various immune cells migrate into the lymphatic channels, they soon enter the lymph nodes." There "they interact with other immune cells, particularly T-cell lymphocytes (which cause or facilitate tissue damage), causing the lymph nodes to enlarge and become repositories of "angry" immune cells. Views through a microscope reveal a condition called reactive hyperplasia, an overgrowth of the lymph node resulting from reactions to environmental factors---including silicone."

"Scientists agree that microscopic quantities of silicone reach the lymph nodes along with immune

cells. But there is disagreement over what happens to this substance once it settles in the nodes. Ultimately, silicone particles may be able to travel throughout the entire body. This may occur via the following process:"

"1. Lymph fluid goes into the chest in a tubelike collecting system called the thoracic duct."

"2. This fluid, and possibly the silicone particles themselves, goes into the right side of the heart and into the lungs via the thoracic duct."

"3. Once it flows past the lungs, the left side of the heart pumps the lymph and silicone particles out to the rest of the body. If this occurs, silicone will enter the bloodstream and may possibly trigger a bodywide immune-system response."

IMPLANTS MAY INCREASE THE RISK OF NEUROLOGICAL DISEASE

"Bernard M. Patten, a neurologist at Baylor College of Medicine in Houston, has found an association between silicone breast implants and serious autoimmune conditions as well as neurological dysfunction. In an August 27, 1992, abstract for a platform presentation to the American Neurological Association, he described several young women with amyotrophic lateral sclerosis (ALS), known as Lou Gehrig's disease and whose typical victims are older men, and many others who showed signs of sensory-motor neuropathy and other symptoms. The average time of disease onset, Patten reported, was about seven years from implantation. In addition, some of these women had peripheral nerve disease, a condition not seen in the natural form of ALS."

"Dr. Patten, in the same abstract submission, also reported on patients with implants who had an unusual form of multiple sclerosis (MS). These patients demonstrated a combination of typical MS symptoms

along with the unexpected manifestation of joint pain and swelling. This highly unusual combination could mean that implants had been a factor in triggering a silicone-specific version of the condition. Symptoms were found to improve in some patients following implant removal. The neurologist's conclusion was that 'silicone may provoke damage to nerve and muscle, probably indirectly promoting autoimmunity.' In the research submitted for publication, he strongly recommends a 'reappraisal of the risk-benefit ratio for {silicone breast implant} surgery'."

FOAM IMPLANTS POSE CANCER RISK

Polyurethane "foam-coated implants were originally designed to help prevent the natural scar tissue around implants from developing into capsular contracture. Studies later showed that the outer layer of foam could break down in the body. A by-product of this breakdown is 2-toluene diamine (TDA), a substance that has been banned in hair dyes and other products because IT CAUSES LIVER CANCER IN ANIMALS." (I had this type of implants)

557

"William J. Pangman, M.D. a prominent plastic surgeon, now deceased, developed the foam used as a filler and the coating for these implants. Dr. Pangman claimed the foam shouldn't break down in the human body. Yet no one seems to have any record of exactly what kind of foam he used"!"

Section Seventeen - Department of Health and Human Services Report on Polyurethane Foam

"DEPARTMENT OF HEALTH & HUMAN SERVICES"

"DATE ????" (This may have been written some time in late 1990 or in 1991) "From Deputy Director, DSRD (HFZ-410)"

"Subject Additional Information on Polyurethane Mammary Implant & Cancer Risk to Director, Office of Device Evaluation"

"Through: Director DSRD"

"This memorandum is an addendum of my April 3, 1989 and May 31, 1990 technical reviews on the same subject.-"

"Our previous reviews did not provide the precise chemical nature of polyurethane (PU) foam used in the implant because at that time we were unable to obtain such information from the manufacturer. Through our review of several in masterfiles from both device manufacturer and foam manufacturer and communication with the foam manufacturer and Device

EIR, we now can reasonably document the exact nature of the PU-foam used in breast implants. This has allowed us to review and compare two previously published results of animal studies on similar PU-foam obtained from different sources."

"THE PU-Foam"

"The stock foam used in the mammary implant is actually made by Scottfoam Corporation of Eddystone, Pennsylvania and sold to the manufacturer as precut washed individual pieces through vendors (either Wilshire foam or by Sirod Corporation of California). The cleaning, packaging, and some testing are also done by the vendor. The foams are cleaned for class 10 laundry by ABA cleaning services for Wilshire foam or by Prudential overall supply (class 10 laundry) using unknown detergents and supplied to the device manufacturer. The PU mother stock is designated as SIP 100 PPI Z MA, which refers to reticulated Scott Industrial foam with 80-110 open pores per linear inch. This is a polyester polyurethane made by using saturated polyester resins (Adipic acid and diethylenc

Glycol, mixture made by Inolex Chemical Company), Toluene diisocyanate (Dow Chemical: Voranate T-80- an 80:20 mixture of isomers of TDI, N-ethylmorpholine (Texacat REM) and catalysts such as n-cetyl, N,

N-dimenthylamine in isoproponal (Lonza or Airproduct) and N-methyldicyelohexylamine (Polycat-12), and commercial surfacant mixtures."

"A recent study performed in the preformed foam characterized the product as a cross-linked polyesterurethane made from diol-terminated polyadipate oligomers containing small amounts of the corresponding amines and amine-isocyaates."

"The foam is made in large industrial quantities and the end process involves quick burning for opening of the pore. The major application of the foam is for use in the air and oil filters. Although the designation MA indicates "for medical applications", no special steps or precautions in the manufacturing is involved."

"The Two Carcinogenicity Studies"

Two published studies have been reported by Heuper from The National Cancer Institute (1961 and 1964). Although the studies are old, results are still valid because these are the only available bioassay results using this type of polyesterpolyurethane foam. The foams used in the first' study were obtained from Mobay Chemical and the second study used foam made at NCI Laboratory. The chemical formulation provided by the author indicates that the PU-foam used in these studies is similar, if not identical, to the foam used for breast implants. These studies used Bethesda black rats implanted with shredded or intact PU-foams and several routes of administration."

"The results of these studies are positive. Without going through the details it can be briefly reported that a significant increase in adenocarcinomas were noted in both studies (8/30 and 6/70). For clarification purposes, several aspects of these results need further comments. Firstly, the shredded PU implants produced

563

tumors, which indicate that no solid-state phenomenon were involved, as such event requires continuous smooth surfaces (generally 0.5 cm.). Carcinogenicity of any solid film under this size is generally taken to be indicative of chemical effect. Furthermore, the tumor types involved in this study included adenocarcinomas, (in addition to local sarcomas), which has never been associated with solid-state carcinogenesis. Secondly, the author indicated that the PU material was partially resorbed. Collectively, these two observations strongly indicate that PU is acting as a straight-forward chemical carcinogen. In the discussion section, the author commented on the unsuitability of PU-foam as a implant in cosmetic surgery." ["It is remarkable that these comments were made in the sixties when the constituent TDI or (TDA) was not known to be a carcinogen."] "(emphasis added)"

"Manufacturer Sponsored Bioassay of PU-Foam"

"The masterfile submitted to F D A by "Surgitek" (device manufacturer) contained an interim report from

Dr. Woodward which indicates that a contract for bioassay was initiated by the company (90 rat study) on June 23, 1987. I was informed that this study has been terminated at 9 months (1 month after the interim report). However, I was unable to obtain either the original protocol or a final report of this study. I have requested OC to follow-up this study through Bioresearch Monitoring Staff (memo attached). The interim report does not contain any reviewable data but contains a set of conclusionary findings. Two of the reported findings are:"

a.   *"Within the connective tissue infiltrating the PU, collections of foamy macrophages containing PAS positive deposits are frequent. This non-hemosiderin pigment may represent a PU breakdown product."*

b.   *"The polyurethane film implants decreased in size at least 50% between two to eight months, although the film is recoverable at eight months This finding is strong evidence for the local degradation of the porous PU film."*

"Conclusion"

1.   "The two reported positive bioassay results correlates very well with our previous conclusion of potential carcinogenicity of PU-foam due to hydrolytic release of TDA.   The composition of PU-foam used in mammary implants is similar to the PU-foam tested in the bioassays.   It is now reasonable to assume that TDA generated form the PU-foam may be the etiologic agent producing the adenocarcinomas in rats (chemical as opposed to solid-state carcinogenesis)."

2.   "The interim report from the sponsor's testing indicates that PU-foam (as used in breast implants) is resorbed in the animal model..   The resorption rate in the biologic system can now be assumed to be at 50% at six months.   This information is consistent with data on the loss of mechanical strength of PU-foam in water and certainly of relevance to patient complaint reports provided in our previous memo."

3.　　"As these reports are consistent with in vitro analytic data demonstrating release of TDA from various experimental conditions (Batish et al, Guidion et al, [OST in-house results]), our previous conclusions regarding the carcinogenicity of PU-coated breast implants were correct. It may be restated again in the words of Dr. Huper as: "Polyurethane foams of different chemical composition are pluripotential carcinogens capable of eliciting cancers in various tissues and organs." "Consequently, PU-foam is not an appropriate material for use in breast implants."

"Recommendation"

"Based on the information we posses, we believe PU mammary implants are sold at the rate of 50-60 thousand units per year, which translates to about 75-800 patients implanted per day. Since polyurethane has been shown to contribute very little to the functioning of breast implants, an additional delay in the resolution of this important safety issue is not justified. I strongly recommend that we proceed *with the CDRH Risk Assessment Committee meeting in a timely manner."*

"Nimual K. Mishra , D.V.M., Ph.D."

"FDA000054916

("As you read the carcinogenicity studies completed in the 1960's on the polyurethane foams I wonder if it was amazing to you that this information has been available for so long! I received my breast implants way after the sixties 1990 STILL there was NOTHING in the published literature which would cause concern about implantation of these devices. I simply TRUSTED my surgeon who stated these Meme™ implants from "Surgitek", "Bristol Myers Squibb", "Medical Engineering Company" were totally safe! Now, I am overly cautious....I suppose as a direct result of this whole issue")

Section Eighteen - F D A Meeting September 11, 2000 - "Platinum Studies"

"Chemically Associated Neurological Disorders, President - Marlene Keeling - was granted a meeting on September 11, 2000, with the F D A, Office of Device Evaluations to present preliminary date from soon to be published research on the release of platinum in a TOXIC REACTIVE form from silicone gel-filled breast implants."

"Fourteen members from the F D A attended as well as Wanda Jones, Office of Women's Health, HHS. Four congressional aides were present including Marc Gonzales, Chief of Staff, and Rosemary Garza with Representative Gene Green's Office, Floyd Gilzow with Representative Roy Blunt's Office, and Emmett O'Keefe with Representative Ron Klink's Office. All of these congressmen are on the Commerce Oversight and Investigation Committee."

"The following agenda was presented":

"STATEMENT OF PURPOSE OF THE MEETING": *"The purpose of the meeting is to present preliminary data documenting significant release of platinum/low*

molecular weight silicones from explanted silicone gel-filled breast implants. New information on additional testing by ion chromatography to establish the valence state of this metal ion has clearly demonstrated this platinum release is PLATINUM SALTS in the reactive valence."

"SPECIFIC OBJECTIVES/OUTCOMES": "This pilot study, with a targeted November, 2000, publish date, will document the release and the potential TOXIC effects of long-term chronic exposure to platinum in genetically susceptible individuals with gel-filled breast implants. Since the health consequences or genotoxic effects are not fully known, as a precautionary approach, WE ASK FOR A HALT TO THE IMPLANTATION OF GEL-FILLED BREAST IMPLANTS AS SOON AS THIS RESEARCH IS PEER-REVIEWED AND PUBLISHED. Upon further confirmation from other independent research or from the manufacturers as part of their PMA application, WE ASK FOR A PUBLIC HEALTH ALERT AS TO BREAST-FEEDING OR PREGNANCY TO AVOID POSSIBLE GENOTOXIC EFFECTS AND ADVICE AS TO

REMOVAL TO AVOID POTENTIAL OR WORSENING HEALTH CONSEQUENCES."

"ATTENDEES:"

"Marlene Keeling - Chemically Associated Neurological Disorders. Brief history of research project. Brief case history of research subjects."

"Arthur Brawer, M.D.,- Rheumatologist and Internist, has documented and photographed over 300 symptomatic patients in research titled: "Chronology of Systemic Disease Development in 300 Symptomatic Recipients of Silicone Gel-Filled Breast Implants", including skin rash in 58%, tinnitus in 20%, and cognitive dysfunction in 64%. Other research includes: "Clinical Features of Local Breast Phenomena in 300 Symptomatic Recipients of Silicone Gel-Filled Breast Implants", "Silicon and Matrix Macromolecules: New Research Opportunities from Old Diseases From Analysis of Potential Mechanisms of Breast Implant Toxicity", and "Amelioration of Systemic Disease after Removal of Silicone Gel-Filled Breast Implants"

(link to skin rash and dermatitis, tinnitus, cognitive dysfunction, improvement upon removal).

Jerremiah Levine, M.D., Professor Of Pediatrics, Gastroenterology & Nutrition. Research includes: "Esophageal Dysmotility in Children Breast-Fed by Mothers with Silicone Breast Implants", "Lymphocyte Response to Silica Among Offspring of Silicone Breast Implant Recipients", Sclerodermalike Esophageal Disease in Children Breast-Fed by Mothers With Silicone Breast Implants", and abstract: "Perinatal Aspects of Reproductive Casualty After Silicone Device Implantation". (link to potential DNA changes and breast-feeding or transplacental passage of toxic platinum.)

Michael Harbut, M.D., M.P.H., Board Certified In Occupational Medicine, WHO HAS LIMITED HIS PRACTICE TO THE DIAGNOSIS AND TREATMENT OF DISEASES CAUSED BY OCCUPATIONAL AND ENVIRONMENTAL TOXINS, concludes breast implants contain 500 to 1500 TIMES the federal standard of safe levels of platinum salts allowed. Part of his research was published in 1999, entitled: "Asthma in Patients with Silicone Breast Implants:

Report of a Case Series and Identification of Hexachloroplatinate Contaminant as a Possible Etiologic Agent". His research is also presented in a body of work: Plaintiffs' Supplemental Submission on the Chemistry and Toxicology of Platinum" requested by Judge Pointer after Dr. Harbut identified faulty work on the part of the science panel. Dr. Harbut quotes Dr. Niezborala and Dr. Garner who state, "At no stage should a (industrial) worker be able to come into contact with a solution or a solid containing these particular complex platinum salts". Furthermore, platinum salts are considered so toxic that the consensus opinion in Occupational Medicine is that platinum allergy exists in a worker presenting with classic allergy symptoms (who is exposed to platinum salts) until proven otherwise. (link to asthma, etc.)

Ernest Lykissa, Ph.D., Forensic Toxicologist and Researcher, documented new equipment and methods of measuring low molecular weight silicone/platinum release.   Data points with significant amounts and speciation of platinum was reported (human link to disease after chronic platinum exposure).

Other treating physicians, who have actually examined breast implanted patients, and have published research or data collections include the following:

Patricia Salvato, M.D., Internist, data on over 633 women with silicone breast implants were presented indicating the natural killer cell number ranged from 8 to 256, or a median of 110.   The main symptoms that these patients presented with were: memory loss, severe fatigue, muscle and joint pain, and neurologic complaints of burning and stinging sensations consistent with neuropathy.   136 (One hundred and thirty-six) healthy controls showed natural killer cells in the range of 320 to 550, with a median of 410. From this data it can be postulated that silicone has a direct and toxic effect on natural killer cell numbers in patients with silicone breast disease.   It has been reported in the medical literature that natural killer cell activity may somehow impinge on the central nervous system. Natural killer cells are capable of crossing the blood brain barrier and are present in the brain and certain pathologic states. It has also been reported that natural killer cells express receptors of neuropeptides and hormones. It has also been shown that products of activated natural killer cells are damaging to the neurons. Some of the activated natural killer cells infiltrating normal tissue might cause local damage that would impinge on cells of the central nervous system of patients, thus manifesting as a cause of neuro-endocrine abnormalities. This research lends more evidence to the growing medical literature supportive of silicone's toxic effects on the immune system, central nervous system, and peripheral nervous system. There are also many symptoms. (link to immunosuppression)

Andrew Campbell, M.D., "Suppressed Natural Killer Cell Activity in Patients with Silicone Implants: Reversal Upon Explantation" Toxicology and Industrial Health 10: 3, May-June, 1994. The Institute of Medicine (July 1999) noted "consistent with animal toxicology studies, it appears that NK (natural killer) cells in humans might be affected by exposure to silicone gel, since removal of silicone breast implants was followed by an increase in NK-cell function in 50% percent of women". (link to immunosuppression)

Arthur Dale Ericsson, M.D., Neurologist, documents over 87% percent of symptomatic patients have demyelinating and axonal neuropathy in his published research: "Syndromes Associated with Silicone Breast Implants: A Clinical Study and Review". (link to peripheral and demyelinating polyneuropathy).

CONCLUSION: The manufacturers of implants agree "platinum salts" cause both toxicity and systemic hypersensitivity reactions in humans but contend there are no "platinum salts" in silicone gels and elastomers. At this meeting we were able to prove that platinum salts remain or revert to platinum salts in silicone gels and elastomers cured with a platinum catalyst. Human health consequences after exposure can range from asthma, rhinorrhea, tinnitus, conjunctivitis, urticaria, fatigue syndromes secondary to impaired oxygen *exchange, neurotoxicity, sicca syndrome, and macular rashes. If no action is taken by the F D A within a reasonable time after publication of this important new research, in light of F D A's own research documenting gel (presumably including toxic platinum) found outside the scar capsule in 21% percent of cases and previous warnings of human health consequences to platinum toxicity and hypersensitivity by Dr. Ray Biagini (NIOSH) in 1993, Omar Henderson (CDC) in 1996, Dr. Michael Harbut in 1993, 1996 conference call, and 1998 IOM (Institute of Medicine) presentation, and Ernest Lykissa, Ph.D., 1997 F D A meeting, we will be left with no alternative but to ask for a CRIMINAL INVESTIGATION AND A CONGRESSIONAL HEARING.*

For the women who have been called hysterical and greedy, for the physicians and scientists whose research has been coined "junk science", for the attorneys who have truly tried to help those of us who have been toxically poisoned by the chemicals in these implants....This new research is a vindication for all that we have experienced! Knowing the TRUTH ourselves and actualization of the TRUTH for the general public is a milestone indeed. Now finally, all modes of media will report this and the manufacture of these toxic devices will CEASE!

SUBSEQUENT to this meeting: (Just TWO DAYS LATER) "On September 13, 2000, Representative Gene Green, Democrat from Texas, was recognized on the Floor of Congress and delivered the following statement: "Regarding": "H.R. 1323", the "Silicone Breast Implant Research and Information Act"

Representative Green Says:

"Mr. Speaker, today I want to talk about legislation that I have been working on." "It is "H.R. 1323". "H.R. 1323 deals with breast implants, an issue that has been the subject of many court cases now for a number of years." "On Monday, (September 11, 2000), the Food and Drug Administration, hosted a meeting to discuss research on silicone gel-filled implants, and I am grateful for the F D A in their willingness not only to meet with my own constituents but also, other people and my staff on this issue and hopefully will continue to dialogue with the F D A to ensure that women get the information they need on the safety of the implants."

"However, the research indicates that platinum salts have been released by silicone gel-filled implants." "This is significant information because the platinum salt in certain form, is known to be TOXIC." "New technology has allowed scientists to determine that the platinum used as a catalyst in making the gel and the shell of the gel-filled breast implant is being released into the body of women in a HARMFUL TOXIC FORM."

"Last week, the F D A released information on their web site citing breast implant complications." "This is a victory for the consumer advocates who have been working to provide more information to women who are considering implants;" "However, the information provided in this web site does not include the recent findings on the TOXICITY of PLATINUM SALTS FOUND IN GEL-FILLED IMPLANTS."

"Women need to know how HARMFUL THE RELEASE OF PLATINUM IN THEIR BODY CAN BE and what it can do to their children who may be nursing." "It has come to my attention that children breast-fed from mothers' with silicone implants may also experience *HARMFUL TOXIC SYMPTOMS* from exposure to platinum salts."

"Symptoms of exposure to platinum in a reactive form can include fatigue, dry eyes, dry mouth, joint inflammation, hair loss, and rashes."

"As a sponsor of the :Silicone Breast Implant Research and Information Act"' "I believe that the need for more research is especially compelling in light of the F D A's own study on the rupture of silicone breast implants".

"On May 18, of this year (2000), Dr. Lori S. Brown's research showed that 69% percent of the women with implants had at least one ruptured breast implant." "The F D A concluded that the rupture of silicone breast implants is the primary concern although the relationship of the free silicone to the development of progression of the disease is unknown."

"We do know there is a rupture of silicone into the body, but we do not know the impact." "That is why we need more research by the F D A".

"I heard from my own constituents over the last number of years and literally women across the country," "Mr. Speaker", "Who have suffered from the long-term consequences of reconstruction and cosmetic surgery." "They have experienced": Infections, chronic pain, deformity and implant rupture, inaccurate mammography readings due to the implant concealing breast tissue and difficulties in getting health insurance to pay for the high cost of repeated surgeries." "The cost of faulty implants is paid by all of us in the system even if it is covered by insurance."

"The Institute of Medicine estimated that by 1997, 1.5 Million to 1.8 Million American Women had breast implants with nearly one-third of these women being breast cancer survivors." "The American Plastic and Reconstruction Surgeons cited breast augmentation as the most popular procedure for women ages 19 through

34." "In 1988, nearly 80,000 women in this age bracket received breast implants for purely cosmetic reasons." "By 1999, an additional 130,000 women received saline breast implants."

"In spite of the escalating numbers, very little is known about the long-term effects of silicone or platinum in the body." "Few patients understand that even when they opt for saline breast implants, the envelope of the implant is made of silicone."

"Following the F D A's decision to approve saline breast implants, the agency did warn women of the potential risk." "F D A officials called upon implant manufacturers and plastic surgeons to ensure that thorough patient information is provided to women before they undergo the surgery"

"Mr. Speaker", "With the F D A approval process behind us, the only course of action to safeguard the future of women is that of an informed consent document." "Somehow, a piece of paper cannot make up for a manufacturer's insufficient data or the retrieval

analysis." "It cannot make up for inaccurate labeling and even risk estimates."

"There is so much we do not know, and yet the one government agency mandated to safeguard the public's food, drug, and medical devices is moving so slow on this issue that could jeopardize women with a medical device that has alarmingly high failure rates."

"In spite of the agency's call for post-market studies, the F D A approval of saline breast implants provides no incentive for the manufacturers to make data better or a safer medical device."

"Mr. Speaker, hopefully the F D A will continue their research."..........!

There are thousands of "court gagged" documents somewhere in a depository in Alabama which contain many **research** *studies on silicone gel breast implants, as well as actual court documents from the early breast implant litigations in which women received huge amounts of money because of the PROOF of poisoning* these documents contained. Somehow, someway I intend to find these documents and bring them forward to the public

Postscript: **My Story** with Silicone Polyurethane Breast Implants from the beginning to the present time, including: further "PLATINUM" studies; Knowledge of tissue, hair, finger and toe nail sample analyses proving multiple chemical and heavy metal poisoning; Sweat, urine, and blood studies; as well as; Results of actual bone marrow biopsies, and the latest news from the F D A..............will be coming soon!

About The Author

Written by a woman whose life has been drastically and profoundly affected by breast implants. A professional woman by trade whose career was marketing, management and research in the medical area; steaming with desire to bring forth the actual stories about breast implants and the women affected by them.

LaVergne, TN USA
28 October 2009
162271LV00001B/5/A

9 781418 421915